Object Relations

A DYNAMIC BRIDGE
BETWEEN INDIVIDUAL AND FAMILY TREATMENT

Object Relations

**A DYNAMIC BRIDGE
BETWEEN INDIVIDUAL AND FAMILY TREATMENT**

SAMUEL SLIPP, M.D.

Jason Aronson, Inc.

New York

London

An earlier version of Chapter 6 appeared in *Family Process*, Volume 12, pages 377-398, in 1973.

An earlier version of Chapter 7 appeared in the *Journal of the American Academy of Psychoanalysis*, Volume 4, pages 389-409, in 1976.

An earlier version of Chapter 8 appeared in the *Journal of the American Academy of Psychoanalysis* Volume 5, pages 359-376, in 1977.

An earlier version of Chapter 9 appeared in Wolberg, L.R., and Aronson, M.L. (Eds.), *Group Therapy: An Overview*. New York: Stratton Intercontinental, 1979. The material was originally presented at a panel discussion, "Holocaust Survivors and Their Children," at the Annual Meeting of the American Academy of Psychoanalysis, Atlanta, Georgia, May 1978.

Library of Congress Cataloging in Publication Data

Slipp, Samuel.
   Object relations.

   Includes bibliographical references and index.
   1. Family psychotherapy. 2. Psychoanalysis.
I. Title. [DNLM: 1. Family therapy. 2. Object attach-
ment. 3. Psychoanalytic therapy. WM 460.5.02 S6330]
RC488.5.S57   1984   616.89'156   83-15557
ISBN 0-87668-747-1

Manufactured in the United States of America

To my wife, Sandra,
and my daughter, Elena

"Children have the compulsion to smooth over all kinds of disorders in the family, that is to say, to take onto their tender shoulders the burdens of all others; naturally, in the final analysis, not out of pure unselfishness but to regain the lost peace and the tenderness that is part of it."

Sandor Ferenczi (1932)

CONTENTS

Development • Self-Differentiation and Symbiotic Relatedness • Intrapsychic Undoing as a Mirror of the Family Dynamics • Case Illustration • Evidence Confirming a Double Bind
on Achievement • Psychodynamic Activation Studies • Summary

PREFACE

Over the years psychoanalysis and family therapy have each accumulated a great amount of knowledge and therapeutic skill related to working with individuals suffering from emotional disorders. Although both disciplines employ psychological means to help patients, a growing rift between the practitioners of the two has developed. Family therapists accuse individual dynamic therapists of working with the patient as if in a vacuum, ignoring and also disrupting the family system. Psychoanalytic practitioners view family therapists as paying attention to the family system and forgetting that the patient is a unique individual.

This polarization seems both unfortunate and unnecessary. Each approach has a distinct contribution to make, yet until now there has been no way of bridging the gulf that exists between them. Object relations theory is offered as the means not only to surmount the theoretical differences, but also to enable the two therapeutic methods to be employed in a complementary fashion. Using object relations theory, a typology of family interaction is developed which takes into account the intrapsychic influences on family patterns, which in turn affects the patient's personality. The understanding coming from this intrapsychic-interpersonal approach can be used to evaluate the appropriateness of a form of treatment for a particular type of disorder at a given point in time. If we can surmount the hurdles of distrust and criticism, psychoanalysis and family therapy can complement each other in a number of ways. The result will be an enlargement of the theoretical understanding in both fields, as well as a treatment approach that is dependent not on the theoretical orientation of the therapist but, rather, on the needs of the patients and the significant others who surround the patient.

The present volume begins with an exploration of the conflicting theoretical foundations and current clinical practices of psychoanalysis and family therapy. It then describes how object relations theory can be employed to provide an encompassing framework for the two fields. This framework provides a rational basis for deciding which approach is more appropriate at the beginning of treatment, and which may be indicated during later phases of therapy.

Chapter 2 deals with epistemology, which is defined as the theory of science or the method and grounds of knowledge, especially with respect to its limits and validity. Since its introduction by the anthropologist Gregory Bateson into the field of family therapy, epistemology has provided a rationale for studying and treating families. Unfortunately, it is a theory that is often misunderstood or used inappropriately in the field of family therapy. A clearer understanding of modern theories of knowledge is provided, as well as an investigation of their effects on the work of Sigmund Freud, the father of psychoanalysis, and Don Jackson, one of the co-founders of family therapy. The means by which the two fields can be integrated are then discussed.

Chapter 3 provides a general review of object relations theory and the ways in which it can be adapted to produce an interactive, interdependent system that bridges the individual and familial dynamics. Because child development has been neglected in the field of family therapy, it is discussed here. I will offer an exposition and critique of Melanie Klein's and Margaret Mahler's developmental phases, and will present a comparison to the phases as described by Sigmund Freud, Otto Kernberg, and Heinz Kohut. Because the concept of the primitive defense of projective identification is used differently in my work than in that of Melanie Klein, who introduced it, I present her definition as well as my own interactional modifications. Chapter 4 provides an understanding of the newer concepts of countertransference that have evolved in recent years, as well as a discussion of the uses of countertransference in therapy.

The second section of the book is devoted to presenting the family typology in which specific family dynamics are related to specific forms of psychopathology. Chapter 5 presents the first core concept of this system, that of adaptation and survival for the individual and for the family. The second core concept concerns what I consider to be the paramount cause of developmental arrest: the paralleling of the child's intrapsychic fantasies with the actual family interaction. In such a situation, the family interaction does not provide an opposing reality to permit differentiation, growth, and development. Instead, the similarity of the family interaction to the child's fantasies perpetuates the child's omnipotent fantasies through negative feedback.

Chapter 6 presents an intrapsychic-interpersonal theory of the

pathogenesis of schizophrenia. A number of studies have demonstrated the genetic basis for schizophrenia; other studies, however,
have indicated the importance of family interaction in the development and maintenance of this disorder. Biology may be necessary,
but it is not sufficient. It is not either nature or nurture, but the combination of the two, that must be understood. The chapter reviews
the work of several family investigators and then presents the concept of the symbiotic survival pattern as it is found in families with
a schizophrenic patient.

Chapter 7 describes a clinical study of family interaction in depression and discusses the "double bind on achievement" that exists in
the families of depressives. Two studies that provide validation for
the theory of a double bind on achievement are described. In these
studies, which employ Silverman's laboratory technique of psychodynamic activation of unconscious fantasy, a tachistoscope is used
to provide subliminal visual stimulation. Specific subliminal messages
trigger unconscious fantasies that produce cognitive and emotional
responses that can be measured on psychological tests. These studies
provide additional evidence of the effects of family interaction on
unconscious fantasy and personality functioning.

Chapter 8 discusses hysteria, which was the first disorder studied
in psychoanalysis. The chapter reviews the historical descriptions of
this disorder, dating back to ancient Egypt, and describes the most
current controversies concerning the validity of hysteria as a diagnostic category. A discussion of the first theory to explore the pathogenic influence of the family on the patient, Freud's seduction theory, together with a critique of Freud's famous case of Dora is
presented. The continuing importance of seductive binding and exploitation is described, as well as the particular forms of splitting and
projective identification that occur in families with a hysteric or borderline patient.

Chapter 9 outlines a controlled clinical research study of some of
the factors involved in the intergenerational transmission of psychopathology, and provides further empirical evidence to attempt
to validate the existence of a double bind on achievement in the families of depressives. In this pilot study, the subjects were all children
of Nazi Holocaust survivors.

Chapter 10 summarizes and integrates the previously presented concepts of family interaction in schizophrenia, hysteria-borderline conditions, and depression into a cohesive whole. In addition, one form of delinquency, that in which a parent is overinvolved with a child, is included to complete the classification of family interaction. Specific types of splitting and projective identification are shown to occur in each of these pathological conditions. These primitive defenses form the basis for homeostasis in the family as well as for the internalization and structuralization of the patient's personality.

The third section of the book demonstrates the actual clinical application, using object relations theory as a bridge between individual and family therapy. Chapter 11 illustrates the application of the family typology system to the initial evaluation of a family, as well as to the family treatment process itself. Clinical case material is provided to add greater understanding. Chapter 12 shows how the family typology system can enrich individual therapy. Here again, clinical case material is employed to provide an added dimension.

The concepts presented here draw on the richness of psychoanalysis, with its emphasis on early development and conflict, and the dramatic findings of family therapy, which have concentrated on here-and-now interaction. A scientific basis for theory and treatment is presented that integrates these two approaches through the use of object relations theory. It is my hope that this integration will prove beneficial to family therapy, to psychoanalysis, and to psychiatry, but most of all to those suffering from the pain of emotional disorders.

ACKNOWLEDGMENTS

This book represents the culmination of a life-long goal of integrating family therapy and psychoanalysis. Most of my clinical and experimental work has been performed with this objective in mind. Having been trained in both psychoanalysis and family therapy, I have always felt that each discipline could be enriched by the insights of the other. A number of people have assisted me in this journey. I was inspired to learn family therapy by Don Jackson. My first teacher at the Mental Research Institute was Virginia Satir. She employed many of the concepts of psychoanalysis, in particular ego psychology, in her family work. My first analyst was William Bellamy, who had been analyzed himself by Abraham Kardiner. I believe that Kardiner's interests in enriching psychoanalysis with the insights of cultural anthropology must have subtly come through. Bill became a close personal friend after I completed my analysis in San Francisco, and I still prize his friendship. My analytic training at New York Medical College was both excellent and eclectic. Included in my course work were lectures on family therapy by Ian Alger and a group therapy experience with Alexander Wolf. I owe a great deal to the rich legacy left by a number of people who stimulated my professional and personal growth: Jean Hershon Slipp, Peter Hogan, Jack Royce, and Sheldon Selesnick.

The opportunity to establish the first family and group therapy unit at New York University was provided me by Samuel Wortis, who was then chairman of the Department of Psychiatry. Sam was very supportive in providing me with staff and funds so that we could develop our research, teaching, and clinical activities. This support was continued by Morris Herman, the acting chairman, and Robert Cancro, the current chairman of the deparment.

I wish to express my deepest gratitude to my editor, Joan Langs, for encouraging me to write this book, and for her kindness and generosity of spirit in making this book a reality. I also want to acknowledge the enthusiastic assistance and saintly patience of my secretary, Marie Smitelli. Most of all, I am grateful for the continued love of my wife, Sandra, and my daughter, Elena, who gave me the courage to persist through all the difficult labor of writing this book.

1

THE DEVELOPMENT OF THEORIES IN INDIVIDUAL AND FAMILY THERAPY

THE DICHOTOMY BETWEEN INTRAPSYCHIC AND ENVIRONMENTAL FORCES

Since the turn of the century, the thrust of psychoanalysis has been to evolve a comprehensive theory of human behavior and a system of therapy for the individual patient. This approach is based on inner personality development and its vicissitudes during *childhood*, with particular emphasis on the first five or six years of life. The pathogenesis and the focus of analytic treatment has been on early intrapsychic conflicts for neurotic states and on developmental arrest for borderline and psychotic conditions. Simultaneously, over the past decade family therapists have made great strides in recognizing and working with the external, current effect of the family on the pathology of the identified patient. This has been particularly true for patients with low levels of self-differentiation, who remain symbiotically bound to their families. Here, before individual therapy is possible, it is often essential to work first with the family therapeutically, to diminish the forces that originate in the family and bind the patient. Only then can the patient separate and individuate.

Family therapy, partly because of the lack of a unifying theoretical foundation, has evolved into a large and rather confusing variety of therapeutic approaches. Some of these approaches completely ignore early childhood developmental needs and deny or minimize intrapsychic difficulties within the individual. In treatment, these family therapy approaches concentrate solely on here-and-now interaction between family members. No matter how dramatically effective such treatment may be in reducing overt symptomatology and releasing the patient from the family system, it is only a beginning.

1

Continued work with the individual patient is essential in order to consolidate the gains and to achieve inner growth and autonomy. Similarly, psychoanalysis could benefit from greater consideration of the ongoing impact of the family in maintaining pathology in the patient. Instead of polarizing these approaches, the present volume will emphasize the potential complementarity of psychoanalysis and family therapy. We will demonstrate the significance of early childhood development as well as the effect of ongoing family interactions on the genesis and maintenance of psychopathology.

LACK OF AN INTEGRATED THEORY IN FAMILY THERAPY

Despite the rapid growth of family therapy over the past decade, no encompassing theoretical framework has yet evolved. In fact, the field of family therapy is probably more fragmented today than it was in 1970, when the Group for the Advancement of Psychiatry (1970) conducted an extensive survey of the theoretical orientations of family therapists. In the 1970s at one extreme were the psychoanalytic family therapists, and at the other the pure systems family therapists. In the 1980s the therapeutic approaches have multiplied, with the addition of paradoxical, structural, problem-centered, experiential, interactional, and a variety of other approaches. Thus, the field has become even more fragmented, without any encompassing framework linking these various forms of family therapy. This book will attempt to provide such a theoretical framework, as well as a typology of family relationships that is associated with specific forms of pathology in the patient.

A large number of clinicians have recognized family therapy as a therapy in search of a theory. Murray Bowen (1982), on stepping down as the first president of the American Family Therapy Association, commented in its newsletter that in the rapid rush into family therapy, theory and science had been bypassed. Many so-called family therapy experts jumped on the bandwagon, becoming almost like circuit riders converting followers to their own brand of gospel and dogma. Bowen stated, "In the chaos of the 1970s, people never understood the difference between natural systems and general systems theory, between the facts of science and the truths of philosophy, or the baselines on which the various disciplines were founded. . . . The words paradigm and epistemology, formerly used with some precision by Gregory Bateson, have been distorted to fit the subjectivity of the speaker." Bowen's hope had been that family therapy would prove to be *the* way to observe and study human behavior and to enable all of psychiatry to achieve the status of a science. Sharing these concerns and hopes regarding the field of family therapy, I attempt in this book to bring together the polarized and diverse positions in the field through a review of the scientific basis of knowledge and the development of an encompassing theoretical framework. Object relations theory will be used as the bridge to unite these diverse positions and to connect the intrapsychic with the interpersonal and family-as-a-whole levels of functioning.

OBJECT RELATIONS THEORY AND FAMILY THERAPY

Object relations theory is an existing general framework in psychoanalysis and psychiatry that has provided us with the means for understanding the earliest developmental phases of childhood. It studies the attachment and differentiation from others, a process of great importance not only for individual personality functioning but also for familial and social adaptation. The lack of differentiation of family members has become one of the cornerstones of Murray Bowen's work in understanding sick families, as well as of Helm Stierlin's work (1976b) studying the functioning of larger social groups.

Until recently the main thrust of object relations theory has been the psychoanalytic study and treatment of borderline and narcissistic personality disorders. The ways in which the internalized self and object influence the transference-countertransference relationships in individual therapy have received special emphasis. My own work has used object relations theory differently, broadening its focus to include other patient populations and applying its concepts to family studies to search for pathogenic factors in the family that influence the identified patient. Thus, diverse patient populations and their families have been studied to explore the interaction and interdependence of individual dynamics and family systems functioning. The ultimate goal of these studies has been to apply an integrated understanding to family treatment.

This book will elaborate on the four major forms of pathological family relationships found in these studies. These relationships proved unresponsive to the developmental needs of the child and nonenhancing to the personality growth of other family members. Instead, they are an unconscious attempt by the parents to externalize and master, in their actual current family relationships, past traumatic relationships from childhood that have become internalized. The primitive defense mechanisms of splitting, projective identification, denial, and idealization, as delineated in object relations theory, were found to be operative in these families. A family typology was developed for various psychiatric disorders, in which specific forms of splitting and projective identification within the family are seen as resulting in a particular form of pathology in the identified patient. Family therapy has long searched for a typology that classifies certain forms of family interaction with psychiatric conditions. The typology that will be presented here encompasses the predominant family interactions in schizophrenia, depression, and hysterical/borderline conditions, as well as delinquency. How identification of each of these patterns can be helpful in treatment, to decipher and change family interaction, will be discussed.

THE GROWTH OF FAMILY THERAPY

Individual psychotherapy can trace its origins to Breuer's treatment of Anna O. over 100 years ago (Freud and Breuer 1895); family therapy has existed only for a little more than 25 years. Despite its youth, family therapy has grown into one of the most widely used forms of psychotherapy. A number of factors have contributed to this rapid acceptance. Clearly a good deal of groundwork for the psychological treatment of emotional disorders had already been laid by individual psychotherapy and psychoanalysis. Family therapy built on this foundation, and growth occurred more easily and rapidly. This is not a sufficient explanation for the acceptance of family therapy, however. Another factor is the accumulation of a large amount of clinical evidence showing that not only are emotional disorders developed in childhood, but the current maintenance and even the prognosis* of these disorders are closely related to the patient's relationship with the family. Freud made the monumental discovery that the child's early experience with the family forms the soil from which neurosis grows. Freud's emphasis remained within the patient, however, particularly the ways in which the child managed unconscious sexual and aggressive instincts and fantasies toward the parents. It was not until the development of family therapy that the full impact of the parents' influence on the child was appreciated, particularly the importance of current, ongoing interactions. Thus, treating the patient together with the family, and working with the family interaction, developed as a logical consequence.

Another reason for the acceptance of family therapy is more pragmatic: its effectiveness as a treatment modality. Family therapy is a powerful form of treatment that produces fairly rapid improvement in patients. This fact has been amply demonstrated by the large number of family therapy outcome studies, reviewed comprehensively by Wells, Dilkes, and Trivelli (1972) and Epstein and Vlok (1981). Family therapy has shown itself to be an extremely potent form of treatment, even more effective with certain types of disorders than is individual therapy.

CONTRIBUTIONS OF PSYCHOANALYSIS TO FAMILY THERAPY

Interestingly, individual psychoanalysis played a crucial role in the birth and development of family therapy. Psychoanalysis was the first form of therapy to employ psychological means to understand and treat mental illness, a tradition that is carried on by family therapy. In addition, most of the pioneers in family therapy, such as Nathan Ackerman, Ivan Boszormenyi-Nagy, Murray Bowen, Henry Dicks,

---

* See the work of Julian Leff (1976), wherein relapse rates of schizophrenics are closely related to critical and intrusive interactions of the family with the patient.

James Framo, Don Jackson, Theodore Lidz, Norman Paul, Virginia Satir, and Lyman Wynne, had psychoanalytic backgrounds. They built on the heritage of Freud to establish the field of family therapy. Family therapy as a field would likely have been established earlier had Freud not abandoned his initial theoretical formulation, the seduction theory (Freud and Breuer 1895). The seduction theory was the first psychiatric theory to involve family dynamics, emphasizing the pathological influence of one person on another. Because of an actual traumatic event, the seduction by an adult or older sibling, the child developed hysterical or obsessional symptoms. Unfortunately, Freud did not nurture this theoretical creation. He abandoned it shortly after its conception, although he did not publicly renounce it until eight years later. Some of the events shaping his decision to abandon an interactional theory will be discussed later. The result of this abandonment for psychoanalysis was a turning away from traumatic events in the family—actual interaction—and a focusing on unconscious fantasy and instinctual drives within the patient. Although Freud had initially touched on the exploitation of the child for others' needs, he turned away from this and focused on the child's inner motives and conflicts.

In treatment of the individual, Freud generally restricted himself to seeing the patient alone and avoided seeing the family members. This framework for psychoanalytic treatment was maintained in order to prevent contamination of the patient's transferential relationship to the analyst. Unfortunately, however, it deprived Freud of the opportunity to explore the real impact of the parents on the child and of the child on the parents. Thus, the child's fantasies could not be evaluated against the reality of the familial context. This limitation is strikingly evident in the case of Little Hans, who was treated by Freud (1909). Freud totally ignored the very real sexual stimulation of the mother, who repeatedly invited Little Hans into her bed and then threatened that his penis would be cut off. Clearly, the mother's conflicting messages of stimulation and inhibition—her seductive influence and her threat of castration—had a powerful effect on Little Hans's unresolved oedipal conflict. Interestingly, Freud did not always follow his own rules about not seeing other family members in individual treatment. In fact, he concurrently (although in separate sessions) analyzed James and Alex Strachey, who were married. Freud also concurrently treated the spouse of a patient who was in analysis when a divorce was threatened (personal confidential communication 1982).

SANDOR FERENCZI'S AWARENESS OF FAMILY INTERACTION

One of the most gifted of Freud's pupils, Sandor Ferenczi (1920), maintained that Freud's original seduction theory was correct and should never have been abandoned. It was not the distortions of reality caused by the patient's fantasies and instincts that produced psychiatric illness, as Freud held, but, rather, actual parental neglect and trauma. Ferenczi's "active" approach in treatment attempted to recreate the early parent–child interaction so the patient could relive and master the parental deprivation. During this regressive reenactment of the parental relationship in treatment, the therapist's empathic responsiveness encouraged resumption of the patient's growth and development. Ferenczi believed that maintaining a passive and abstinent approach with sicker patients, as Freud advocated, only recapitulated and reinforced the patients' experience of neglect and emotional abandonment by the parents. Ferenczi was also keenly aware of the interpersonal relationship of the therapist and patient and used his approach to avoid a negative transference and a resultant poor therapeutic outcome.

Considerable conflict between Freud and Ferenczi arose over these theoretical and therapeutic differences. Ferenczi's influence on psychoanalysis has only recently been adequately appreciated, and he is probably the most creative of any of Freud's original pupils. He was the first to note that a child could act out the unconscious conflicts of a parent, and to recognize the importance of countertransference reactions of the therapist in the treatment relationship. One of Ferenczi's analysands, Melanie Klein, using many of his ideas, initiated her own approach in child analysis, out of which grew the object relations school in Britain. Another analysand, Clara Thompson, strongly influenced Sullivan and other neo-Freudian thinkers in the United States to explore the actual effects of familial, social, and cultural relationships on personality development.

THE DEVELOPMENT OF FAMILY THERAPY IN ENGLAND

The growth of psychoanalytic theory, in particular the British object relations school, provided further impetus for the development of family therapy. How an individual forms an internalized world of self and object determines later adult interpersonal relations. In the 1940s Henry Dicks established a family psychiatric unit at the Tavistock Clinic in London to attempt to reconcile couples referred from the divorce court. Using object relations theory, Dicks (1963) noted that one basis for mate selection was that the other's personality unconsciously matched split-off aspects of the self. Projective identification was employed, so that unacceptable aspects of the self could be externalized and acted out by the partner. These marriages thus established an unconscious complementarity. Usually these couples were unable to give up the hated partner (much like the internalized bad object) and had difficulty divorcing despite sadomasochistic relations. Dicks was later joined by Michael and Enid Balint, who headed the family discussion bureau at the Tavistock Clinic. Michael Balint (1968) was one of the major object relations theorists, contributing much understanding to preoedipal development. In 1949 John Bowlby (1969), known for his studies of childhood attachment and separation, also employed conjoint family interviews at the Tavistock child guidance clinic.

THE DEVELOPMENT OF FAMILY THERAPY
IN THE UNITED STATES

In the United States during the 1940s, David Levy (1943) studied and described the pathogenic effects of certain types of mothering on children. He was able to correlate each of several pathogenic traits in the mother (overprotectiveness, dominance, and indulgence) with certain disturbed behavior in the child. Frieda Fromm-Reichmann (1948) coined the term *schizophrenogenic mother* to describe mothers who were cold, aggressive, domineering, and rejecting. The emotional or schizoid withdrawal of the child as a consequence was believed to contribute to the schizophrenic reaction. Later, Mabel Blake Cohen, Grace Baker, Robert A. Cohen, Frieda Fromm-Reichmann, and Edith Weigert (1954) also studied manic depressive patients and reported in their classic paper the impact of the family on the development of the patient's illness. During this same time Adelaide M. Johnson and Stanislaus A. Szurek (1954) wrote on the subtle transmission of superego defects from parents to their delinquent children. Unwittingly these parents fostered antisocial behavior in their child. The child acted out the unconscious antisocial impulses of the parents, who achieved vicarious gratification through identification with the child. Pathogenesis was never truly established in these clinical studies, but they did markedly change the focus from study of the patient in isolation to exploration of the context of pathological interactions.

This shift in focus, away from the internalized world of the patient to the actual world of relationships, had its effect on treatment. In 1924, Alfred Adler had already initiated the procedure of having one therapist see the parents and child in separate sessions. The parents' session generally focused on providing counselling on how to deal with the child. Not until 1931, however, was the first paper on marital therapy presented by Carl Oberndorf to the American Psychiatric Association. René Laforgue, at the Ninth International Congress of Psychoanalysis in 1936, then presented his experience of analyzing the spouses of one family concurrently (during the same period, but in separate sessions). He demonstrated how each spouse unconsciously communicated to support the other's complementary neurosis. At the same psychoanalytic conference, Leuba attempted to develop a system of family diagnosis. In 1948 Bela Mittelman reported on the individual psychoanalyses of twelve marital couples treated concurrently. He did conduct several joint sessions to resolve conflicting issues. The first instance of a family treated together in the same session on a regular basis was reported in 1954 by Nathan W. Ackerman. In this bold step forward, Ackerman pioneered the use of family therapy in treating emotional problems. He also had the courage to film as well as write about actual family sessions and thus did much to promote popular acceptance of treating the family together as a group.

As more individuals have entered the field of family therapy, the number of therapeutic approaches has increased rapidly. Although the basic schism still is that between the psychoanalytic and systems approaches, there has been considerable proliferation within each. It is virtually impossible to list all the types of family therapy practiced today, but the most popular ones are Bowenian (systems), contextual, experiential, interactional, problem centered, psychoanalytic, structural, and strategic. Each approach has been spurred by a particular individual: Murray Bowen, Ivan Boszormenyi-Nagy, Carl Whitaker, Don Jackson, Nathan Epstein, Nathan Ackerman, Salvador Minuchin, and Mara Selvini-Palazzoli, respectively.

SUBJECTIVITY OF THEORIES IN THE BEHAVIORAL SCIENCES

No theory, nor the therapeutic technique based on that theory, can ever be divorced from the life experiences and personality of its originator. Scientists concerned with the sociology of knowledge, such as Remmling (1967), have challenged the existence of objective, value-free research and theory in the behavioral sciences. Social and personal variables, including cultural value orientations stemming from class, race, ethnicity, nationality, sex, and religion, strongly influence and shape theory building. They all affect the particular way in which an individual perceives and interprets events. Simply focusing on the external observed events, as if these indeed represented objective truth, has been termed *naive realism* and stems from the dualistic splitting of Descartes. Modern epistemology has demonstrated the subjectivity of our knowledge of reality. We need to know as much about the observer, and the act of observing, as the object observed. Who were the mentors of a particular theory builder? Upon what past knowledge was the approach built? Besides the forces that served as a foundation for and stimulated growth of a theory, certain other forces constricted or shaped the direction of the investigator. Were there traumatic life experiences that impinged on the investigator that brought forth certain emotional biases or defenses? Honesty and candor concerning these latter factors are difficult to come by and indeed may even be outside the conscious awareness of the individual. Careful study of the forces shaping the investigator is necessary in order to achieve a greater understanding of the theory and the context of its development.

INFLUENCES ON THEORY BUILDING

To begin this process of examining the context in which a theory developed, I shall start by recounting some of the factors that influenced my own perspective in family therapy. My persistent goal was to integrate individual and family dynamics. Using general systems theory as a base, individual and family dynamics were viewed as interactive and interdependent forces, each influencing the other. The intrapsychic dynamics of each individual and the processes of the family were seen as isomorphic, not as separate and polarized from each other. Thus, all my theoretical formulations in schizophrenia (1969, 1972, 1973), depression (1976), and hysteria (1977) combine intrapsychic and interpersonal dynamics.

I have been influenced by many of the leaders in family therapy, as well as a number of innovative thinkers in psychoanalysis and psychiatry. My thinking began to be shaped by my teachers during my residency training in psychiatry at the Langley Porter Clinic of the University of California in San Francisco. My mentor in psychoanalysis was Emanuel Windholz. I was introduced to the new epistemologies in communications theory by Jurgen Reusch and Gregory Bateson (1951), and in general systems theory, cybernetics, and philosophy by Gregory Bateson (1972). Frieda Fromm-Reichmann was another strong and memorable teacher. I read her classic papers on the influence of the family in schizophrenia (1948) and later, with her co-workers, on manic-depressive illness (Cohen et al 1954). I was also taught by Stanislaus Szurek, who had written with Adelaide Johnson (1954) on the unconscious transmission of superego lacunae by parents to their child that sanctioned delinquent behavior.

My first encounter with the theories of the British object relations school was through Donald Shaskan, who reviewed the group work of Wilfred Bion. Bion (1959) emphasized how the shared unconscious fantasy (one of three basic assumptions: dependency, fight or flight, or pairing) held by members of a group affected their individual functioning and interfered with accomplishing the task of the group.

At Stanford University School of Medicine, I first met Don Jackson, who presented his work with the Bateson group studying schizophrenics and their families. He gave me his manuscript on family rules, which I critiqued, and that was published several years later (Jackson 1965). In 1960 I enrolled for family therapy training at Don Jackson's Mental Research Institute in Palo Alto, California, where Virginia Satir was my principal instructor. The double-bind theory of schizophrenia was being revised at the time by Gregory Bateson, Don Jackson, Jay Haley, and John Weakland (1956, 1962).

In 1965 I was invited by Heinz Wolff, who was head of psychotherapy at the Maudsley Hospital in London, to present a series of lectures on family therapy. During my stay in London, I had the opportunity to meet with Ronald Laing, who had written on "mystification" of the schizophrenic in the family (Laing and Esterson 1964); with Elliot Mishler and Nancy Waxler (1968), who were researching communication in families of schizophrenics; and with Carstairs, Brown, and Wing at the Maudsley, who were conducting a family research project in schizophrenia (see Leff [1976] for a review). I also reencountered Malcolm Pines, who at the time was affiliated with the Cassel Hospital in a suburb of London. The Cassel Hospital had been organized by Tom Main in such a way that the entire family was hospitalized along with the patient and treated by psychoanalytic individual and group therapy. I was impressed by the openness of British psychoanalysts to group and family approaches.

I was privileged during this visit to get to know Michael Balint. Through him, my interest in Ferenczi's contributions to psychoanalysis was stimulated. It was Ferenczi who was the progenitor of modern object relations theory. Ferenczi was interested in the earliest relationships of the child, when the distinction between the self and the outside world occurs and the individual's sense of identity takes form.

APPLYING OBJECT RELATIONS
THEORY TO FAMILY THERAPY

Although I had come to London to teach family dynamics, I left having learned a great deal from my exposure to the British object relations approach. My attempt to understand the relationship between individual and family dynamics began here. Having learned general systems theory from Gregory Bateson, I began by looking for isomorphisms, that is, similar structures and connections. It was only a small additional step to employ object relations theory as a bridging or coupling concept between the family interactional and the individual intrapsychic levels. Splitting and projective identification became the touchstones that brought together for me the work of Stan Szurek, Frieda Fromm-Reichmann, and Don Jackson and served to explain the manner in which one individual influences another.

My initial interest in schizophrenia was stimulated by the work done at the Mental Research Institute, as well as by the studies of Theodore Lidz (Lidz, Fleck, and Cornelison 1965). Lidz noted the forms of triadic relationships, including breaching of generational boundaries, in families with a schizophrenic member. I began by studying 125 schizophrenic patients and their families at the New York University–Bellevue Medical Center. My publications stemming from these studies (1969, 1972, 1973b) were among the first using object relations theory in the field of family therapy in the United States.

In the late 1960s and early 1970s, object relations theory was not popular in psychoanalytic circles in the United States. The very mention of Melanie Klein or the British school frequently triggered skeptical comments. Likewise many leading family therapists rejected psychoanalytic concepts. I persisted despite the heavy crossfire at times.

I developed friendships with other psychoanalysts who were involved in family therapy. These included Ian Alger and Peter Hogan (1969), who had done work with videotaping of families; Al Scheflen (1964), who studied the kinesic (nonverbal) regulation of interaction in families; Ted Lidz (Lidz, Fleck, and Cornelison 1965)

and Helm Stierlin (1969) both of whom had contributed to the understanding of family dynamics in schizophrenia. My interest in hysteria grew also out of my clinical research work at Bellevue.

Family studies had first investigated schizophrenia; the origin of
psychoanalysis lay in the study of hysteria. These events greatly influenced my selection of these two areas as those in which to begin
developing my own theoretical and clinical perspective. My work in
depression drew its theoretical foundations from the writings of Edith
Jacobson (1967, 1971).* The family concept of a double bind on
achievement in depression received its impetus from my enriching
contacts with Frieda Fromm-Reichmann, Don Jackson, and Gregory
Bateson, to whom I am gratefully indebted.

---

* This connection is reviewed in Slipp (1981).

2

KNOWING INTERNAL
AND EXTERNAL FACTORS

THE THEORY OF KNOWLEDGE
FROM ANCIENT TO MODERN TIMES

An understanding of the theory of knowledge is essential if we are to arrive at an encompassing, scientifically based theory of family therapy.

Scientific inquiry had its beginnings in ancient Greek philosophy. The universe was viewed as orderly, and human reason could discover its working laws. Aristotle explained natural phenomena through deductive reasoning, proceeding from general conclusions to the specific. Through speculation, metaphysical constructs* were formulated. A closed system of thought, based on syllogisms, resulted.

Galileo's discoveries in physics represented a revolt against deductive doctrines and theories superimposed on phenomena. He established experimentation as the basic tool of science for both developing and validating hypotheses. In the post-Galilean era, science became characterized by inductive thinking, which begins with the particular and proceeds to the general. This is the empirical method, based on direct observation.

Early investigators, however, looked for the properties of external

---

* A construct is a mental organization that interrelates a number of concepts. We invent it in order to make sense out of the phenomena we observe. Examples of constructs are the ego, id, and superego in psychology, and latitude and longitude in physical science. They have no denotative value in that there is no observable referent in external reality to which one can point. Because the construct cannot be verified experimentally, one cannot use it to identify a causal agent. Using a construct as if it had literal meaning is termed *reification*. Attempting to explain that an individual eats too much by stating that he has an oral fixation is an example of reification. The oral fixation here is only a construct, which is useful but cannot identify a causal relationship. Reification allows for premature but false closure, because one may come to feel at rest by dispelling ambiguity.

referents as if they were "things-in-themselves." In the 19th century the philosopher Kant challenged logic further, stating that it committed the error of "substantialization" by considering an abstraction or reason as if it were an entity. Empiricism was not free of human ideation; the mind was not simply a passive receptacle for the collecting of facts. Initially how the mind conceived external referents determined our perception of reality. Theory penetrates the empirical method, because it determines the perceptual set of the observer and influences which data will be isolated and analyzed. One cannot see without isolating and selecting.

Current scientific inquiry incorporates both deductive and inductive reasoning, speculation and empiricism. Theories derived speculatively can be tested for validity by the empirical method; empirical findings can be brought together to derive meaning through deductive reasoning. Theory itself is always an abstraction of reality. It is based on our ability to draw inferences from a limited number of facts to determine some order or meaning, to predict, control, and clarify the relationships among phenomena. Thus, all theory is indeterminate, inconclusive, conditional, and always open to revision.

The first person to develop the theory of the interdependence of all sciences was the early 18th-century philosopher Giambattista Vico. Vico believed that progress in one field resulted in progress in all the sciences. Generally, it was physics that served as the cutting edge for the other sciences. Vico's ideas can best be seen in operation in the great leap forward that occurred not only in the natural but also in the social sciences following the discoveries of Newton in physics. Newton's findings reinforced our reliance on reason to understand and master nature. This advance in the physical sciences culminated in the 18th-century Age of Enlightenment. The guiding hope of this period, as expressed by Condorcet, was that science and education would disrupt the infantilizing dependence on social authorities, who had exploited humanity's ignorance, fear, and superstition for their own selfish interests. This challenge to collective, authoritarian forms of society in favor of individualistic, democratic, and more humane social structures found political expression in the American and French revolutions. The dethroning of kings was accompanied by the reduction of theories to the status of servants of humanity, not its masters. In America, C. S. Peirce founded the philosophy of pragmatism, which considered all theories to be only instrumental rules for action, not final answers. William James (1907) extended pragmatism by accepting concepts not as entities but only as helpful processes having "cash value." Although we need mythologies and theories to impart meaning to data, these are only tools. Theories have value only insofar as they have working value and produce practical effects.

The next and most profound influence on all scientific inquiry occurred with the development of atomic physics in the 20th century. This influence was reflected in the change from theories using linear causality and simple determination to a more sophisticated, multidetermined systems theory. Matter was found not to be discrete, static, and permanent but, rather, changeable and able to exist simultaneously in different forms. Thus, the concepts of Newtonian physics concerning the nature of matter and causality were superseded. Max Planck's quantum theory abandoned simple determinism, and Heisenberg's principle of indetermination questioned static concepts concerning measuring atomic particles and focused on statistical probability. The very concept of the detached "objective" observer was challenged, since the act of observing influenced what was observed. Einstein's relativity theory further demonstrated the interaction and interchangeability of energy and matter, which were related to the speed of light. Thus, instead of being static, permanent, and mutually exclusive of one another, these opposing states coexisted and could evolve from one another in nature.

According to Aristotelian logic, two contradictory propositions could not at the same time and in the same reference be true. One was true and the other false. In quantum mechanics, however, it was impossible to verify statements according to a simple true-or-false dichotomy. Verbal language itself is based on Aristotelian logic and is limited; symbolic, multivalued logic was therefore developed by such mathematical logicians as Boole, DeMorgan, Russell, and Whitehead to express complex relationships in modern physics. One of the persistent traps in the behavioral sciences has been that language, following Aristotelian logic, splits the universe into nameable parts and delineates boundaries. Thus, language tends to be static, uses linear thinking, and sets up artificial dualities or dichotomies.

Following these findings of atomic physics, Whitehead (1948) introduced into philosophy the concept that all phenomena in nature are essentially relevant to one another. He considered the splitting of nature along dualistic, "either-or" lines the "fallacy of bifurcation" and criticized the concept of simple determinism, which dealt with a limited number of variables using linear causality. Phenomena cannot be extracted and immobilized from their context in nature but, rather, should be studied as processes and relationships.

Following this same line of reasoning, Dewey and Bentley (1949) proposed a field theory to explain relationships. According to the theory, transactions occurring between interrelated systems result in phenomena. Thus, there is a need to study combinations of systems in science, and how they occur, in order to attempt to reconstruct phenomena as they exist in nature. Change in one system reverberates in other systems; systems are interrelated and interdependent; wholes and parts are complementary. Actions can occur because of self-initiation, as a result of the interaction of separate individuals, or from transactions emanating from the system as a whole without separation of its individual components. Linear logical procedures are limited and restricted to the first two actions, whereas transactions are circular, much like reverberating feedback loops.

General systems theory was formulated by Ludwig Von Bertalanffy (1968) in 1945, based on his work in biology, as a general scientific theory whose principles are valid for living as well as nonliving systems. Systems are defined as a grouping of elements that possess a wholeness and in which the various levels or subsystems stand in relation to one another. The aim of general systems theory is to find general isomorphisms in systems, i.e., to look for the general organization or structure of the various subsystems. This goal involves a search for similarities and relationships instead of dichotomies. Each subsystem is part of an integrated hierarchy of levels. Each subsystem has a boundary and a degree of autonomy but is interactive with and dependent upon general control by the suprasystem of which it is a part.

All systems tend to remain in a dynamic steady state, a condition of equilibrium within certain limits. This balance is achieved through two forms of feedback loops. One is a negative feedback loop that regulates the functioning of the system to maintain a general continuity of function and structure. It is a deviation-correcting mechanism and has been termed *morphostasis*. The other is a positive feedback loop that permits growth, development, and adaptation but can produce breakdown of the system if the limits are breached. This is a deviation-amplifying mechanism termed *morphogenesis*. It is through these two forms of feedback loops that control and organization of the system are maintained.

An example of morphostasis, with deviation correction through negative feedback, is the construct of family homeostasis devised by Don Jackson. Here the family delimits deviant behavior and thought by its role structure and rules, which may at times require that one person be the identified patient to preserve this equilibrium. General systems theory has also been applied in general psychiatry. Each individual is seen as a system ecologically suspended in multiple systems. This perception is based on a wholistic view of personality instead of a linear, mechanistic, stimulus–response theory. The goal of this approach is to integrate the various concepts at all levels of the system that influence human personality and behavior.

SIGMUND FREUD AND CLASSICAL PSYCHOANALYSIS

Freud's first theory (Freud and Breuer 1895) can easily be termed a family theory. It dealt with the trauma and subsequent psychopathology produced in a child by physical seduction by a family member (parent, older sibling, maid, or relative). This original theory of Freud begun in 1892 evolved out of his treatment of 18 patients with hysteria. All these patients reported during their treatment traumatic experiences of actual sexual seduction during childhood. Despite the great risk involved in presenting such a theory, Freud reported his findings in April 1896 before the prestigious Vienna Society for Psychiatry and Neurology. This was Freud's first major public lecture,* and he delivered it without notes in a flow-

---

* Freud had delivered an earlier lecture in 1886 before a smaller group, the Society of Psychiatrists, about his work with Charcot in Paris. It had been received coolly.

ing, poetic style. He boldly compared himself to an explorer who had discovered the head of the Nile ("Caput Nile"); he had discovered the root cause for hysteria. It was that an actual traumatic seduction, not a fantasy about sex, had occurred during childhood. This seduction was so incompatible with the patient's values that its memory and the associated feelings were repressed into the unconscious. Freud believed that the feelings about the event persisted in a conflictual state in the child's mind. The conflict consisted of the attempts by the conscious to repress the traumatic memory and the unconscious pushing for the return of the repressed material. A compromise solution occurred, in which the unconscious trauma was converted into symptoms. Freud stated that the hysteric suffered from "reminiscences," and that the recovery of these memories from repression into consciousness and the release of the associated affect would result in cure. In a letter to his friend Wilhelm Fliess after the meeting, Freud told of the "icy reception" by the audience, who arose and left the room silently. His report was met with skepticism by Baron Richard von Krafft-Ebing, professor of psychiatry at the University of Vienna and chairman of the meeting, who stated sardonically, "It sounds like a scientific fairy tale." Subsequently, Freud was met with scorn and isolation in the professional community (Jones 1953), even being referred to as a Jewish pornographer. After having taken such a bold risk to his professional career and suffering humiliation, Freud discovered that the memories of his patients were unfounded in reality; the physical seduction had not actually occurred! Only a year later, he wrote to Fliess on September 21, 1897 and confessed that he no longer believed in the seduction theory (his "neurotica," as he termed it). The trauma of this discovery and his sense of betrayal and inner turmoil must have been devastating.*

---

* Masson (1984) claims Freud gave up the seduction theory to protect his friend Wilhelm Fliess. Fliess, who had evolved a theory connecting the turbinate bones of the nose with female sexuality, in February 1895 performed nasal surgery on Emma Eckstein, a patient of Freud who suffered hysterical symptoms. Fliess inadvertently left gauze in her nose which caused a nearly fatal hemorrhage. According to Masson, Freud denied the reality of Fliess' mistreatment and believed instead

Others have attributed Freud's rejection of the seduction theory to another occurrence. In October 1896 Freud's father, Jacob, died at the age of eighty-one. Klein and Tribich (1982) quote from the work of the Germans Marianne Kruell and Marie Balmary, who believed that Freud abandoned the seduction theory to protect his own father. The seduction theory of neurosis considered fathers to be the main seducers. Because Freud himself suffered neurotic symptoms, the theory would implicate his own father. However, this assumption is not substantiated by the facts. During his self-analysis, Freud clearly stated in a letter to Fliess on October 3, 1897 that "the old man [Freud's father] plays no active part in my case," and he was seduced as a child by an "elderly" and "clever" maid.

Certain information about Freud's relationship with his father is available. We know that Freud's father had been a failure in business as a wool merchant, necessitating the family's move from Freiberg, Czechoslovakia, to Vienna, Austria. Jacob apparently was the warm and nurturant but weak and vulnerable parent. Freud's mother, Amalie who was twenty years younger than her husband, was the stronger, and ambitious parent. She openly favored her first born son, Sigmund, and pressured her "golden Sigi" for achievement to regain the family's lost social status.* Because of this overinvolvement with his mother and the symbolic oedipal triumph over his elderly father, Freud had difficulty resolving his oedipal conflict. In the summer of 1897, about nine months after his father's death, Freud began his own self-analysis. From examination of his dreams and free associations, Freud discovered his own unconscious oedipal fantasies toward his mother. He also experienced his unconscious patricidal wishes, as well as a desire to identify with his dead father.

Freud had difficulty, however, in both these areas concerning his

---

that Emma had hemorrhaged out of an inner need for attention. The validity of this argument seems doubtful. Freud did not publicly present his seduction theory until April 1896, more than a year later, and he advocated it in a letter to Fliess as late as December 1897. In The Interpretation of Dreams (1900), Freud discusses the Dream of Irma's Injection, which occurred in July 1895, Freud describes the operation on Emma (called Irma in the dream), and openly accuses Fliess (called Otto in the dream) for his rashness, carelessness, irresponsibility, and incompetence.

* Freud's family dynamics in some ways fit those of depressives, which will be described in Chapter 7.

father. Not only had Freud's unconscious, omnipotent death wishes for his father seemed capable of actually happening earlier because of his father's age, weakness, and vulnerability; but when Freud was less that two years of age, his younger brother, Julius, had died. In a letter to Fliess in 1897, Freud admitted to guilt over his jealousy and the death wishes he had had for his brother. Thus, the sharp delineation of fantasy from reality concerning his death wishes for his brother was obscured by the brother's actual death, undoubtedly creating a similar problem with his father. Also, Freud had difficulty in identifying with his father as an adequate masculine model, especially in a Viennese culture that was markedly anti-Semitic. Not only was his father a failure economically, but spiritually and physically Freud perceived him as a coward. Freud recounts in his work an incident in which his father's new fur cap had been knocked off by a Gentile who shouted, "Jew, get off the pavement!" The father had not fought back but, rather, had submissively complied and retrieved his cap from the gutter. Freud's ambivalence toward his father was expressed in his dreams, in the book *Moses and Monotheism* (by making Moses non-Jewish), and in his search for idealized, strong father figures such as Brücke, Charcot, Breuer, and Fliess. Freud also admired a Jewish medical colleague, Carl Koller, who had fought and won a duel after being called a "Jewish swine," and sent a letter to Theodore Herzl praising his work in establishing Palestine as a homeland for the Jews. Thus, Freud identified with strong father figures who took courageous stands and fought for their beliefs.

During this time a series of events occurred in Vienna that undoubtedly shaped Freud's professional life and the decisions he made. In January 1897, Dennis Klein (1981) states, Freud considered resigning from the University of Vienna, where he had been a privat-dozent—the lowest appointment, equivalent to an instructor—for the past 12 years. He delayed this decision, however, because Professor Herman Nothnagel, Chief of the Internal Medicine Clinic, proposed him for a promotion to professor. Unfortunately, in April 1897 Karl Lueger, a rabid anti-Semite and head of the Christian Social Party, was elected mayor of Vienna. Emperor Franz Joseph had attempted to block the appointment of Lueger four times previously but finally gave in to pressure from Rome. Anti-Semitism was now officially validated, and laws were enforced to limit drastically the appointment of Jewish individuals to university positions. Because of this policy, Freud's promotion was rejected by the Ministry of Education. It was at this point that Freud dreamed of being Hannibal and conquering Rome. In September 1897 Freud joined the B'nai B'rith, a Jewish fraternal organization, and until 1902 when he established his own Wednesday night circle of professionals,* Freud presented many of his early works before this audience. Until 1904 Freud essentially did not present papers before professional societies, and he discontinued his teaching at the university until 1903. Evidence thus shows that Freud courageously persisted in his views concerning the importance of childhood sexuality as the cause of neurosis despite anti-Semitism and the rigid Victorian sexual mores that existed at the time.

FREUD'S REJECTION OF ENVIRONMENTAL FOR INTRAPSYCHIC PROCESSES

Freud renamed the seduction theory his "old trauma theory," which indeed it was for him personally. Because of the personal and social problems that Freud experienced, he did not publicly reveal his abandonment of the seduction theory for about eight years, until the publication of his "Three Essays on the Theory of Sexuality" in 1905. A profound reversal in Freud's theoretical position had occurred. The emphasis was now on fantasy rather than external reality and on inborn instinctual drives rather than environmental seduction by others. Unconscious fantasy was now considered to be as potent as an actual traumatic event in the genesis of neurosis. It was the child's sexual instincts that caused distortions in the perception of external reality and produced these unconscious fantasies. The origin of these fantasies was now considered to be infantile sexuality, a theory that challenged Victorian mores even more than the seduc-

---

* The original Wednesday night circle consisted of Adler, Kahane, Reitler, and Stekel, to be joined shortly by Federn, Rank, Ferenczi, and Sachs, increasing to 22 members by 1908.

tion theory. In December 1896 Freud had posited the existence of erogenous zones that gave rise to autoerotic sexual instincts that sought discharge. This conceptualization of infantile sexuality also remained Freud's primary theory of child development throughout his life. It was not until Melanie Klein brought the focus back to the infant's relation to the mother (in particular her breast) and the child's need for nurturance and environmental mastery ("the epistemophilic instinct") that change occurred in the psychoanalytic theory of child development.

One of the problems in the therapeutic application of Freud's new theoretical formulation soon became apparent in the case of Dora. Dora was treated by Freud in 1899 after he had abandoned his seduction theory; the case was written up in about 1900* but not published for five years. In his treatment of Dora, Freud (1905a) insisted that she focus on her own instinctual drives and fantasies and not on the actual external events that occurred in her family. Freud's treatment goal was in direct opposition to the wishes of Dora, who insisted on validation of her perception that she had been deceived and exploited by the adults around her. Dora precipitously dropped out of treatment with Freud but returned later. In the meantime, she had confronted her family about their secrecy and deception and forced an admission from them that confirmed her own perception of reality. (Such a technique of renegotiating an actual familial relationship is currently employed by Bowenian family therapists). Dora was then ready for treatment, armed with the truth of her perception. Freud, however, interpreted Dora's confrontation of her parents as a vengeful piece of acting out (Jones 1955) and was not supportive of this action. On reexamining the case, Erikson (1964) found Dora's behavior to be not only adaptive but essential for her identity formation. It was important that Dora not experience what had actually happened to her as simply a product of her own fantastic distortion of reality, which is what her parents and father's mistress

---

* The Standard Edition states that Freud gave the wrong year for his treatment of Dora three times in his writings, (i.e., 1900 instead of 1899) and that Dora's later visit was in 1902.

had encouraged her to believe. Inadvertently, Freud supported this denial of reality by focusing on Dora's unconscious fantasies. Dora had indeed suffered environmental abuse, betrayal, and exploitation. She needed to share her perception of this truth in outside reality with Freud in order to arrive at a condition of "mutual trustworthiness" and honesty. Only then could she develop a therapeutic transference. Unfortunately, Freud, by ignoring external reality (because of his disillusionment with the seduction theory), prevented this development of a therapeutic alliance. Had it occurred, Dora subsequently could have felt safe enough to explore her own sexual strivings. In Chapter 8 the case of Dora will be reviewed further.

FREUD'S DEVELOPMENT OF THE
MECHANISTIC LIBIDO THEORY

Freud had been strongly influenced by his medical school teacher and mentor, Ernst Brücke. Freud worked in Brücke's physiology laboratory for six years and subsequently obtained his fellowship with Charcot in Paris in 1886 through the direct efforts of Brücke. Brücke, along with Hermann von Helmholtz, was a member of the circle of progressive scientists who believed in the necessity of applying the principles of physics and chemistry to the understanding of human beings. Brücke served as an idealized father figure for Freud and is acknowledged by Freud as having had the most influence on his intellectual development. In keeping with this intellectual heritage, Freud (1905) evolved his libido theory of instinctual drives to explain neuroses. This theory relied on 19th-century theories of Newtonian physics and called upon the principle of conservation of energy. Human personality was viewed by Freud as a closed system with a fixed amount of libidinal energy as the fuel for the human machine. The first law of thermodynamics, that the total amount of energy in its various forms remains the same, found expression in Freud's principle of constancy. Intracerebral excitation had to be maintained at a constant level, therefore, it was necessary to liberate excess energy through sensory, motor, or ideational activity. Freud believed that if the excess energy could not be discharged, as occurred in "hypnoid" states (dreamy, vacant states of mind) or as a result of conflict, the energy or affect was cut off from the idea and could be diverted into other channels. It could then find expression in somatic symptoms. The psychic structure of the individual, considered to be closed relatively early in childhood, contained an inherently fixed amount of energy, which was then transformed and shifted. The sexual energy was either "bound" (fixed) or "free" and distributed. Freud devised the term *cathexis* to describe the investment of sexual energy at particular points in the system. Besides these pseudophysical constructs, Freud employed others, such as neutralization, desexualization, fusion, and diffusion. According to this linear, deterministic, and mechanistic framework, if one area of the personality became enriched with libidinous energy another became impoverished.

Kardiner, Karush, and Ovesey (1959) criticized the mentalistic constructs of Freud's libido theory and suggested it be abandoned in favor of an adaptational framework. They considered its assumptions to be derived from fictitious concepts unrelated to clinical data; it was a return to pre-Galilean science, to deductive reasoning, to a theory that could not be scientifically validated. Klein and Tribich (1982) have presented the compelling hypothesis that Freud developed the libido theory precisely because it could never be disproved by clinical data. Proof was built into the theory a priori; all behavior could be traced back to libidinal development. For Freud this inherent validity served as a defense against being proved wrong and traumatized again as he had been with the seduction theory. Freud turned away from exploration of family dynamics in the remainder of his writings. Even though he recognized and mentioned the severe pathology and traumatic interaction with parents in his case studies of Dora, Little Hans, the Rat Man, Schreber, and the Wolf Man,*

---

* See *The Schreber Case* by William G. Niederland (1974) for a detailed description of Schreber's father, who advocated rigid child-rearing practices including the use of torture-like apparatuses into which children were strapped at night to ensure proper posture and prevent "bad" habits. These were used on Schreber as a child by his father. The Rat Man also was terrified by a sadistic and brutal father. The Wolf Man's father, sister, and grandmother all committed suicide, and his masochistic mother stimulated identification with the sufferings of Christ.

Freud gave these no etiological significance. He focused only on the child's inborn instinctual behavior and fantasies that distorted reality. It is interesting that Freud's original seduction theory was never abandoned by Sandor Ferenczi. Although Ferenczi had a close personal relationship with Freud, in some respects similar to Freud's with Fliess, Ferenczi sacrificed the friendship because of this theoretical difference. Ferenczi (1920) continued to explore the impact of actual pathological actions of the parent on the child's development, though not limiting these to seduction. His "active" psychoanalytic technique evolved as an effort to undo the parental neglect and trauma he considered pathogenic for the patient, and thus to permit continued growth and development.

Despite Freud's earlier neglect of environmental factors, his genius was to blossom again; in the last phases of his life, he demonstrated a remarkable degree of openness and creativity. At the age of 64, Freud (1920) formulated a new and revolutionary theory concerning mental functioning in "Beyond the Pleasure Principle." In this book Freud deemphasized the primary importance of the libido theory and combined it with his earlier traumatic view of the pathogenesis of neurosis as espoused in his seduction theory. At the very end of this book, Freud presents his credo, as well as what might be considered an apology. He states:

> We must be ready, too, to abandon a path that we have followed for a time, if it seems to be leading to no good end. Only believers, who demand that science shall be a substitute for the catechism they have given up, will blame an investigator for developing or even transforming his views. We may take comfort, too, for the slow advances of our scientific knowledge in the words of the poet: What we cannot reach flying, we must reach limping. The book tells us it is no sin to limp. (p. 66)

It seems that even though Freud's new theory was couched in the language of instincts and remained within an intrapsychic sphere, he had revised his psychoanalytic theory from a linear, mechanistic, stimulus–response model to one more in line with modern epistemology, which would evolve 25 years later.

In his earlier works, Freud had emphasized the role of the id and proposed that the pleasure principle was the primary motivation for behavior. The mind attempted to reduce excessive excitation from a stimulus that created unpleasurable tension, so as to return to a constant internal state. During the child's development, the pleasure principle was replaced by the reality principle, because of the ego's instinct for self-preservation. The conflict between these two forces was seen by Freud as operating in neurosis.

In "Beyond the Pleasure Principle" and his subsequent writings, Freud radically changed psychoanalysis from an id psychology to an ego psychology. Freud postulated the existence of a protective shield in the ego that served as a first line of defense against excessive excitation. In traumatic neurosis this shield was breached by the overwhelming intensity of the stimuli. The second line of defense against such excessive and overwhelming stimuli was unpleasurable dreams, which attempted to master the stimuli retrospectively. Thus, dreams were not simply wish fulfillments of id impulses under the sway of the pleasure principle but, rather, representations of work by the ego for mastery.

Freud noted that patients also attempted to achieve mastery through an unconscious compulsion to repeat traumatic events, as in neurosis and children's play. During psychoanalytic treatment this repetition compulsion was manifested in the transference and served as a resistance to change. Traumatic events from childhood were repressed and acted out without conscious awareness of them. This mechanism served only to reinforce psychopathology. If a trauma was not remembered, the patient was doomed to repeat it. Only by a loosening of the repression and a remembering of the unconscious material, along with the associated feared unpleasurable consequences, could change occur.

Although the idea of the repetition compulsion had been mentioned by Freud before "Beyond the Pleasure Principle," he now suggested that its origin lay in the death instinct, which he termed *Thanatos*. This was an instinct in the ego that was regressive, restrictive, and repressive. It represented a "conservative" force, tending toward stability, inertia, and death. Paradoxically, Freud even viewed the instincts of self-preservation, self-assertion, and mastery in the ego as component instincts of Thanatos. Their function, according to Freud, was to ensure that the organism followed its own predetermined pathway to death. In opposition to this catabolic instinct was an anabolic instinct that Freud termed the life instinct, or *Eros*. This was a sexual instinct that pressed for prolongation of life, progress, new forms, and change. Thus, Freud postulated that there existed a dialectic between the life and death instincts, between Eros and Thanatos.

Considerable controversy has existed within the psychoanalytic movement concerning the validity of these life and death instincts. Although Freud's views antedate the development of general systems theory and cybernetics by 25 years, his new theory bears striking similarities to them. Freud's new theory, like modern epistemology, concerns homeostatic equilibrium. This equilibrium involves the maintenance of a dynamic steady state with an optimal level of functioning and simultaneously allows for growth and adaptation through two mechanisms. Freud's life instinct, Eros, which brings about growth and development can be equated with positive feedback, which is deviation amplifying. The death instinct, Thanatos, which serves as a stabilizing and adaptive force, can be equated with negative feedback, which is deviation correcting. The next chapter and later portions of this book will amplify the role of negative feedback, which Freud equated with the death instinct and the repetition compulsion, in the perpetuation of psychopathology. Three additional steps are required to effect this transition from Freud's life-death instincts to modern epistemology: (1) a purely biological and instinctual perspective must be abandoned; (2) one cannot restrict oneself, as Freud did, to a purely intrapsychic level of functioning; and (3) interpersonal relations, particularly the responses to others, must be viewed as the feedback loops that perpetuate intrapsychic functioning.

Neurotic patients project intrapsychic conflict onto others, who are perceived and responded to accordingly. Thus, the transferential reaction of the patient serves as a negative feedback loop to reinforce intrapsychic functioning. With preneurotic patients, who use more primitive defenses, internalized aspects of the self or object are placed into another person through splitting and projective identification. The other is then unconsciously induced into feeling, thinking, or behaving in accord with the patient's internalized world of objects. Thus, if the patient is successful in manipulating the external world, it will be perceived as paralleling and reinforcing the intrapsychic world. This pattern serves as a negative feedback loop to prevent change. Change is always difficult, because it produces a degree of identity crisis and instability. For the preneurotic individual, with an unstable core of identity to begin with, change is experienced as a profound threat to survival. Only if this negative feedback cycle is disrupted through an intervention which introduces information into the system and also provides the patient with the necessary security of a positive emotional relationship with the therapist, can the patient risk and accomplish change. Freud was aware of these phenomena that produce change, and his later contributions in ego psychology can be viewed as a predecessor of modern epistemology.

DON JACKSON AND NEO-FREUDIAN PSYCHOANALYSIS

Until about 30 years ago, the mainstream of American psychiatry looked primarily within the patient to understand psychopathology. This approach was readily understandable, because psychiatry had grown out of the medical model, which concentrated on diagnosing and treating illness within the individual. Viewed from a broader perspective, the medical model itself grew out of the philosophy of the Enlightenment that emphasized individualism and rationality. This perspective was reinforced by the natural sciences, which concentrated on the search for presumably "objective" entities and structures. With the development of social psychiatry, family and group therapy, and transcultural studies, this outlook has begun to be replaced by an interactive, interdependent systems model that searches for processes and relationships with multiple determinants in order to understand the development of psychopathology.

Although Freud was the first to note the importance of familial dynamics in the development of pathology and did explore the role of culture in his later writings, it rested with neo-Freudian psychoanalysts to study and elaborate how familial, social, and cultural environmental factors influenced normal and pathological personality development. Adler (1917) stressed the competitive nature of society and the evolution of the individual's personality out of relationships with others. Jung (1927) wrote about the importance of folklore, myths, and social patterns in culture that influence personality development. Horney (1937) noted how cultural forces can corrupt and bury the spontaneous real self of the individual. Kardiner (1939) emphasized the reciprocal interaction of culture and personality, the ways in which each reinforces and perpetuates the other. He noted that the techniques of child rearing in a given culture tend to produce similar personality constellations. Sullivan (1953) abandoned the linear, mechanistic libido theory and viewed the personality as developing out of interpersonal relations with parents, peers, and the culture. The self was a reflection of interpersonal relations. The self was not a static entity but a process, which Sullivan termed the self-system. Sullivan even defined mental health as the awareness of one's interpersonal relations. Thus, psychiatric pathology was viewed less as a static, structural entity isolated within the patient and more as a product of the interaction of the individual with the family, group, society, and culture. Some of the theoretical underpinnings of this perspective can be found in general systems theory, cybernetics, communications theory, game theory, field theories, and the behavioral sciences in general.

JACKSON'S REJECTION OF INTRAPSYCHIC FORCES FOR RELATIONSHIPS

Don Jackson was probably the most influential thinker in the growth of family therapy, introducing modern epistemology to provide much of the theoretical basis in this field. His work represents the opposite end of the spectrum from classical psychoanalysis and is even a radical departure from neo-Freudian thinking. Jackson abandoned the exploration of the development of the individual as a self and totally rejected the medical model of illness. Pathology was viewed as residing only in the relationship; it did not even exist within the individual. To Jackson, emotional dysfunction was primarily the outcome of the family interaction. He totally rejected the intrapsychic concepts of psychoanalysis, especially the role of instincts and fantasy, and focused solely on the actual, observable family interaction. The part played by the patient in the interaction was also ignored.* It was as if the patient were a black box or victim of pathogenic family interaction. His theoretical foundation was thus a radical departure from both psychiatry and psychoanalysis. From this theoretical vantage point, Jackson (1957) concluded that if the therapist simply changed the pathogenic relationship patterns in the family, the patient's behavior and symptomatology would change. As a consequence, Jackson's interactional therapy revolved around developing strategic interventions to change these ongoing relationship patterns in the family. The patient was simply the individual in the family who demonstrated the manifest symptomatology, whom he labelled the identified patient. Jackson considered all the family members as patients. This, then, represented the rationale for treating the entire family as the patient. Jackson coined the term *conjoint family therapy* to describe the process in which all the family members are treated together at the same time.

Jackson's approach to studying pathological phenomena was also at the opposite end of the spectrum from Freud's. Instead of using deductive reasoning, as Freud did in the libido theory, he attempted to reason inductively only from observed and quantifiable data. Jackson believed it essential to minimize the level of inferences he made and to rely only on empiricism. This approach was an extension of the empirical stance taken earlier by Harry Stack Sullivan. Jackson therefore developed research of families that studied manifest communication and behavior, which he termed interactional exchanges. Unfortunately, the result was a vast collection of quantified data that stemmed from direct observation but that could not be brought together under a general hypothesis to provide some meaning and order. The observed behavior patterns could not be organized to de-

---

* Even current psychoanalytic theory views the internalization of the parent in the child's superego as a reflection of the actual parental characteristics as well as distortions resulting from the child's projected fantasies onto the parent.

velop a family typology, as he had hoped. Jackson had employed reductionism to such an extreme extent that he became hopelessly trapped by meaningless particularism.

ANTIPATHY FOR PSYCHOANALYSIS

How did this departure from psychoanalytic concepts occur? Even with personal knowledge of Jackson, and some familiarity with his background, only certain inferences are possible. He had a searching mind and was gifted with unusual creativity. He was also a rather sensitive and private individual. Jackson took his psychiatric residency from 1947 to 1949 at Chestnut Lodge in Maryland, where he was exposed to the psychoanalytic teachings of Frieda Fromm-Reichmann. It is clear that at that time he was influenced by the interpersonal theories and approach of Harry Stack Sullivan. From 1947 until 1951 he was a candidate at the Washington-Baltimore Psychoanalytic Institute. In 1951 he returned to Palo Alto, California, where he became chief of the psychiatric department of the Palo Alto Medical Clinic. He continued his psychoanalytic training as a candidate at the San Francisco Psychoanalytic Institute, which was known for its conservative position among classical institutes. In 1954, however, Jackson discontinued his candidacy, after having completed seven years of psychoanalytic training. There undoubtedly were strong feelings involved in this move, because none of his subsequent work contains theoretical constructs derived from psychoanalysis. Indeed, there was a deliberate effort to avoid psychoanalytic theory and therapy altogether. Jackson focused on immediate, here-and-now behavior, made no genetic reconstructions, did not consider intrapsychic conflict as significant, and did not look for transference phenomena or make interpretations. Insight was not considered by him as a curative factor, as it is in classical psychoanalysis.* Thus with Jackson's rejection of his own psychoanalytic train-

---

* His colleague Virginia Satir (1964), however, did use insight and relied on concepts derived from psychoanalytic ego psychology.

ing came a rejection of psychoanalytic constructs. Because Jackson and some of his close collaborators were critical of psychoanalytic theory, a polarization of attitudes occurred in the family therapy movement. *

It is likely that Jackson's association with Gregory Bateson strongly contributed to Jackson's move away from psychoanalysis. Bateson was a brilliant cultural anthropologist and philosopher who was on the faculty of Stanford University and also taught at the University of California Medical School. His theoretical orientation derived from Von Bertalanffy's general systems theory (1968) and Whitehead and Russell's theory of logical types (1910). The latter theory dealt with hierarchies of classifications and paradoxes. In 1954 Bateson invited Jackson to join him (and his associates Jay Haley and John Weakland) in his research project on communication patterns in families with a schizophrenic member. The double-bind theory of schizophrenia advanced by Bateson, Jackson, Haley, and Weakland (1956) grew out of this project. In the double bind the patient is exposed to two negative messages, communicated simultaneously but at different levels (verbal and nonverbal), that are mutually contradictory. The patient is threatened with punishment by the parent for not complying with both of these contradictory messages, creating a paradox. Furthermore, the patient is prevented from leaving the field or commenting (metacommunicating) on this no-win dilemma. In many respects this theory resembles that of Fromm-Reichman (1948) concerning the "schizophrenogenic" mother. In the former the child is

---

* For example, Watzlawick, Beavin, and Jackson (1967) saw psychoanalysis as discontinuous with systems theory because energy concepts, rather than information, are used as a unit of exchange. Here all of psychoanalysis is erroneously subsumed under the libido theory, which used energic concepts. Except for some classical analysts, who still adhere to the libido theory, most of psychoanalysis has moved beyond this conceptualization to relationships and issues of adaptation. The intrapsychic level is not a closed system, as Watzlawick and colleagues claim, but interacts with and determines the interactional level, as will be demonstrated later in this book.

also a victim, not of a rejecting mother but of a double-binding mother.

Jackson was also influenced by the work of Norbert Wiener (1954) in cybernetics. Wiener focused on communication and control, positing that behavior is governed by feedback. Messages that are communicated change the behavior of the recipient; information determines an individual's adjustment. In 1957 Jackson published his paper on family homeostasis, which viewed the family as a rule-governed system that maintained a balance or constancy of internal interactional processes. The family resisted any change in this ongoing relationship system, which was achieved by an error-activated negative feedback system. Family members monitored one another's behavior to correct deviation from the family rules.* Jackson compared this process to a furnace thermostat that maintains a constant temperature. The theory of family homeostasis was a particular example from general systems theory of morphostasis. Jackson postulated that in dysfunctional families, to sustain this homeostatic balance of relationships, one member would be induced to play the role of the identified patient. Only the identified patient manifestly presented symptoms. The identified patient contained the pathology of the system and preserved the personality integrity of the others in the family. Other family members bought their mental health at the expense of illness in the patient.

---

* Some of the actual nonverbal (kinesic) physical cues used to prevent deviation from rules in families were studied by Al Scheflen (1963). Scheflen carefully undertook microanalysis of films of families and noted specific nonverbal methods employed to control deviant behavior. He postulated that kinesic regulation of interpersonal relationships occurs by mutual, often simultaneous and complementary, bodily signals which are out of the conscious awareness of the participants. Standard configurations, which are culturally specific, include quasi-courtship behavior (grooming), similarities of postural positions (parallelism), leg blocking, and gaze holding and aversion. These serve to regulate the intimacy, direction, and speed of the interaction. Scheflen used the term *monitoring* to indicate signals that warn participants of deviation from the group rules of behavior. For example, disapproval can be indicated by nose wiping or brush-off movements with the hand. Scheflen was able to identify dominance patterns, coalitions, degrees of alienation, limitations on closeness, support, and symbiotic relationships.

PROBLEMS IN USING GENERAL SYSTEMS THEORY AND CYBERNETICS

In accordance with cybernetics, Jackson saw individual personalities and behavior as governed and sustained by feedback. In family treatment, therefore, Jackson designed specific techniques to produce either deviation-correcting (morphostatic) or deviation-amplifying (morphogenetic) feedback. In devising these techniques, however, Jackson fell into a linear and dualistic distortion of the use of cybernetics. He viewed the observer as outside the system and considered the observer thus able to manipulate and control the system.* According to cybernetics and other modern epistemologies, the observer is part of the system and is affected by its part-whole constraints.

Jackson can also be criticized as using a simple linear determinism in viewing the individual as merely a product or victim of family relationships. This viewpoint was part of both the double-bind and his homeostatic theory. Insufficient attention was paid to the patient's role in the interaction. Later, Bateson and his colleagues (1962) corrected the erroneous linear causality concept of the double-bind theory, replacing it with one of mutual causality. The patient was an accessory in the process, not simply the bound victim or passive recipient. The family homeostasis concept however was never modified. Jackson also did not explore the intrapsychic system within the individual, nor did he establish the relationship of the family system as a whole to the culture and society. He did not employ general systems theory to look for isomorphisms and relationships among the various levels of the system but, rather, restricted himself primarily to the interactional level. This single level of the system was viewed as if it were a separate, closed system. Indeed, certain of Jackson's colleagues set up an either-or dichotomy between psychoanalysis

---

* Jay Haley, Jackson's collaborator, comments on Gregory Bateson's reactions to their interventionist form of therapy in an interview reported in the *Family Therapy Newsletter* in 1982. Haley came under the influence of Milton Erickson's directive style of therapy, which viewed therapy as a power struggle between the therapist and the patient for control. Bateson strongly opposed this type of therapy, especially if it sought legitimacy in modern epistemology. Bateson (1979) had clearly stated earlier that issues of power and control arose from a linear, Newtonian epistemology and not from cybernetics.

and family interactional processes. Instead of searching for bridging concepts, looking for relevance or isomorphisms among various levels of the system, and trying to determine how these levels might be coupled, they simply dismissed psychoanalysis as old fashioned. Psychoanalysis became totally identified with only one aspect, the libido theory, and was totally rejected as being linear and mechanistic.

Ironically, this is the very charge that can also be leveled at Jackson's form of treatment and his theory of homeostasis. Bateson (1972) stated that considering family homeostasis to be the cause of the patient's illness was dualistic and epistemologically incorrect. Indeed, Bateson later lamented the misuse of modern epistemology generally in the behavioral sciences (1979). The laws of physics, he believed, could not simply be imposed on living systems. In physics the second law of thermodynamics applies: All structures run down into disorder (entropy). In a closed mechanical system, because work is not performed with 100 percent efficiency, the amount of available energy diminishes. In the living world the opposite is true: Structures tend to build up and fit together or couple to become more orderly (negentropy). Living systems are open, so energy, in the form of information, can enter, leading to greater organization of the system. Dell (1982), amplifying Bateson's thoughts, considers the entire concept of family homeostasis to be unnecessary because living systems tend to create internal consistency. The interactional system simply results from the structural coupling that arises from the individual's fit into the system. Thus, Dell states, family rules or homeostatic mechanisms to force the system to hold together and to prevent change are not needed at all. This statement is not necessarily valid for all families, and especially dysfunctional families. The latter operate more like a closed system, barring the entry of information, so that greater organization cannot naturally occur.

Thus, based on insufficient and biased information, psychoanalysis, the major conceptual system for understanding behavior was negated by Don Jackson. Just as classical psychoanalysis may be faulted for its excessive concentration on intrapsychic processes, Jackson's family theory, as well as his therapy, can be criticized for ignoring the individual as well as the family's relationship to the society and culture. People are seen simply as black boxes, manipulated by communication and behavioral interaction between people. Child development is totally ignored, and intrapsychic processes are treated as nonexistent; defenses and conflict have no place in this brave new world.

The work of John Spiegel (1971) has been extremely helpful in developing bridging concepts between the family and the society and culture. The philosophical basis of Spiegel's overall framework is the field theory of Dewey and Bentley. As a bridge between culture and the family, Spiegel utilizes Florence Kluckhohn's ideas of cultural value orientation. As a bridge between society and the family, he uses George Meade's role theory. Each family is seen as a collection of individuals involved in small group dynamics, taking part in the social system, and transmitting cultural orientations and traditional belief systems to one another. Spiegel has used this approach not only in studying dysfunctional families, but also in examining the cultural value orientations and conflicts of various ethnic groups and in investigating role complementarity, conflict, and resolution. In the following chapters object relations theory will be used as a bridging concept between the individual and the family. It is hoped that this approach will provide a deeper understanding of the fit of the individual in the system and of the ways in which interpersonal relations can induce pathology in one member of the family.

3

OBJECT RELATIONS THEORY
AS THE BRIDGE

GENERAL SYSTEMS THEORY AND
OBJECT RELATIONS THEORY

In the previous chapter, problems in the theoretical underpinnings of both psychoanalysis and family therapy were discussed. Sigmund Freud, who had been influenced by his research in Brücke's laboratory in physiology, believed it essential that psychology be firmly rooted in science. The science and epistemology of his times, however, and that which he employed, were derived from Newtonian physics. With newer scientific knowledge, Freud's emphasis on the libido as the source of motivational energy has been criticized, and the libido theory is no longer universally accepted in psychoanalytic circles. Don Jackson's work, in contrast, was based on cybernetics and general systems theory, modern epistemologies stemming from newer findings in atomic physics. Jackson's theory of homeostasis, however, can be viewed as having some of the same flaws as Freud's libido theory. Although Jackson uses circular feedback loops, which Freud did not, both theories are mechanistic, both are closed systems, both employ the stance of the detached, objective observer, and both use simple linear causality.

The theoretical system that will be presented here is, I believe, more consistent with the work of Gregory Bateson. It is a theory and therapy based on general systems theory, in which the individual, the inter-personal, and family-as-a-whole levels are viewed as interactive and interdependent. Object relations theory will be used as a bridging concept between the individual system and the family system. It will serve to indicate the fit of the individual into the system and the effect of the individual on the system. Similarly, the therapist treating the family will not be viewed as a detached observer; instead, the dynamic interaction of the therapist with the family will be explored. The same interdependent interaction has already been developed in psychoanalysis by Robert Langs (1976a), who looks at the "bipersonal field" in therapy. This consists of the interaction between the patient and the therapist, between transference and countertransference. Thus, the constraints and effects of each system on the other are taken into account, in accordance with modern epistemologies. It is first essential to review newer developments in psychoanalysis and to discuss child development, usually deemphasized and at times misunderstood in family therapy.

MOVEMENT AWAY FROM AN INTRAPSYCHIC FOCUS IN PSYCHOANALYSIS

Although Freud never abandoned his libidinal drive theory, in his later works he did change psychoanalysis from an id psychology to an ego psychology. In "Beyond the Pleasure Principle" (1920), the concept of the repetition compulsion was developed. This was a state of organization in the personality that needed to re-create past emotional trauma in the current environment in order for the ego to achieve mastery over instinctual drives. The concept represented a shift away from simple tracking of libidinal energy within the person and toward a focus on the adaptation of the individual with the environment. It was the beginning of Freud's development of an open system in psychoanalysis. In his structural model, Freud (1923) divided the personality into ego, superego, and id. This division recognized not only internal libidinal forces, but also actual environmental demands. The ego mediated these two pressures and established defenses to facilitate adaptation. In addition, the new theory of anxiety formulated by Freud (1926) viewed anxiety as developing in response to threats to the ego. Anxiety was not simply the result of repressed emotions pressing up from the unconscious, as Freud had previously held. Anna Freud (1936) extended her father's work in ego psychology and considered the ego to be an ally in the treatment process. The patient and the therapist formed a therapeutic alliance and joined in analyzing the patient's defenses and transferences. Hartmann, Kris, and Lowenstein (1951) later postulated a "conflict-free sphere" of the ego, in which cognitive controls determined what was perceived and expected, leading to constancy and reliability of behavior. Hartmann (1939) delineated the concept of the self as a separate structure in the ego that contained self-representations and object representations of others from the external world. He postulated that a model of external reality became internalized, functioning like a cognitive map, which he termed the "inner world." Throughout the work of Freud and the other ego psychologists, however, only one perspective is elaborated. The theoretical emphasis remains intrapsychic, focusing on the ego's own autoplastic responses in order to adapt to the environment. The ego modifies itself in response to the external world through defenses and distortions. Ego psychology does not truly develop an interactional framework that deals with the interdependence of intrapsychic and interpersonal forces.

Object relations theory comes closest to being an open system. In this book, it will be modified to be a nonlinear, circular, interactional theory. The term *object relations* is an unfortunate choice, because the word *object* has mechanized and dehumanized connotations. It is a remnant of Freud's libido theory that has continued to be used, albeit with a meaning considerably different from the original. Freud coined the term in an effort to make psychoanalysis scientific and precise, using a physical system instead of a living system. As Freud used the term, an object was the aim of an instinctual drive and could be a person, an idea, or anything inanimate that was cathected or valued. Ironically, Freud's earlier seduction theory, which was truly an interpersonal theory, forms the basis of current object relations theory.

FERENCZI ON FAMILY INTERACTION IN THE GENESIS AND TREATMENT OF DISORDERS

Sandor Ferenczi continued to use the seduction theory in his work with patients, examining the traumatic effects of parental neglect on children. Ferenczi concentrated on the emotional conflicts of early childhood that had resulted in patients' unfulfilled dependency cravings. In the sicker patients whom Ferenczi treated, developmental arrest had occurred because of actual traumatic events in the patient's childhood. This state stood in contradistinction to the intrapsychic conflicts in neurosis noted by Freud. In treatment Ferenczi encouraged the patient's regression, thereby reliving, and restituting for, this early deprivation. In this "active" approach, Ferenczi (1920) believed, the therapist needed to be emotionally available, warm, and responsive, even touching and caressing the patient. Such an approach was at variance with Freud's, which permitted no physical contact with patients and advocated an abstinent emotional stance by the therapist. The therapist was not to gratify or even be judgmental of the patient's impulses. Freud was concerned that in Ferenczi's active approach the therapist might become emotionally overinvolved, act out, and exploit the patient for the therapist's own emotional or sexual needs.*

Whereas Freud avoided dealing with countertransferential feelings and emotional interaction with the patient, Ferenczi believed that with sicker patients there were always countertransferential feelings that could not and should not be avoided. The analyst needed to be aware of and deal with these feelings. Emotional interaction between the patient and the analyst did occur and had to be worked with in a controlled fashion in treatment. Therapy thus became a dyadic system, rather than one in which the therapist was a detached, objective observer. Ferenczi was also the first to report that patients projected their internal fantasies onto the analyst and others in an attempt to use these persons to fulfill their needs. Such reports were the forerunner of the concept of projective identification. Ferenczi is generally considered to be the father of object relations

---

* This abstinent therapeutic framework of Freud's stemmed from Breuer's experience in the case of Anna O. Although Freud himself never treated Anna O., he was keenly aware of Breuer's difficulty in handling his own emotional responses to this patient. Breuer felt forced to discontinue treatment with Anna O. abruptly, because of the sexual atmosphere that developed, and this resulted in a negative therapeutic outcome for the patient. The current emphasis on the therapist's empathic connection and its role in providing needed narcissistic supplies to restore the self has become important in Kohut's theory of the treatment of narcissistic patients (1977).

theory, even though Karl Abraham also stressed the interaction with objects in his conception of the developmental stages of early childhood.

MELANIE KLEIN ON EARLY MOTHER-CHILD INTERACTION AND FANTASY

It was Melanie Klein, who was analyzed by Ferenczi and Abraham, who brought together these insights into a systematic theory. Klein (1948) focused on the earliest years of life in studying her adult and child patients, and she contributed greatly to our awareness of the interaction of the infant and the mother. Whereas Freud saw the infant as primarily concerned with trying to master its own internal id drives, Klein viewed the infant as object oriented from birth. Through the interplay of projection and introjection, the infant attempts to relate to the mother, who is seen as good and bad, as a part and, later, as a whole object. Object relations theory encompasses many schools of psychoanalysis, yet its basic foundation is Klein's work, particularly the subjective dialogue between the self and projected or introjected objects.

Klein's major contribution to the understanding of infantile development is the role played by fantasy. Fantasy, not instinctual discharge, was seen as the main force for psychic development. Klein even considered instincts to be simply another fantasy in the context of the mother–child dyad. This approach is a complete reversal of Freud's position; whereas he believed that instincts created fantasies, Klein saw fantasies as creating instincts. Fantasy is the method the infant uses to regulate itself and to become attached to objects. The infant employs fantasy to explore its world and to communicate with the mother.* The infant is not a passive receptacle to outside input, nor a being cut off from its environment. Instead, it uses fantasy as the basis for two primitive mental mechanisms, splitting

---

* Jean Piaget (1954, 1963) also explored experimentally the ways in which children use fantasy to relate to others and to perceive reality.

and projective identification. The infant splits its experience of sensorimotor bodily sensations according to the pleasure principle—i.e., into pleasure and displeasure, pain and comfort, and good and bad.

According to Grotstein (1981), splitting is a fundamental defense mechanism, the forerunner of repression, in which

> the ego discerns differences within the self and its objects, or between itself and objects. In the perceptual or cognitive sense, an act of discriminative separation is involved, while in the defensive sense splitting implies an unconscious fantasy by which the ego can split itself off from the perception of an unwanted aspect of itself, or can split an object into two or more objects in order to locate polarized, immiscible qualities separately. (p. 3)

Projective identification is defined by Grotstein (1981) as

> a mental mechanism whereby the self experiences the unconscious fantasy of translocating itself, or aspects of itself, into an object for exploratory or defensive purposes. If projective identification is defensive, the self may believe that through translocation it can rid itself of unwanted, split-off aspects; but it may also have the fantasy that it can enter the object so as to [actively] control it, or disappear into it [passively] in order to evade feelings of helplessness. (p. 123)

Projective identification in essence can be viewed as the infant's attempt to control or return to the mother's body. The mechanism was first described by Melanie Klein (1948) and was seen as occurring during the "paranoid-schizoid" phase of infantile development, during which there is lack of differentiation between the self and objects. In order for the infant to preserve the good mother introject, which is essential for the ego's survival, the aggressive, "bad" parts of the self are split off and disposed of by being projected into another person. Thus, the "bad object," which threatens to destroy the ego from within, is projected out into another person. The infant entertains an omnipotent fantasy of control and taking possession of the object.

The infant masters painful feelings by getting rid of them, removing them from the inside to an outside object, which is experienced as a bad object. The effect of this defensive maneuver is then internalized by the infant. For example, when the infant is hungry, the pain, frustration, and rage are attributed to the object. The mother's breast is fantasied as a bad object, which is then internalized and experienced as a dangerous internal bad breast biting the infant. Thus, the infant egocentrically interprets its world on the basis of the fantasies of splitting and projective identification in response to stimuli from its own sense organs. This mechanism is an example of exploratory projective identification. When the infant regresses to oneness with the mother during sleep, it is an example of projective identification used as a defense. In neither of these uses of projective identification does the infant lose contact with the external object.

During this time the infant feels persecuted by bad objects that cause pain; Klein termed this the paranoid-schizoid position. This phase lasts for the first four months of life and corresponds to Mahler's autistic and symbiotic phases. These formulations of Klein's also correspond to the concrete-operational phase of the sensorimotor period described by Jean Piaget (1954, 1963), during which the infant develops schemata of the environment based on sensory input.

KLEIN ON INFANT DEVELOPMENT

Fantasy creates the first internal world of self and object for the infant. This world is archaic and conflictual, and yet it is through this world that the first attempts are made to understand the self in relation to the outside world. Fantasy thus is the first method used for adaptation, just as myths are employed in primitive cultures. Klein considers the infant during the paranoid-schizoid phase to be part object related—that is, not to see others as whole and separate beings—and to feel magically omnipotent. Klein's next developmental stage is the depressive position, which corresponds to Mahler's stage of separation-individuation. Klein postulates that the infant gives up the fantasy of magical control of the internal and external object and transfers its omnipotence to the mother through projective identification. The mother thus becomes idealized, and the infant seeks to merge with her symbiotically. Thus, the child copes with its helplessness by the magical fantasy of being one with the omnipotent mother. Besides this identification and unification, the infant uses manic defenses and repression during this period and begins to relate to others as whole objects.

It is only recently, with the advent of more scientific, empirical infant observation, that the importance of Klein's theoretical work has been fully appreciated. Although Klein's use of pathological terms, such as *schizoid-paranoid* and *depressive*, in labeling the stages of infant development has been criticized, her work is now proving to be more accurate than Mahler's in its descriptions of the very earliest stages. Mahler (1958, 1975) had postulated an autistic stage for the first four to eight weeks of life. Mahler's concepts are in keeping with Ferenczi's postulation (1913) that the infant continues its fetal condition of oneness with the mother through hallucinatory wish fulfillment and seems to be in an unconditional omnipotent, autistic orbit after birth. (Peterfreund [1978] also criticizes the use of a pathological state—autism—by Mahler.) According to Mahler (Mahler, Pine, and Bergman 1975), during the autistic phase the infant is shut off by a stimulus barrier from the external world and is concerned with reducing inner physiological tension; the infant is in a closed, monadic system that is self-sufficient and unaware of the mother. In contrast, Klein postulated that the infant simultaneously is merged with the mother in a state of oneness and exists as a separate individual from birth onward. The infant is object directed from birth, needing to know and to master its environment in order to adapt. Klein termed this the *epistemophilic instinct*.

SUPPORT FOR KLEINIAN THEORY
FROM DIRECT OBSERVATIONAL RESEARCH

Emde and Robinson (1979), in reviewing 300 observational studies of infants during the first two months of life, found results to contradict the assumption that the infant is passive, cut off, and concerned only about drive reduction. The infant is programmed from birth to attempt to acquire knowledge of its environment and to regulate itself. The infant was found to be active, stimulus seeking, and creative in its efforts to construct its world. These findings of individuation beginning from birth were confirmed by Thomas and Chess (1980) in their extensive review of infant studies. Brazelton and Als (1979) found that the newly born infant will organize itself around a stimulus, such as a human voice. Daniel Stern (1980) also noted, from microanalysis of slow-motion films, that infants have preferences for certain facial expressions and even tonal ranges in speech. Infants as young as 2 weeks were found to be able to discriminate the mother.

At the 1982 Conference on Indicators of Mental Health Disturbances in the First 18 Months of Life, sponsored by the National Center for Clinical Infant Programs, Stanley Greenspan, Alfred Scheuer, and T. Berry Brazelton noted early infantile milestones and the problems associated with them. During the first two months of life, problems in self-regulation (e.g., calming) may occur, to be followed by problems in human attachment. These problems do not simply disappear but, rather, remain and are added to, creating later psychological difficulties. Stanley Greenspan at the Clinical Infant Research Unit of the National Institute of Mental Health, as well as others, is able to diagnose and offer specific treatment intervention for infants found to be at risk. The infant's capacity for self-regulation serves as a foundation for the process of human attachment. Indeed, the foundation for personality development appears to be laid during the first three to four years of life. When the mother's responses are appropriate to the infant's temperament and needs, a positive feedback loop is developed, which then enables the infant to move on to more advanced developmental tasks. If the mother's responses result in the infant's overstimulation or understimulation (for example, if the mother is depressed) or are overly intrusive, the infant may not progress to the next stage of development.

DONALD WINNICOTT ON MOTHER-INFANT INTERACTION

The importance of the mother–infant interaction for normal growth and development had been noted by Piaget (Flavell 1963), Spitz (1945), and Bowlby (1958) in their studies. In psychoanalysis, however, Donald Winnicott (1965), one of the major British object relations theorists, was the first to emphasize the effect of early mother–infant interaction on personality development. Winnicott, although not a Kleinian, had been strongly influenced by Klein's work. He differed in not viewing the death instinct or greed and envy as significant to child development. Whereas Klein focused on intrapsychic mechanisms, Winnicott focused on the interaction of the infant with the mother.

To Winnicott it was the mother's devoted responsive sensitivity to the infant's needs, which he termed "good enough mothering," that was important. The infant is fed when hungry, comforted and soothed when anxious, and so forth. In this way the infant is able to maintain the illusion of omnipotent control over and fusion with the mother. There is no distinction between the self and the mother, between inside and outside, nor between fantasy and reality. This concordance creates sufficient basic trust and security for the infant to internalize the good mother function. The infant then can give up magical control and use what Winnicott termed a "transitional object," onto which the infant transfers its dependent attachment. This object—for example, a blanket or a teddy bear— provides texture and warmth. It serves as a substitute mother, maintaining the fantasy of fusion with mother and defending against separation anxiety by being endowed with soothing and tension-relieving properties. The transitional object is not internalized, however, it remains an external, "not me" possession that can be controlled by manipulation. When it loses its meaning, it is not mourned. The transitional object serves as a root for symbolic functioning, enabling fact and fantasy, inner and outer objects to become differentiated. This capacity leads to reality testing. Winnicott notes that the acceptance of reality is never complete throughout life, and strain persists between inner and outer reality. By using real external objects to help build a creative illusory world, the individual can relieve this strain between the subjective inner world and the constant external world. Winnicott notes that these traditional phenomena occur later in life in play, art, and religion.

Because the mother's adaptation to the infant's need can never be complete, disillusionment occurs, in which the separateness and reality of the object become evident. If the mother's adaptation were too exact, reality would reinforce the infant's magical omnipotent control, resulting in a lack of differentiation of subjective from objective perception (i.e., reality testing). Winnicott further noted that when the infant experiences frustration, the mother is perceived as a bad object and becomes the target of aggression. When she provides a "holding environment" that contains the infant's aggression without retaliation or abandonment, further individuation and separation can occur. In this "good enough environment," the infant experiences the fact that its hatred does not destroy the object; thus, external reality modifies the infant's fantasy. The infant is enabled to relinquish its omnipotence and to learn that the object has a separate existence. The child can then accept the object, as well as the self, as separate and constant. After the child discovers "I am," it can learn "I am responsible," moving out of a narcissistic position to one of concern for others.

If the mother is unresponsive or impinging, this sequence of normal infantile development does not occur. Continuity and survival are threatened, and the result may be that the infant experiences "unthinkable anxieties," such as the dread of the self falling apart or being annihilated. Later such patients still fear being alone. There is a lack of (not a conflict in) the organizing capacity of the ego, resulting in insufficient ego integration and a "false self" that is imitative and compliant. This developmental arrest, according to Winnicott, leads to psychopathology when the appropriate mother–child interaction has not occurred.

Balint's "basic fault" (1968) and the "schizoid split" of Fairbairn (1952, 1954) and Guntrip (1971) are similar formulations, based in the tenet that ego strength depends not on instinctual gratification but on the appropriate responses of the mother. Developmental arrest, not conflict, is emphasized. This position is also in agreement with the theories of Heinz Kohut (1977), who sees a weakened or defective self with insufficient self-cohesion as the core of psychopathology. Such a state results when the self has not been confirmed by the parents, whom Kohut refers to as "selfobjects," causing a lack of self-differentiation from the object during early childhood. Only through satisfaction of the "mirroring" (admiring responses) and "idealizing" needs of the child by the selfobjects (parents) can an authentic and capable self be built. If the self of the child is not appropriately responded to, the child cannot individuate and

separate; it retains its archaic grandiosity and its desire to merge symbiotically with an omnipotent selfobject.

MARGARET MAHLER ON PHASES
OF INFANTILE DEVELOPMENT

Mahler's child developmental stages (Mahler and Furer 1968, Mahler, Pine, and Bergman 1975) bear great similarities to those of the
Kleinian and object relations theorists. Mahler describes the symbiotic phase, from four to six months of age, as characterized by a
lack of differentiation of self and object representations. The infant
deals with its helplessness by experiencing the self as merged with
the mother, possessing a common ego boundary. The infant borrows
confidence and power by feeling part of or at one with the omnipotent mother. The next phase, separation-individuation, lasts until
three years of age and is subdivided into the hatching, practicing,
and rapprochement subphases. Just as during the earlier symbiotic
phase the mother must be responsive to the infant's developmental
needs, the mother in this phase needs to let go and to encourage
the toddler to venture forth to explore its world. As the child ac-
quires motor skills and masters its environment, the mother is still
available as an anchor to reality and as a refueling station to provide comfort and security when needed. If the mother is not responsive to these needs, resolution of the symbiotic phase does not occur and developmental arrest ensues. Mahler defines individuation
as equivalent to the development of intrapsychic autonomy; separation deals with differentiating the self from the object, distancing,
and structuring boundaries between the self and the mother. If these
processes are successful, during the rapprochement subphase the
mother becomes internalized. The child can trust that the mother's
love will continue even in her absence. The child is able to evoke
an image of the mother in its memory that is psychologically available when needed, just as the actual mother previously was present
to supply comfort, nurturance, and love. Object constancy can now
occur, as well as the development of a separate cohesive self that is
relatively autonomous. The child can thus assume the equilibrium-
maintaining functions of the mother within itself, providing sooth-

ing and self-regulation of narcissistic supplies to sustain self-esteem. The child also learns to tolerate ambivalence, so that the defense of splitting is no longer necessary and the child relates to others as whole and separate individuals who are seen as both good and bad.

During the rapprochement subphase, accompanying the loss of omnipotence and the awareness of the helplessness and separateness of the self, there develops concern with displeasure and the loss of the love of the object. Structuralization of the ego occurs, with the internalization of rules, demands, and ideals that serve to develop a superego. The child masters speech and learns to express itself verbally, through symbolic play, and art in order to maintain human contact and to master developmental tasks.

If developmental arrest occurs, so that symbiotic relatedness continues, the individual remains overly sensitive to the regulation of self-esteem by others in the environment. In narcissistic disorders, in which separation and a cohesive self, but not autonomy, have been achieved, others are experienced as need-satisfying objects to maintain self-esteem. These patients feel entitled to make demands and resent any limits that arise out of the other person's separate motivation. Borderline patients, who have neither been able to rely on a transitional object as an auxiliary soother to separate nor to internalize the mother, have not even achieved a cohesive self. Loss of the object not only results in the loss of narcissistic supplies to sustain self-esteem, but also threatens the organization or cohesion of the self. Both these types of patients attempt to maintain control over the external object and extract what is needed to preserve their own self-esteem and psychological survival. Lacking internal tension-relieving mechanisms for sustaining narcissistic equilibrium in their psychic structure, they remain excessively sensitive to environmental selfobjects to relieve tension and modulate their self-esteem.

THE APPLICATION OF A CHILD DEVELOPMENT PERSPECTIVE TO FAMILY THERAPY

In the following chapters we will see how these issues of developmental arrest involve not only the patient but also the parents, who use other family members to regulate and stabilize their own personalities. The parents, also, have not established firm identities, and they maintain identities that are reactive to and sensitive to others' thoughts, feelings, and behavior. In sicker individuals not only self esteem but the very sense of psychological survival of the self is dependent on sustaining these symbiotic relationships. Essentially, the glue that holds the self together and continues to regulate self-esteem is this external relationship, which is termed here the *symbiotic survival pattern.*

Normally, during adolescence there is a disengagement from familial object relations and a redirection of interests to love objects outside the family. To facilitate this shift, the adolescent may again borrow the identity and power of the peer group, much as the symbiotic infant merges with and shares the omnipotent power of the mother. By submerging one's ego identity in that of the group, the strength to emancipate oneself from the family is achieved. Ideally, the adolescent's developmental process will continue to evolve into a strong and independent individual identity. Even though eventually a relatively firm core of self-identity does evolve in the normal adult, self-esteem still is affected by events and selfobjects throughout life: losses or gains in personal relationships, support groups, achievements or failures, and physical wellness or disease. If one has a firm identity and the internal ability to regulate one's narcissism, "the slings and arrows of outrageous fortune" are less devastating and a return to a healthy narcissism is more likely to occur.

CHILD DEVELOPMENT SCHEMATA

All psychoanalytic investigators consider the fixation points for various forms of mental illness to occur during the infantile developmental stages. Melanie Klein places the fixation point for schizophrenia in her paranoid-schizoid position, whereas Mahler puts it in the autistic and symbiotic phases. Affective disorders have a fixation point in the early to middle part of Klein's depressive position or Mahler's separation-individuation phase. The later part of the depressive position, which corresponds to Mahler's rapprochement subphase of separation-individuation, is considered the fixation point for borderline and narcissistic disorders. Neurotic disorders occur after object constancy develops. Figure 1, which is taken from Rinsley (1981) and modified to include the work of Melanie Klein, compares the child development schemata of Freud, Klein, Mahler, Kernberg, and Kohut, and notes the fixation points for various psychiatric disorders. In Kernberg's schema (1975) the self and object are initially fused (S–0) and seen as either all good (G) or all bad (B). Kernberg's second stage involves separation of self and object, with each seen either as all good or all bad. In his third stage, ambivalence has been integrated and the self as well as the object are each seen as both good and bad. Employing retrospective clinical studies, Kernberg (1975) has identified specific phases of developmental arrest during childhood that result in deficiencies of identity and pathology, using the phenomenology of self and object. The third stage is the phase of object constancy and is characteristic of neurotic disorders. In borderline patients self-object differentiation has occurred, but these patients have not integrated their ambivalence or achieved object constancy. They continue to use the primitive defense mechanisms of splitting and projective identification. In summary, the essential psychological tasks of child development are self-object differentiation, internalization of the good-bad mother, integration of ambivalence, development of object constancy, and structuralization of the psyche.

THE INTERACTION OF FANTASY AND REALITY IN PERSONALITY DEVELOPMENT

Whereas Melanie Klein focused on the preoedipal period and found that the infant's fantasy created the internal world of reality, Sigmund Freud concentrated on the oedipal period and noted that the child's fantasy distorted external reality (Table 1). Freud found that unconscious fantasy, shaped by instinctual drives and affects, influences the way the child perceives reality. The external world that becomes introjected by the child thus has been modified by the child's instinctual endowment. After abandoning the seduction theory, Freud noted that fantasy was as powerful as actual reality in the

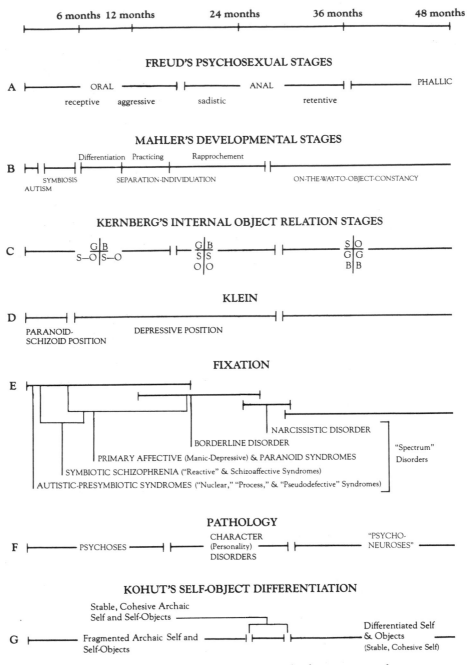

FIGURE 1. Child development schemata, showing the fixation points for various psychiatric disorders. (Adapted from Rinsley [1981, p. 121]. Used by permission.)

TABLE 1. The Effects of Fantasy and Reality on Personality

THEORIST	PERIOD EMPHASIZED	RELATIONSHIP BETWEEN FANTASY AND REALITY
Klein	Preoedipal period	Fantasy creates internal world reality
Freud	Oedipal period	Internal fantasy distorts external reality
Slipp	Childhood	External reality influences internal fantasy
		a. Normally, internal fantasy comes closer to external reality through positive feedback
		b. If external reality in the family parallels the child's internal fantasy, developmental fixation occurs; fantasy is not differentiated from external reality
		c. After developmental fixation, projective identification is employed to attempt to shape external reality to again parallel internal fantasy; if this attempt is successful, external reality is then internalized as a negative feedback loop to perpetuate the fixation

patient's psyche. The goal of his treatment, then, was through id analysis to diminish the patient's fantastic view of reality, to make it less distorted by instinctual drives. Klein accepted this formulation as a developmental stage that followed hers. As the child continues to grow, its internal reality, which is based on fantasy or distorted by fantasy, has an opportunity to be reworked as new information is perceived and processed.

Studies of the adolescent and young adult patient in the context of the family can lead us to another formulation: external reality shapes internal fantasy. External real objects modify and shape the child's internal world of objects through the processes of projection and introjection to approximate reality more closely. In the terms of general systems theory, external reality is seen as a more differentiated organization that is internalized through positive feedback in order to facilitate adaptation. If the actual functioning of the family corresponds to the child's internal world of fantasy, however, fixation occurs, because there is a lack of differentiation between fantasy and reality. For example, if the family itself fears aggression and sees it as destructive, the child's omnipotent fantasy about the destructiveness of its own aggression will be reinforced. It is here that negative feedback loops (deviation-correcting cycles) can be seen as operating to prevent change in the internal world of the child. Similarly, if the family uses the primitive defenses of splitting and projective identification, the child will likely continue to employ them as well. Not only is the fixation initiated by this process, but it is perpetuated by negative feedback in the here and now of the ongoing family interaction. Thus, the family interaction, when it parallels the child's unconscious fantasy, serves as a deviation-correcting, negative feedback loop to sustain the child's primitive internal world of objects. In turn, the child's participation perpetuates the existing form of family interaction. Later, as an adult, the patient will attempt, through the use of projective identification, to shape significant others to parallel their internal fantasy. Thus the process is repeated and this shaped external reality is then internalized, as a negative feedback loop, to perpetuate the fixation.

DIFFERENCES IN THE USE OF CONCEPTS DERIVED FROM THE WORK OF MELANIE KLEIN

Melanie Klein considers Freud's death instinct to be the motivating force for splitting. As mentioned earlier in this book, the death instinct, however, can also be viewed not simply as an intrapsychic mechanism but, rather, as a form of negative feedback that involves interpersonal processes. We can posit in addition that it is not always the bad part of the self or object that is split off and placed into another person. For example, in depression it was noted that it is the good self of the parent that is projected onto the child. The parent then identifies with the child's successes and achieves vicarious gratification. Klein also uses projective identification as a one-person monadic phenomenon, with little recognition of external reality and its impingement on the person. An alternate formulation of projective identification (Slipp 1973b) involves either dyadic or triadic relations. Klein employs projective identification primarily as an intrapsychic phenomenon, but it can also be used in the interpersonal sphere to understand schizophrenia (Slipp 1973b), depression (Slipp 1976), and hysterical-borderline conditions (Slipp 1977) in the context of family relations. Not only do schizophrenic, severely depressed, and hysterical-borderline patients blatantly demonstrate splitting and projective identification, but their families employ these primitive defenses as well.

Bion (1959), noting that patients make efforts to manipulate the therapist, was one of the first to indicate that interpersonal factors exist in projective identification. Bion considered projective identification to be an extremely important factor in inducing countertransferential reactions in the therapist. If the therapist cannot contain the patient's projective identification, he or she may be manipulated into playing out an assigned role by the patient. Many of these ideas have been further elaborated on by Kleinian analysts concerning the use of countertransference in therapy. Recently, Langs (1976a) noted that the therapist as well as the patient participated in this phenomenon. The interchange of transference and countertransference was seen as crucial to treatment which takes place in what Langs terms the "bipersonal field."

It is here considered that for projective identification to occur, the ego boundaries of the patient must be fluid, so that good or bad aspects of the self or the object can be put into another. In addition, pressure is exerted to induce the other to think, feel, or behave in a manner that is congruent with the internalized self or object. (This may be either the self or the object, or may flip back and forth between them.) Such manipulation and control of the object is usually accomplished through nonverbal forms of communication (use of particular voice tones, and bodily and facial gestures). For example, a narcissistic patient may speak in a monotonous, unrelated tone of voice that may bore, put the therapist to sleep, or in general tend to induce the therapist to feel distant or even nonexistent. Finally, a close, continuing relationship between the projector and the object is needed, so that the evoked behavior of the object can be reinternalized through identification. Langs (1976b) has pointed out that the evoked behavior does not simply reflect what has been put in by the projector but, rather, has been metabolized or processed through the personality of the object.

This formulation of projective identification presented here is different from that of Grotstein (1981), who does not differentiate it from pure projection. We can conceptualize pure projection as a state in which firm ego boundaries exist, and in which the other is perceived and experienced only in terms of the inner feelings and images that are transferred. The projector does not feel connected to the object; rather, the other is seen as a separate, distant, even threatening individual. In addition, no significant efforts are made to induce or control the other's behavior, feelings, or thoughts.

We can view the goal of the projector in projective identification as being the manipulation of external reality so that it is congruent with internal fantasy. In essence, the projector does to another what was done to him or her by the family. External reality is made to parallel internal reality. The processed responses of the other are then internalized, providing a negative feedback loop to reinforce the internalized world of object relations. This process is similar to that used in early infancy to create an original internal world through fantasy. The process thus perpetuates an archaic form of symbiotic adaptation to the world and perpetuates the omnipotent fantasy that one can enter the object, manipulate it, and control it. If all members of a family use projective identification, the result is a mutually controlling, intrusive form of interaction that will be termed the *symbiotic survival pattern*. This pattern will be elaborated on more fully in Chapter 6.

Thus, we can conceptualize projective identification to be (1) a primitive intrapsychic form of adaptation and defense based on fantasy and normally used during infancy; (2) an interpersonal defense to sustain the integrity of the family through what we have termed the symbiotic survival pattern; (3) a form of object relations by which one can live through others as part objects; (4) a method of manipulation and control of another, based on omnipotent fantasies; (5) a form of communication, usually nonverbal, to induce responses in another; (6) a method of ridding oneself of certain aspects and inducing pathology in another; (7) the source of the ongoing negative feedback loops that originate and perpetuate developmental fixation in the identified patient; (8) the source of one type of countertransference in therapy, the type Winnicott (1965) has termed objective; (9) a means of modifying internalized objects by external reality and psychotherapy, and (10) part of the brain's wholistic functioning.

4
COUNTERTRANSFERENCE

COUNTERTRANSFERENCE AS RESISTANCE
AND AS A TOOL IN TREATMENT

Probably the most significant contribution of object relations theory to psychotherapy has been the newer understanding and use of countertransference. Freud first mentioned the occurrence of countertransference in "The Future Prospects for Psychoanalytic Therapy" (1910):

> We have become aware of the countertransference, which arises in the physician as a result of the patient's influence on his unconscious feelings... We have noticed that no psychoanalyst goes farther than his own complexes and resistances permit, and we consequently require that he shall begin his practice with a self analysis and continually carry it deeper while he is making his observations on his patients. (p. 144)

In this paper and persistently thereafter, Freud viewed countertransference basically as a resistance in the analyst caused by unresolved past conflicts that limited and interfered with the capacity of the analyst to understand the patient. Countertransference was defined as the *therapist's unconscious transference* to the patient based on the therapist's own unresolved intrapsychic conflicts and unconscious fantasies.

A revolutionary revision in the understanding and use of countertransference subsequently occurred, initiated by members of the British object relations school. Donald W. Winnicott (1949) was the first psychoanalyst to expand the traditional definition of countertransference to include all the reactions of the therapist to the patient. He believed that with more disturbed, non-neurotic patients, countertransference difficulties were often based on so-called objective reactions to the patient, and not simply on subjective intrapsychic conflicts within the therapist. Indeed, these patients seemed compelled to evoke repeatedly certain responses in others, and receiving feedback to these responses represented a maturational need. For example, many sicker patients attempt to gain omnipotent control

59

over the therapist, and through projective identification to re-create their early mother–infant, symbiotic relationship in the treatment dyad. Treatment provides these patients with a unique opportunity to repeat and master their developmental arrest and to grow. Thus, Winnicott radically shifted the focus, viewing countertransference not as a resistance that interfered with progress in treatment but as a source of information for the therapist about the developmental needs of the patient. Countertransference, therefore, could actually facilitate therapeutic progress. The therapist's responses were viewed not as separate and isolated from the patient but, rather, as strongly interactive and as an integral part of the treatment.

Many of the further developments in the understanding and use of countertransference were initiated by Kleinian analysts. Paula Heimann (1950) recommended that the therapist attempt to become aware of these countertransference reactions and then use them as a therapeutic tool. Heimann considered these reactions of the therapist to constitute a method for empathically understanding the patient's unconscious that was superior to one based purely on conscious intellectual judgments. "The analyst's countertransference is an instrument of research into the patient's unconscious," Heimann stated, and using it in this way provided important material for the therapist concerning the patient's conflicts and defenses. Margaret Little (1951) believed, as did Ferenczi earlier, that with severely disturbed patients countertransference feelings were unavoidable and omnipresent. The countertransference that was provoked in the therapist through projective identification by the patient was often a repetition of the patient's early relations with his or her parents. In treatment such a patient was extremely sensitive to the therapist's unconscious countertransference, which in turn strongly influenced the patient's transference. When the therapist behaved as did the patient's parents because of an induced countertransference reaction, a repetitious negative feedback cycle was established, perpetuating the patient's pathology and making interpretation of the patient's transference almost impossible. If the therapist simply interpreted the patient's transference, without dealing with his or her own induced countertransference, the therapist denied the patient's perception of the therapist as behaving similarly to the parental objects. This denial of reality for the patient disrupted the possibility of a genuine relationship with the therapist. Little, therefore, believed that the therapist's induced responses had to be openly revealed, so that the patient's perception of reality and sense of trust could be bolstered. Only then could the distorted transference responses in the patient be explored and worked through. If this countertransference/transference block was not resolved, progress in treatment was halted. Openly revealing the therapist's reactions to the patient was a revolutionary position in psychoanalysis, because self-revelation by the analyst had been prohibited. This prohibition was probably a direct extension of Freud's limiting himself to studying the intrapsychic factors within the patient after abandoning the seduction theory, thereby avoiding any confrontation of the interactive effect of others (i.e., the parents previously or the therapist currently) with the patient. Nevertheless, Little recommended openly admitting and interpreting the countertransference reaction to the patient, but only after the therapist had carefully attempted self-analysis and had resolved the reaction to as great an extent as possible.

Subsequently, two seminal papers were published by Heinrich Racker (1953, 1957) that described in considerable detail the manner in which the transference and countertransference interacted. Each influenced the other in a reciprocal manner, and the input of the therapist was crucial. Not only did the patient's transference distort the perception of the therapist, but the therapist's countertransference distorted the perception of the patient. In turn, the therapist's responses influenced the image that the patient had of the therapist. Just as a transference neurosis developed in treatment, a countertransference neurosis also occurred, which then had to be analyzed. The therapist needed to be keenly aware of his or her own responses to the patient's projective identification. Racker pointed out that if the therapist rejects what he termed the "concordant" identification, consisting of the therapist's empathic responses to the thoughts and feelings arising from the patient's ego and id, the opposing, "complementary" identification becomes intensified. In the latter, the therapist abandons a neutral position and identifies with the patient's dissociated, unwanted aspects of the self or superego objects. For example, the therapist may reject the patient's aggressiveness and identify with the patient's persecutory parental object internalized in the superego. The therapist thereby also becomes judgmental or condemning and acts out the "complementary" countertransference, thereby functioning similarly to the original bad internal object. The patient's past infantile trauma is then re-created and will be acted out in the therapy. This forms a negative feedback cycle, in which external reality again reinforces the patient's pathology to prevent change.

Racker further described how certain types of transference evoke corresponding countertransference reactions. When in the transference the patient projects a superego object into the therapist and the therapist identifies with this superego object, the therapist then experiences and may express punitive countertransference feelings. The patient experiences himself or herself to be dominated and accused externally, much as in past experiences with the parents. This reaction corresponds to the past internalization of this interaction, which caused the ego to be treated punitively by the superego. Racker termed this a depressive-paranoid transference. Alternately, the patient may identify with his or her own superego object and utilize a manic defense to project unacceptable aspects of the self in the transference. The patient then proceeds to persecute the therapist, who may in turn develop a depressive-paranoid countertransference. Here the therapist may experience feelings of being accused, subjugated, and denigrated, just as the patient had as a child.

Thus, Racker believed that the countertransference response of the therapist was helpful in understanding the patient's transference. It could aid in determining whether the self or object was being projected in order to re-create in the treatment relationship a traumatic interaction from childhood. This information could be used in making interpretations to the patient. Racker was hesitant, however, to recommend directly revealing these countertransference feelings.

CONTAINING AND WORKING WITH COUNTERTRANSFERENCE

Wilfred Bion (1959, 1970) pointed out the importance of the therapist's serving as a "container" during treatment, holding and not simply responding behaviorally to the patient's projective identifications. This function provides the patient with the necessary conditions of safety and security essential for further growth. Balint (1953, 1968) also emphasized that during periods of regression in the patient the therapist needs to accept and experience the patient's projective identifications without acting them out or even interpreting them. Searles (1965) also considered it to be essential with more disturbed, non-neurotic patients to establish a controlled therapeutic symbiosis between the analyst and patient. According to Searles, the ability to be open to the patient's projective identification, to function genuinely as a part of the patient and yet be separate enough to observe and analyze, allows the patient to differentiate self and object representations and to individuate. Similarly, Kohut (1977) stressed that it is important for narcissistic patients to find confirmation of the self through the development of idealizing and mirror transferences. Here the therapist provides security by functioning as an idealized object with whom the patient can merge, yet also encourages initiative and autonomy through positive (mirroring) responses. This interaction compensates for the past deficit of inappropriate, negative, or absent responses on the part of the parents to the child's developmental cues. Thus, reliving, reconstructing, and correcting developmental interactional patterns facilitates greater self-cohesion. The therapist functions as a selfobject whose empathetic responsiveness and support for individuation and separation help the patient develop an independent and cohesive self.

Langs (1976b) has pointed out that the failure of the therapist to contain and adequately process the patient's projective identifications can result in a "therapeutic misalliance." Here the therapist and the patient use each other for gratification and for defensive purposes. Unfortunately, the patient's pathology is only further consolidated, because the therapeutic misalliance recapitulates the original destructive parent–child interaction. The analyst is unresponsive to the patient's separate needs, and uses the patient much as the parents did, i.e., as a container for projective identification of their own psychopathology. Thus, the patient may be caught up in attempting to cure the therapist, just as he or she attempted previously in childhood to cure the parents. For example, a noninsightful countertransference cure might occur, with temporary relief of the patient's symptoms, for the benefit of the therapist. Such a cure occurs at the expense of the patient's own needs for growth and development. Langs stresses that psychoanalytic therapy is a bipersonal field, with circular and reciprocal influences arising from intrapsychic and interpersonal mechanisms of both the patient and the therapist. Because the therapist's countertransference can strongly influence the patient's transference, resistance, defenses, symptoms, or even regression, it is essential for the therapist to be alert to any unusual changes in these areas, as well as to the therapist's own feelings and fantasies. Ideally, in treatment the therapist can contain, metabolize, and interpret the projective identifications coming from the patient, so that they are not acted out but, rather, discussed at a symbolic verbal level, leading to cognitive insight and mastery.

In work with narcissistic patients in individual treatment, considerable controversy has arisen regarding the relative importance of interpreting the patient's aggression versus maintaining a holding environment. Modell (1976) indicates that both are important but that the timing of each is crucial for successful treatment. During the first phase, the narcissistic patient attempts to maintain the grandiose self as a defense against dependency, and expresses the illusion of self-sufficiency by his or her nonrelatedness. Modell terms this defensive phase the "cocoon." Others have employed other metaphors, such as Volkan's "plastic bubble" (1973) and Guntrip's "sheet of glass" (1968). Likewise, Giovacchini (1975) and Green (1975) have noted that the therapist may be treated as an inanimate object or as nonexistent. Kernberg (1975) details how narcissistic patients project their omnipotence into the therapist and idealize and fuse with the therapist in the transference. In alternation with this process, the patient may project devalued aspects of the self into the therapist and attempt to demean and render the therapist helpless. Modell (1976), following Winnicott and Balint, states that the therapist needs to provide a "holding environment" for projective identifications, offering acceptance without interpretations during the initial phase. The rationale is that the patient does not have sufficient separateness to establish a therapeutic alliance. We can also postulate that the therapist's interpretations are experienced as an impingement from an external, controlling, intrusive source (much like the parents during childhood), or as criticism and abandonment. The therapist needs to function as a "transitional object" and as an idealized selfobject, empathetic and also responsive to the patient's needs for growth. This reciprocal, interpersonal interaction, which was lacking in childhood, provides sufficient safety to permit further ego consolidation (i.e., self and object constancy). The therapist's responsiveness to the cues for growth initiated by the patient fosters separation and autonomy. In the middle phase of treatment, rage emerges. If it is contained and not acted out in the countertransference, the patient does not feel helplessly controlled by external omnipotent forces or by his or her own powerful instincts. The result is further self-differentiation and the development of a therapeutic alliance. The therapist then can become more confrontational and interpretive of the patient's defensive grandiosity and fantasies of self-sufficiency. The third phase approximates a classical analytic case; a transference neurosis emerges and can be interpreted along with defenses. Such interpretation must be done cautiously, because the potential for regression still exists.

Langs (1976b) offers some guidelines for detecting the therapist's disruptive countertransferential reactions. The therapist may employ uncharacteristic behavior with a patient, offer incorrect interventions, or deviate from the analytic framework. In addition, cues may be obtained from the patient's associations, dreams, unexplained resistances, acute disturbances, symptoms, regressions, acting out, or disruption of the therapeutic alliance. Langs recommends self-analysis by the therapist to foster awareness of the countertransference. When derivative material from the patient suggests disruptive effects stemming from the countertransference, the therapist can acknowledge the patient's perception as correct, thereby sensitively and honestly supporting the patient's reality testing.

USING THE FAMILY TYPOLOGY
IN WORK WITH COUNTERTRANSFERENCE

Combined with the understanding derived from family studies, the countertransference may be helpful in determining the form of projective identification a patient in individual therapy has employed. The patient will either attempt to induce the therapist into the role of the internalized parental figure, or do to the therapist what the parent did to the patient. These mechanisms provide the therapist with important clues that concern the transference of object or self and that can be used in reconstructing genetic material from the patient's family of origin. If the therapist is open to experiencing what the patient likely felt as a child, the therapist can gain empathic understanding and consolidate the therapeutic alliance with the patient. Knowledge of family interaction from family studies can also be helpful. For example, there is a patient commonly called the "help-rejecting complainer" who is typically a self-defeating masochistic depressive. The help-rejecting complainer comes from a family where he or she was exposed to a "double bind on achievement" during childhood.* The patient attempts to satisfy the narcissistic demands of a parent, yet any action taken is not rewarded and is insufficient. As an adult, the patient repeats this process with others, demanding others do something, but what is done is never enough. The patient asks for help, yet if the therapist responds, whatever is suggested is negated with a "Yes, but." The result is often a negative countertransference. After establishing a sufficient therapeutic alliance with such a patient and receiving enough clues about the patient's background, one can comment, "I know it is difficult for you, and I do want to respond to your requests for help, yet I find myself feeling helpless and frustrated. No matter how hard I try to help, it never seems good enough. I have a strong suspicion that you often felt like that yourself as a child. Something was expected of you, but no matter what you did, it was never good enough, and you yourself wound up feeling helpless and frustrated."

Here the therapist maintains a neutral position and interprets the manic defense of projection of the bad self into the therapist, as well as its genetic background, while maintaining empathic connection. In this interpretation of the double bind that is experienced, the therapist processes the projective identification differently from the way

---

* See Chapter 7 for further elaboration.

the patient did with the parents. The therapist is not taken over by it, nor does he or she act it out by masochistic compliance, passive-aggressive maneuvers, or by attacking or abandoning the patient. Instead, the therapist retains autonomy and encourages an alliance with the patient's observing ego in order to bring the countertransference response out in the open for further exploration with the patient. This empathic understanding diminishes the patient's omnipotence in manipulating the therapist and encourages differentiation, emotional catharsis, and working through. The emotionally rich, here-and-now relationship with the therapist becomes therapeutic and is not a repetition of the past. Ideally, this pattern can be extended to those relations outside of treatment that have served as negative feedback to perpetuate the patient's pathological fixation. Achieving clear distinction between the past and the present, between the internal object and the real external person, between unconscious fantasy and reality, in a safe holding environment that sustains empathic connection, is what allows growth and change to occur.

COUNTERTRANSFERENCE AND FAMILY HOMEOSTASIS

Once the patient overcomes the resistance to change, it is important for the therapist to be aware that others in the patient's family may manifest their own resistance to this change. Because the patient may have been the container for the projective identifications of other family members (to disown their own conflict by placing it into the patient or by living through the patient to enhance the self), the homeostatic balance of the family may become disrupted. Thus, at the point at which the patient has enough autonomy to stop acting out the induced countertransference, the therapist may need to recommend treatment for a spouse or other members of the family. This will prevent disruption of the patient's individual treatment and the development of pathology in another family member. The spouse or other family member(s) may be referred to another therapist or may be brought in for conjoint family therapy.

Psychoanalysis has explored in considerable depth the use of primitive defenses, such as projective identification, splitting, primitive idealization, devaluation, and denial, in borderline and narcissistic patients. The primary focus has been on the expression of these primitive defenses in individual therapy, which usually manifest themselves through the transference-countertransference reactions that develop. Not only borderline and narcissistic patients use these primitive defenses, however; other patients with pregenital developmental arrest, such as hysterics, depressives, and schizophrenics, employ them as well. Three major questions arise at this point: First, how do the families of these types of patients contribute to the developmental arrest, and does the family play a role in its perpetuation? Second, how is our understanding of transference-countertransference of use in our attempts to comprehend marital and familial conflict? Third, how can this knowledge be employed, at a very practical level, in family therapy?

Because these patients have not internalized the mothering function during the separation-individuation phase of early development, they are unable to regulate their own narcissistic equilibrium. They thus continue to function symbiotically, using others in their environment as need-satisfying objects to sustain their self-esteem or even their self-cohesion. They remain excessively dependent upon, and need to control, the responses of important others, who function as selfobjects to sustain their precarious narcissistic equilibrium. Self-object differentiation remains low, and they employ primitive defense mechanisms, particularly in intimate relationships. These mechanisms find their clearest expression in marital and family relationships and are powerfully operative from the very moment of inception of a relationship. The very selection of a marital partner is largely unconsciously determined by them. Murray Bowen (1978), the eminent family systems theoretician, notes that individuals who marry usually have the same level of self-differentiation. In the terms of object relations theory, if one spouse has a developmental arrest and employs primitive defenses as a way of relating, the spouse generally does so also, or at least is willing at an unconscious level to accommodate. Otherwise, the relationship cannot sustain itself. Each spouse needs to accept and identify with the projective identification from the marital partner of unwanted aspects of the self or of an internal object. Thus, a complementary transference-countertransference relationship, in which defensive structures mesh, can become established that stabilizes one or both of the personalities.

In addition, as the marital relationship progresses, there is a continual shaping of the spouse through projective identification that induces certain countertransferential responses. The externalization of the internal world of object relations allows for a recapitulation of early parental relationships that played a role originally in producing the developmental arrest. Instead of being relived and mastered in the marriage, however, this old trauma unfortunately is used to sustain a defensive equilibrium or homeostatic balance within and between the spouses. Family homeostasis thus can be explained by the mutual transference-countertransference balance that becomes permanently established between the spouses. A form of unconscious collusion occurs that serves as a negative feedback cycle to perpetuate pathological functioning. This collusion might be compared to what existed in the family of origin, in which members used one another to sustain their self-esteem and identity. In the marriage, also, each partner influences the other's self-esteem and identity in a reciprocal manner through projective identification, sustaining a defensive equilibrium. Thus the external marital relationship that develops serves to reinforce the internalized object world of both partners. Old conflictual relationships stemming from childhood become resurrected, recapitulated, and acted out in the marital family.

PRIMITIVE DEFENSES AND FAMILY TRIANGULATION

Because of the defense of splitting the internalized self or object into all good or all bad parts, a third family member tends to be triangulated into the interaction. Thus, as children are born into the family, they may become induced to fulfill a part object role. Because of this unconscious process, their own developmental needs are not responded to, inhibiting their own growth. Splitting and projective identification are the core processes that can be considered responsible in the family for the development of psychopathology in the child. For example, one person, because of splitting and projective identification of an internalized object, may induce a second person to act out the all-bad object and a third person to act out the all-good object. Thus, symptomatology in the identified patient can be viewed as arising out of an induced countertransference reaction. The patient has accepted and identified with the projective identification of a part self or object placed into him or her, and acts out this acceptance behaviorally.

In viewing the entire family as having a problem, and not limiting it to the identified patient, family therapy has made one of its major contributions. Despite the pragmatic value of this approach in family treatment, however, there has been a lack of sufficient understanding of the causes of this familial situation. We can postulate that the previously discussed processes of splitting and projective identification, by which split aspects of the self or internal object are placed into two other family members, are involved. The couple and the triangulated child become locked into an overly close relationship, which we have termed the symbiotic survival pattern. They are functioning as if they were one personality, with each member of the triangle taking a component part of self or object, either good or bad. This phenomenon has variously been termed by others in family therapy as the undifferentiated family ego mass (Bowen 1978), pseudomutuality (Wynne, Ryckoff, Day, and Hirsch 1958), and enmeshment (Minuchin 1974). A further discussion of the symbiotic survival pattern that arises out of splitting and projective identification can be found in Chapter 6.

THE EFFECTIVENESS OF FAMILY THERAPY FROM AN OBJECT RELATIONS VIEWPOINT

Even though the driving force for the compulsion to repeat old conflicts in current family relationships may be a desire for mastery and growth, the conservative forces to sustain self-esteem and self-cohesion by controlling external object relations are more powerful. Hence, resistance to change is the stronger element. Change is frightening for these individuals; because of a lack of self and object constancy, it threatens their self-definition and psychological survival. Nevertheless, precisely because the internalized conflict is externalized and reenacted in the family relationship, it is on the surface and can be worked with effectively in family therapy. This may be one of the reasons that manipulating the external relationship in family therapy can be so effective in influencing the underlying pathological interaction.

Perhaps the greatest contribution of family therapy has been to remove the focus away from the symptomatology of the identified patient, thereby altering the pathological processes of splitting and projective identification. The patient is only the container for the family pathology, or the manifest expression of more widespread pathology in the family system of interaction. This shift away from the patient, which is in direct opposition to the medical model, tends to neutralize the splitting and projective identification, instead of reinforcing these defenses. When the patient is taken out of the role of scapegoat in the family, the countertransference of the patient is profoundly diluted. The patient is taken out of a demeaning role, and his or her identity is enhanced and redefined. This change is furthered by the provision of paradoxical instructions to the family. Here the patient's functioning is reframed from a negative role into a positive role, in which the identified patient is seen as curing or saving the family. The patient's role is to prevent or heal narcissistic injuries in the parents. When this aspect of the patient's behavior is brought out into the open, the entire transference-countertransference balance is disrupted. For example, telling a patient he or she ought to continue to fail, because in that way the father will be helped, reveals the underlying projective identification. The patient may have identified with the bad self or object projected from the father. The patient, by containing unacceptable aspects that the father wanted to be rid of, preserves the father's self-esteem. The father's feeling like a success depends on the patient's being a failure. Once this pathological interaction is revealed, it is difficult for the father not to own this aspect of himself. In addition, the patient's self-definition is changed from a negative to a positive one, resulting in enhancement of the patient's self-esteem.

CONGRUENCE OF TRANSFERENCE-COUNTERTRANSFERENCE IN ALCOHOLISM

Probably the most striking example of a sadomasochistic relationship, with a permanence that defies the imagination, is that of an alcoholic and his or her spouse. Despite great mental suffering, anguish, and even physical abuse, the alcoholic and spouse seem to be bound together by some strong, invisible bond. This binding is a result of the collusive defensive structure, a misalliance, in which each spouse employs projective identification, so that simultaneous transferences and countertransferences operate.

As a hypothetical example, we shall use a marriage in which the husband is the alcoholic. Usually the wife has some awareness of the mate's alcoholic problems even during the courtship. Likewise, the husband has some awareness of the wife's excessive sense of responsibility. The wife usually believes that she can cure her partner, that through her love and strength she can reform him. It is well known that the alcoholic has a rigid superego structure, with a punitive, controlling internalized parental object. This superego object is projected onto the wife, and she is perceived in the transference as a controlling parent. The wife in turn may have many of the same residual conflicts from her own childhood with a controlling parent, who has also become internalized as a punitive superego object. The wife, however, uses a manic defense to identify with this internalized parental object, and through projective identification places her dependent, devalued self into her husband. The husband identifies with this projection, and thus his own transference is reinforced by a similar induced countertransference from the wife. He experiences a depressive-paranoid transference, which is reinforced by his induced depressive-paranoid countertransference. Not only does he expect his wife to dominate him in the transference, but his induced countertransference, coming from her, corresponds to this expectation. The husband will experience himself as dominated and will blame the wife for his drinking. Similarly, the wife's own transference, in which she relates to her husband as if she were his parent, is reinforced by her induced parental countertransference, coming from the husband.

Thus, the wife will deny her own problems and see only her husband as sick.

A vicious cycle of mutual control becomes established, in which each partner's pathology reinforces the other's. It is the congruence of the transference and the induced countertransference in each of the spouses that makes them inseparable. Each partner serves an indispensable defensive function for the other. A reversal in the sadomasochistic roles of this relationship can occur when the husband is drinking. The wife's acceptance of parental responsibility, blame, and guilt for the husband's drinking leaves her vulnerable to abuse when the husband is drunk.

If one partner changes through therapy or group support, a rupture of this collusive defensive structure occurs. The husband may assume responsibility for himself or shift his dependency to the group and no longer develop the same sort of parental transference with his wife. The transference and induced countertransference no longer are congruent and reinforcing of each other. The husband may relinquish his transference and not identify with the wife's projective identification of the unwanted devalued aspects of herself. Thus, if the husband gives up drinking, the wife's manic defense, which had externalized her own problems, is no longer effective. The wife may then decompensate and become severely depressed or alcoholic herself, because her self-esteem and identity are no longer maintained by the relationship.

Marital and family therapy have been more effective in treating the alcoholic than has individual therapy. This is probably due in large part to the complementarity and reinforcement of each of the marital partner's defenses, which cause the spouses to function as if they were merged. Both members must be treated in order to break the vicious cycle of mutual projective identification that has perpetuated the drinking. In addition, working with both partners prevents the well spouse from decompensating or sabotaging the treatment once the alcoholic partner begins to change. Some of the same factors seem to operate in Alcoholics Anonymous to dissolve this pathologically binding relationship. The alcoholic assumes responsibility for his drinking, and control does not rest with the wife. Group support is offered, and the stigma of alcoholism is lessened by considering it a physical disease. The alcoholic may also take on the role of helper for others, to lessen further a negative self-image. The wife and children also become involved in therapeutic groups, so that they are provided with a support network as well.

THE THERAPIST'S SUCTION INTO THE FAMILY SYSTEM AS COUNTERTRANSFERENCE

Awareness of the phenomenon of countertransference is extremely useful for the therapist conducting family therapy. Most prominent family therapists have commented on the great danger, when working with sicker patients and their families, of being "sucked into" the system. Although this occurrence has been observed to be clearly disruptive of treatment, no deep understanding of this process exists in family therapy. Why does the family apply this suction, and why is this occurrence so destructive to treatment? Essentially, being sucked into the system is equivalent to developing an induced or objective countertransference. It is similar to the individual therapist's being induced through projective identification to feel or behave in a way that corresponds to the patient's internalized world of object relations. The difference is that in family therapy the induction comes from more than one individual and is essential for the defensive equilibrium of the family.

Induction of the therapist will only reinforce the existing externalization and acting out of the internal world of objects that is reflected in the transference-countertransference balance or homeostasis in the family. If the therapist also reacts with his or her own projective identifications into the family, a therapeutic misalliance will be created, just as in individual therapy. The collusive interaction already existing within the family, in which each member uses the others for defensive purposes, will be reinforced.

Many family therapists attempt to deal with the force of this suction, or induction, by insisting that a co-therapist work with them or observe through a one-way mirror. It is hoped that the other therapist will contain the "suction" (the projective identification) that occurs, so that neither therapist is taken over by it. Knowledge about the processes of splitting and projective identification can help the therapist maintain an objective, growth-enhancing position with the family, particularly if he or she has some awareness of what form of these defenses to expect in a given pathological condition. Specific types of splitting and projective identification appear to operate in the involved families in schizophrenia, hysteria and borderline conditions, depression, and delinquency. These will be discussed in the following chapters.

5

ADAPTATION AND FIXATION

HISTORICAL DEVELOPMENT OF FAMILY THERAPY

Family therapy was a product of the 1960s, a time in the United States that was characterized in certain quarters by strong anti–establishment sentiment. It was a time of disillusionment with governmental authority, arising from events ranging from the McCarthy loyalty inquisition to the Vietnam involvement. In many respects, this anti-establishment attitude bears a striking similarity to the development of the existentialist movement in Europe after World War II, in which distrust of governing authority and a philosophy of distrust of theory imposed on phenomena went hand in hand. From its inception, family therapy attracted a group of creative mavericks, therapists who swam against the mainstream of the psychiatric and psychoanalytic establishment. Theory would somehow catch up with practice. This distrust of an encompassing theoretical foundation was experienced by many family therapists as a safeguard against premature closure and control by the establishment. Despite this openness to creative development, however, a price has been paid for this oppositional attitude. Without a unified theory, particularly a theory and a system of typology connected with general psychiatry, family therapy remains in an alienated position. It remains a stepchild, as evidenced by the continuing reluctance of insurance companies to reimburse for family therapy. Family therapy has grown up, has proved its effectiveness, and does not need defensively to establish distance to preserve its autonomy. It is time for it to take its place, along with individual and group therapy, in the family of psychotherapies.

During the 1960s the field of family therapy developed spontaneously in various locations, under the leadership of a number of charismatic therapists. Each established his or her own unique therapeutic approach, and as a result a wide spectrum of theory and practice in family therapy has evolved. These approaches can be grouped into two broad categories, psychodynamic and directive. The psychodynamic approaches explore familial patterns transmitted through two or three generations and include psychoanalytic, family systems, and contextual family therapy. The directive approaches are ahistorical and actively attempt to change overt family behavior in the here-and-now; they include structural and strategic family therapy. Many family therapists pick and choose, at various times and with different families, aspects of each of these two approaches in treatment.

Despite these radically different viewpoints, there are some areas of consensus in these approaches to family therapy. There is an overall acceptance of general systems theory by most schools of family therapy. In addition, both approaches view the identified patient as containing the pathology for the family system, preserving the functioning and continuity of the family as a group. This idea provides the raison d'être for working with the entire family rather than only the individual patient. The family is seen as the patient, and changes in family interaction are sought.

The similarities, however, abruptly end here. The directive (structural and strategic) approaches in family therapy use as a foundation Don Jackson's theory of homeostasis (1957). According to Jackson, the family can be viewed as a self-correcting, rule-governed group that prevents deviation through negative feedback. Dysfunctional families evidence a stereotyped role structure and an overly restrictive and rigid system of rules, with little tolerance for deviation of behavior. In the directive approach, the goal of treatment is to effect a change in the feedback cycles that preserve this rigid homeostasis. Thus, the identified patient is freed from being locked into the sick role.

In contrast, the psychoanalytic approaches in family therapy tend to look at projection processes or projective identification as the method of maintaining defensive equilibrium and inducing pathology in the identified patient. Projective identification is viewed as the mechanism used to establish and sustain the negative feedback cycle. In treatment, however, psychodynamic family therapists believe that change in family interaction should come about through internal personality changes, arrived at by the individuation and growth of family members. As each member achieves insight and greater self-awareness, the need to deny and project conflict and express it behaviorally is diminished. This change permits the patient to function with greater autonomy. The psychodynamic approach requires a longer treatment time than does the directive approach.

In directive therapy, insight is unessential, because change is imposed from the outside onto the family. The structural therapist manipulates the power and communication structure; the strategic therapist prescribes paradoxical instructions or illogical homework. Indeed, to some radical members of the directive group, pathology is seen as existing not within the patient but, rather, only between family members. The patient is only a vehicle to express the family's dysfunction. The aim of treatment is to change the family interaction, which it is believed will automatically eliminate the pathology expressed by the identified patient. Grandiose claims have been made by some directive therapists of "curing" schizophrenia in from one to twelve sessions. This extreme position is at total variance with psychoanalysis and psychiatry in general, which see pathology as existing independently in the patient, even though the family may play a significant role in the development and maintenance of the disorder.

THE FAMILY'S ROLE IN THE GENESIS, MAINTENANCE, AND PROGNOSIS OF SCHIZOPHRENIA

There is a mounting wave of scientific evidence that disputes the claims made by some radical, directive family therapists that schizophrenia is not a mental disorder residing in the patient. This group denies that schizophrenia is an illness at all and sees it as only a manifestation of disturbed family relations. They claim that the pathology is in no one person but, rather, between people. The opposite position is supported by the findings of the Danish adoption studies, which generally disconfirmed the effect of familial relationships on the genesis of schizophrenia. The condition was viewed as a hereditary disease within the patient. This widescale study by Kety, Rosenthal, and Wender (1968) studied children of schizophrenic mothers who were raised by biological and adoptive parents. These genetically loaded children were found to be at greater risk for developing schizophrenia, whether raised by their own or by adoptive parents. Wender, Rosenthal, and Kety (1968) also studied the biological and adoptive parents of schizophrenic children, and the adoptive parents of normal children. They found that the biological parents were significantly more disturbed than the adoptive parents of schizophrenics, who in turn were significantly (but not greatly) more disturbed than adoptive parents of normal children. Wynne and Singer (1972), after reexamining the Rorschach test responses of these parents for communication deviance, were able to identify with 100 percent accuracy the parents of the schizophrenic children, whether adoptive or biological. The adoptive parents of schizophrenics had the most deviant communication, followed by the biological parents, and then the adoptive parents of normals.

These findings led to the collaboration of Lyman Wynne with Pekka Tienari of the Oulu University in Finland. The Finnish adoption study replicated the Danish adoption study, with the additional variable of carefully studying the familial relationships of the adoptive parents. At the International Symposium on the Psychotherapy of Schizophrenia in 1981 and at the 1982 meeting of the Society of Biological Psychiatry, Tienari reported on his controlled study of 200 families. He found that when the adoptive parents were disturbed, the children of schizophrenic mothers were at greater risk for severe disturbance than were the children of nonschizophrenic mothers. This finding supported the results of the Danish study with regard to the importance of genetic loading. Indeed, all children raised in severely disturbed adoptive families were significantly more likely to be severely disturbed themselves than were those reared in healthy or neurotic families. The study also found, however, that when children of schizophrenic mothers were raised in normal or neurotic adoptive families, they were no more likely to be severely disturbed than were the normal children in a matched control group. Thus, although genetic loading seems necessary, it is not sufficient to produce schizophrenia, and the interaction of the genetic potential and familial factors is significant in the genesis of schizophrenia.

That the family interaction can maintain schizophrenia seems indicated by the laboratory findings of David Reiss (1971). He found that schizophrenic patients did worse on problem-solving tasks when tested with their families than when tested alone. Normal subjects did better with their families than alone; i.e., the family enhanced their functioning. In addition, Waxler (1974) found that schizophrenic children were better at problem solving when they were with a normal family. Normal children were not affected by schizophrenic families, however.

In terms of prognosis, Leff's Maudsley study (1976) found that schizophrenics whose families were hostile, critical, and intrusive (termed "high expressed emotion," or high EE), suffered a higher relapse rate than those whose families were not so. Reducing the patient's contact with the family to less than 35 hours a week or changing the family's high EE was helpful in lowering the relapse rate. These studies indicate the significant role played by families in the genesis, maintenance, and prognosis of schizophrenic illness.

THEORIES AND TECHNIQUES IN DIRECTIVE FAMILY THERAPY

The directive group of family therapists does not represent a unified approach, but is beset by conflicting theoretical and therapeutic aims. Fraser (1982) points out that there are contradictory conceptions and targets of change in the structural and strategic approaches. These positions are so divergent, Fraser states, that integration of these approaches in clinical practice is extremely difficult, if not impossible. The structural group attempts to change structure and thereby alter function, whereas the strategic group works directly with actual functioning, which is considered to evolve as an erroneous solution to a problem. The structural therapist becomes actively engaged with the family, joining the system and changing seating arrangements to influence the power and communication structure; the strategic therapist maintains a more distant stance and offers paradoxical prescriptions or illogical homework assignments. The structural approach seeks to create new transactional patterns between members and subsystems of the family so as to disrupt negative feedback (deviation-decreasing) cycles. The goal is, through changing role relationships, to loosen the rigid homeostatic balance that exists in dysfunctional families. According to Minuchin, this balance consists of enmeshment (overinvolvement) or disengagement (alienation) among family members. The strategic group, in contrast, focuses on the processes of the family as a whole and attempts to interrupt positive feedback (deviation-amplifying) cycles. Via alterations in the overall family rules that have evolved as a solution to a problem but that have only created more problems, these existing "vicious" cycles are changed into "virtuous" cycles.

Analogies to a heating system have been useful in understanding these differences in feedback cycles. Negative feedback can be compared to a thermostat that cuts off the furnace as the temperature rises, so as to maintain a steady state of temperature. The thermostat is deviation decreasing, preventing the room temperature from going above a preset level. Positive feedback (deviation amplification) is analogous to the opening of a window to let in cool air when the house becomes too warm. The thermostat then senses the lowered temperature and starts the furnace, which raises the temperature. A second window is opened, and so on, until all the windows are open or the furnace breaks down. Here a repetitive vicious cycle has been created that only escalates the problem.

We can apply these analogies to treatment situations. If the room is too cold, the structural approach might consider the thermostat to be set too low (to be restrictive) and would advocate setting it higher to allow for greater tolerance before the negative feedback becomes operative. In the strategic approach, if the room is too warm, what is needed is not more of the solution (opening windows) but less of it. A change in the rules that determine functioning (not opening windows and lowering the thermostat) is indicated.

Both the structural and strategic approaches employ the theory of cybernetics. They both employ a cause-and-effect form of linear thinking concerning causality instead of an interactional one, however. Also, they both view the therapist as outside the system, able to control or manipulate it. As we mentioned earlier, this is an epistemological error of linear thinking that does not give sufficient import to the part-whole constraints on the observer, who is influenced by the system. Much like the Freudian libido theory, the directive approaches use a mechanistic model based on Newtonian physics, even though it claims not to do so. Merely looking at the interactional level (the role relationships) that determines communication and the power structure, as in the structural approach, or at the family-as-a-whole level that establishes the system of family rules, as in the strategic approach, is not sufficient. The notions of positive and negative feedback, although useful, do not provide us with sufficient information concerning how and why the interactional and systemic levels develop. The individual level must be examined as well in order to provide a greater depth of understanding.* If general systems theory or cybernetics is to be used as the theoretical underpinning for family therapy, all these three levels must be incorporated, and probably the biological, social, and cultural levels as well.

To develop an integrating theory in family therapy that uses modern epistemology and incorporates the individual, interactional, and family-as-a-whole levels is an ambitious undertaking. Suggestions for a theory that brings together some of these aspects of family therapy can be developed, however. The first core concept is the importance of adaptation and survival as an overall framework for the individual and the family. The second core concept integrates the individual's developmental level with the family interaction. According to this concept, developmental arrest occurs in the patient because the patient's level of functioning and internal fantasy correspond to the actual external interaction that exists in the family.

THE FIRST CORE CONCEPT: ADAPTATION AND SURVIVAL

Survival as the first core concept of a theory of family therapy has been discussed in relation to the symbiotic survival pattern (Slipp 1969, 1973b). Such a concern with survival and human adaptation, however, has many theoretical predecessors. In the early 1920s Freud (1923, 1926) changed psychoanalysis from an id psychology to an ego

---

* Disruption of projective identification can be viewed as essential to the therapeutic effectiveness of both approaches.

psychology concerned with human adaptation. He revised his theory of anxiety, developing the structural model and the concept of the repetition compulsion. The ego had to master biological drives as well as cope with external reality in order to adapt. This formulation was the beginning of a shift in psychoanalysis to an open system concerned with the interaction of the individual with others and the world. Anna Freud (1936) furthered this development in her studies of the ego's mechanisms of defense; Hartmann, Kris, and Lowenstein (1951) postulated an internalized cognitive map of the external world, with mental representations of the self and others, as well as an autonomous, conflict-free sphere of the ego. Bowlby's studies of bonding and separation (1969) and Mahler's differentiation of the stages of individuation and separation in child development (Mahler and Furer 1968) were other landmarks.

Although studies of animal group behavior cannot be directly applied to humans, they do provide us with interesting leads. Generally, lower animals are controlled by releasing mechanisms, or rituals, that are genetically determined, whereas higher primates are regulated by the interplay between instincts and learning. Buirski and colleagues (Buirski, Kellerman, Plutchik, and Weininger 1973, Buirski, Plutchik, and Kellerman 1978) noted in their studies of higher primates that baboons and chimpanzees depended for their survival on the integrity of their social group. The social group provided security against predators and other environmental dangers, and regulated biological drives. Individual behavior was highly controlled in order to support the group's cohesion and function. Buirski (1980) postulates that the perpetuation of the species in higher primates, including humans, is dependent on the social group. We know that survival in primitive societies as well as in authoritarian and totalitarian groups involves submersion of the individual's autonomy in the group. In his fascinating book on Adolph Hitler, Stierlin (1976a) discusses how Hitler stimulated merging with the group. Hitler verbally identified himself and the audience as one with Germany and, through the use of music, uniforms, and ritual, broke down individual barriers to promote merging. An analogy can be drawn between the individual who sacrifices autonomy and perhaps his or her life for the group's sake, as in the Jonestown mass suicide, and the schizophrenic patient who sacrifices his or her autonomy to become the identified patient in order to preserve the family group. With authoritarian groups and cults, however, the regression of adults to symbiotic merging with the group tends to be temporary and needs continual reinforcement. In dysfunctional families the symbiotic merging seems more permanent, because of the developmental arrest of the patient during childhood.

The loss of individual autonomy and lack of differentiation of members in sicker, dysfunctional families, particularly in schizophrenia, has been noted by most family therapy investigators. Some of the concepts involving merging with the family group are Murray Bowen's "undifferentiated family ego mass" (1960), Gregory Bateson's and Don Jackson's "double-binding" (Bateson, Jackson, Haley, and Weakland 1956), Ronald Laing's "mystification" (Laing and Esterson 1964), Theodore Lidz's and my own "symbiotic relatedness" (Lidz, Fleck, and Cornelison 1965, Slipp 1969), Salvadore Minuchin's "enmeshment" (1974), David Reiss's "consensus sensitivity" (1971), Helm Stierlin's "parental delegation" (1974), and Lyman Wynne's "pseudomutuality" (Wynne, Ryckoff, Day, and Hirsch 1958). One question remains, however: Why should the schizophrenic patient accept a constricted sick role that involves loss of autonomy and interference with individuation and separation? Is it due to the intensity of the manipulations by the system or the projective identifications of the family, or does the patient unconsciously altruistically choose self-sacrifice in order to preserve other family members? We can suggest that the answer is neither and both. The individual is compelled to comply to the family pressure, and by preserving the group, the other's and one's own survival is felt to be safeguarded. The schizophrenic is fixated, or functioning at, a primitive symbiotic level at which one's survival is experienced as merged with the group's survival, as it was during infancy with the mother. Because the individual has not internalized and separated from the mother, self-esteem and identity remain reactive to the family.

THE SECOND CORE CONCEPT: DEVELOPMENTAL ARREST

The classical psychoanalytic position explains developmental fixation on the basis of a greater amount or insufficient neutralization

of aggression. The object relations theorist Winnicott (1965), however, views developmental fixation at the symbiotic level as a result
of the mother's insufficient responsiveness and the manner in which
aggression is handled interpersonally between mother and child.
When the mother's responsiveness to the infant's needs is "good
enough," the infant sustains the illusion of omnipotent control over
the mother. If sufficient trust and security develop, the infant can
internalize the "good mother function" and can provide its own
soothing and comforting. A "transitional object," such as a blanket
or teddy bear, helps in internalizing the mother, because it serves
as a substitute, maintaining the fantasy of fusion with mother and
diminishing separation anxiety. When the mother also provides a
"holding environment" that contains the child's aggression without
retaliation or abandonment, the child can further relinquish its omnipotence. The child experiences the fact that anger has not destroyed the mother; fantasy and reality become differentiated. The
constancy of the object and the self thus becomes established and
allows for individuation. If the mother is unresponsive, the infant
is too insecure to give up its omnipotence, needs to control the object (so as to feel symbiotically part of it to avoid annihilation anxiety), and is unable to differentiate self from the object. Without having internalized the mother, the child cannot regulate its self-esteem
and identity and remains dependent on others.

Masud Khan (1974) extended Winnicott's conceptualization of the
"holding environment" beyond the mother–child interaction during infancy to include the ongoing care-taking functions of the parents in relation to their developing child. We can further suggest that
the family be viewed as a natural extension of the original symbiotic oneness with mother. The family is the mother group that normally provides the security and strength (a holding environment and
a transitional group) to facilitate the child's individuation and separation from the family and adaptation in society. If the symbiotic
level of relatedness persists pathologically in the family, autonomous
functioning and separation from the family is experienced by the patient to be much like the process of separating from the mother during infancy. Because of a lack of internalization of the mother and
an inability to regulate one's own narcissistic equilibrium, separation

from others in the family is experienced again as abandonment, with loss of self-esteem and fear of lack of survival. The individual has not achieved autonomy; instead, self-esteem and identity remain symbiotically connected with, and need constant reinforcement by, others in the family.

Some of the evidence validating this clinical finding comes from controlled laboratory experiments that have been replicated repeatedly. Using a tachistoscope for subliminal stimulation, it has been possible to activate unconscious fantasies of symbiotic merging with the mother that produce measurable cognitive or emotional responses. For example, Silverman (1975), using the subliminal maternal symbiotic message "Mommy and I are one," was able to produce a significant lessening of thought disorder in schizophrenics. However, loss of the mother through the aggressive stimulation "Destroy mother" produced an increase in pathology. Slipp and Nissenfeld (1981) noted improvement of depressive mood and feelings of well-being in female depressives after presentation of this same maternal symbiotic merging message. These messages were effective in more differentiated patients, in whom a sense of self was preserved. In schizophrenic and depressive patients, registering low levels of self-object differentiation on psychological tests, the maternal symbiotic message was not effective or worsened symptomology. Here, further merging with mother threatened total annihilation of the self. Chapter 7 will go into greater detail about these laboratory experimental studies.*

Additional evidence comes from family studies of schizophrenics. For example, Lidz, Fleck, and Cornelison (1965) noted that parents of schizophrenics were unresponsive to the child's needs for nurturance and personality development. Instead, the child was used to complete the life of one of the parents, often through alliances that breached the generational boundaries. In the families of schizophrenics studied at New York University Medical Center (Slipp 1969, 1973b), the family not only did not provide a "holding environ-

---

* For a more comprehensive review of the use of tachistoscopic studies to validate psychoanalytic theory, see Silverman, Lachman, and Milich (1982).

ment" to contain the child's omnipotent destructive fantasies, but even inadvertently reinforced these very fantasies. Instead of presenting an opposing reality to the child's fantasies, the parents were themselves unable to handle aggression without fear of abandonment. The parents used primitive defenses as well. Through splitting and projective identification, aggression was denied toward the spouse, who remained idealized as the good object, and was displaced onto the child, who became the bad object, the scapegoat. Autonomy was diminished in these families, because each member's self-esteem and survival were experienced as dependent on the behavior of other family members, a pattern we termed the symbiotic survival pattern. When the family fosters this form of magical thinking by making the child feel responsible for the existence of others through his or her own behavior, the child's omnipotent destructive fantasies become again reinforced, interfering with object and self constancy. Internal regulation of one's own narcissistic equilibrium cannot occur, and this regulation remains externalized in the relationship.

In studies of the families of depressive patients (Slipp 1976, 1981), a concordance was again found between the child's intrapsychic processes and the actual family interaction and was considered responsible for the developmental fixation. Jacobson (1971) posited that intrapsychically the parental object is split, with the powerful parent being incorporated in the superego and the deflated parent being incorporated in the self-image. It has been noted that in depressive families (Slipp 1976) one parent tends to be powerful and dominant, whereas the other parent is indeed weak and deflated. This pattern of dominance-submission has also been found by Cohen, Baker, Cohen, Fromm-Reichmann, and Weigert (1954) and Fromm-Reichmann (1959), and in the family research of Lewis, Beavers, Gossett, and Phillips (1976). The actual familial power structure mirrors the child's intrapsychic splitting. The dominant parent also employs splitting and projective identification, with the bad self being placed into the spouse, who is demeaned, and the good self into the patient, who is expected to perform. The dominant parent then lives vicariously through the child's achievement in order to sustain his or her self-esteem. In addition to the overt pressure to achieve, however, there is a covert, simultaneous, and contradictory message to fail.

We can term this the "double bind on achievement," because the child cannot win, either by achieving or by failing. The dominant parent does not gratify the child's achievement; it is never enough, even though the child is exploited to enhance the parent's prestige. This parent is at the same time competitive with the child and jealous of the child's achievement, needing to control the child. The child thus cannot own, and grow more autonomous because of, his or her successes. The result is a pervasive sense of helplessness and a good deal of anger, which is directed against the self or acted out in passive-aggressive, oppositional behavior. There is an arrest in development; symbiotic, merged functioning persists in order to avoid abandonment and to sustain self-esteem.

A similar parallel between the child's intrapsychic structure and the family environmental structure has been found in families of women with hysterical and borderline personality (Slipp 1977). The oedipal wishes of these women seemed capable of realization, because the fathers in these families were narcissistic and emotionally seductive. The fathers used splitting and projective identification, demeaning their wives as the bad maternal image and idealizing their daughters as the good mother. Freud's case of Dora (1905a) clearly exemplifies this pattern of family interaction.

Other factors were noted in family studies by Edward Shapiro (1975) of adolescent borderline patients and their families. The conflicts in these patients were also found to mirror those in the parents. The family shared certain underlying basic assumptions that resulted in conflict over dependency issues. Autonomy was considered a hateful devaluation of the family, yet the patient's dependency was simultaneously viewed critically as demanding and draining. To maintain a defensive equilibrium, the parents had used projective identification to evolve complementary, stereotyped roles. One parent was autonomous and the other dependent. The adolescent then became the container for one of these disavowed aspects of the parents and was punished. Both autonomous and dependent behavior by the adolescent resulted in retaliation and withdrawal by the parents.

Thus, two main concepts have been developed in this chapter. First, the issue of adaptation and survival can serve as an encompassing framework. The mother–infant symbiosis is seen as extending to the normal family group to facilitate social adaptation. In dysfunctional families the patient merges with the group at the expense of individual autonomy. Because of developmental arrest and continued symbiotic functioning, the patient experiences survival of the self as dependent on the survival and integrity of the family group. This pattern can explain why the identified patient sacrifices autonomy and individuation to preserve the family and the self.

Second, the developmental arrest or fixation of the patient does not result from either intrapsychic factors or familial dynamics alone. Rather, it is the paralleling or concordance of the child's fantasies with the actual family interaction that causes the fixation. The child's fantasies are not differentiated from reality. The family of the schizophrenic is unable to handle aggression and lacks a holding environment. In schizophrenic, borderline, depressive, and delinquent patients, the family's own use of primitive defenses such as splitting, projective identification, and idealization has reinforced these same defenses in the patient. In the terms of general systems theory, a cycle of negative feedback from the family prevents change and perpetuates the child's primitive psychic structures. It is the interface between the individual dynamics and the family interaction that is the crucial dimension in the development and maintenance of developmental arrest and psychopathology.

6

SCHIZOPHRENIA:
THE SYMBIOTIC SURVIVAL PATTERN

FAMILY INTERFERENCE WITH INTERNAL REGULATION OF SELF-ESTEEM, INDIVIDUATION, AND SEPARATION

The relational theory of schizophrenia termed the symbiotic survival pattern (Slipp 1969) arose from the study and treatment in the family therapy unit of the New York University–Bellevue Medical Center of over 125 families, nearly 50 percent of which had an adolescent or adult schizophrenic member. The theory was based largely on direct clinical observations, case material, and clinical conferences in the unit. A common pattern of interaction was found in many of these 125 families, but the pattern was present to an extreme degree in families with a schizophrenic member. The essential characteristic of this pattern was that each person's self-esteem and ego identity were felt to be dependent on the behavior of the other family members. Thus, each member felt controlled by his or her overwhelming sense of responsibility and guilt concerning the self-esteem and ego identity of the others, and at the same time each needed to control the others' behavior.

The genesis of this pattern appears to be the parents' need to act out their own intrapsychic conflicts in the interpersonal sphere. In the case of the child, it is inferred retrospectively that this pattern reinforces the form of mental functioning found normally during a crucial phase of infantile development. In addition, this system of interaction contributes to the continuation of disordered patterns of thinking through subsequent phases of childhood development. Although the child does learn secondary process cognition generally, there are lacunae within the ego in which primary process thinking persists, especially in interpersonal relations and personal identity. Because this family pattern exercises such enormous control over personality functioning, the child does not learn to integrate (and

91

cope with) his or her sexual and aggressive feelings, nor to experience a total sense of self or self-sameness apart from the family. Thus, the child does not form a stable, autonomous, and permanent mental self-image and continues to be excessively influenced by the ongoing family relationships. Not having sufficiently developed self-esteem and ego identity, the identified patient is unable to be spontaneous and assertive and remains constantly reactive to others. In addition, such patients need to perpetuate this mutually controlling, symbiotic pattern; otherwise, they fear, they would cease to exist or would be left with uncontrollable, aggressive feelings. (This is the case not only in the family, but in therapy as well.) Thus, to sustain their own and their parents' personality integration, these patients actively participate in perpetuating this pattern of interaction.

The most frequently recurring stress precipitating an overt, psychotic reaction appears to be a crucial period that threatens the patient's participation in this family system. Such a period occurs when the needs for symbiosis and individuation conflict, as normally happens during adolescence. Disruption of the symbiotic relationship is experienced as a loss of the self, as an inability to survive intact alone, and as an act of destruction of one or both parents. Thus, the identified patient's self-definition continues to be *reactive* and *relational*; he or she remains excessively dependent on the family relationships for self-esteem* and ego identity. This symbiotic survival pattern appears to prevent the differentiation in the child of mental images of self and others, of mental images from external objects, and of what is inside and outside (ego boundaries), and hampers the general transition from primary to secondary process cognition in certain areas.

FAMILY STUDIES IN SCHIZOPHRENIA

The unifying concept in family therapy has been that the individual presenting the overt symptomatology, the identified patient, is only part of a larger system of family pathology. Thus, the family

---

* External objects serve as auxiliary ego supports to maintain the self.

became the unit of treatment. In a survey reported by the Group for the Advancement of Psychiatry (1970), however, the underlying theoretical orientations of family therapists were found to represent a rather wide spectrum, ranging between the systems and the psychoanalytic approaches. At one extreme is the pure systems theorist, who views pathology as residing not in the identified patient but, rather, solely in the family interaction. Here there is an implicit assumption that, if the family system of interaction changes, personality change in the patient will automatically follow. This position denies internalization of pathology and fails to explain why a patient remains psychotic when he or she leaves the system or even when the system does change. Other family theorists do consider pathology as internalized in the identified patient, but only as a reflection of a one-way process, i.e., learned from or directly mirroring family pathology. For example, Bateson, Jackson, Haley, and Weakland (1956) state that because of double-binding communication in the family, the schizophrenic is prevented from learning to handle multiple levels of signals, resulting in impairment of discrimination and an inability to categorize perception and thinking logically. The third position, characterized by the work of Lidz, Fleck, and Cornelison (1965) and Wynne, Ryckoff, Day, and Hirsch (1958), combines the psychoanalytic concerns regarding early arrest of ego development with an emphasis on the family's continuing effect on ego functioning and identity formation.* The fourth position, represented by other

---

* Lyman Wynne and Margaret Singer (1972) have investigated styles of family communication and found significant differences between families with a schizophrenic patient and control families. They describe a form of communication deviance that results from the lack of a shared focus of attention among members of the family. The members do not stick to an issue; instead, there are sudden shifts in focus and attention so that communication becomes vague, fragmented, and idiosyncratic. It thus becomes difficult to derive meaning or reach closure on an issue. These investigators posit that this pattern serves to transmit the parents' own disordered patterns of thinking to the child. We can also view this obfuscation of communication as a subconscious attempt to deny separateness, caused by an inability to deal with aggression openly and directly. This subconscious attempt stems from the symbiotic survival pattern, in which separation is associated with loss of self-esteem and an inability to survive alone.

psychoanalytic investigators, acknowledges the family's influence on the identified patient but concentrates on intrapsychic factors, i.e., fixation during infancy and subsequent trauma and regression, with return of primary process cognition.

The symbiotic survival theory further elaborates the third of these positions, which views the family's influence as panphasic and the identified patient's pathology as internalized. Individual personality is seen as shaped by the system during development and reinforced by the system subsequently. In addition, the identified patient, as well as other family members, actively participates in perpetuating the system of interaction. The systems and psychoanalytic approaches deal with phenomena at different levels, but the two intertwine and modify each other. Thus, the child's psyche and the family system of interaction are both considered to be part of a larger interactive, interdependent, theoretical framework.

PROBLEMS IN DEVELOPING
A COMPREHENSIVE FAMILY THEORY

One reason for the slow evolution of an interactive, interdependent family theory is the temptation to provide simple generalizations for complex, multidetermined phenomena, often by analogy to mechanics or learning theory. For example, the concept of family homeostasis (Jackson 1957), which deals with an important phenomenon, uses an error-activated feedback system as an explanation. This same lack of an interactive theory is noted by Levinson (1964) to be the case in the behavioral sciences generally.* He refers to the "mirage" theory in psychology, which assumes that individual adaptation is primarily personality determined. Reality is structured by the individual to suit his or her inner needs. In contrast, the "sponge" theory in sociology sees the individual as passively conforming to group values, norms, and goals.

---

* Dennis Wrong (1964) provides an interesting critique of the concept of socialization in the behavioral sciences. Socialization is equated with superficial learning, even though it derives from Freud's theory of the superego. Socialization does not take into account, however, what the individual brings to the field—his or her unique response, which accounts for subgroup formation, deviance, change, growth, and creativity.

A second factor accounting for the slow development of an inter-active family theory has been the concentration on schizophrenia in theory building. Because the schizophrenic has been able to es-tablish neither a separate and constant mental self-image nor ade-quate ego functioning, he or she continues to require that relation-ships in the family fill these needs. The schizophrenic is therefore so markedly influenced by the here-and-now group interaction that the pathology appears to reside solely in the family system.

THE LACK OF UNDERSTANDING OF CHILD DEVELOPMENT IN FAMILY THERAPY

A greater understanding of ego development, and its integration into family theory, are essential for the construction of an interac-tive, interdependent framework. Freud's original formulations of ego development were essentially intrapsychic and based on the concept of frustration of libidinal needs. Subsequent psychoanalytic inves-tigators, such as Balint (1953), Bowlby (1958), Escalona (1953), Provence and Lipton (1952), and Suttie (1952), have noted an in-born, object-seeking propensity; the infant's ego is dependent for growth upon interaction with significant objects. Harlow's studies of monkeys (1958) also suggest that object relations have primary sig-nificance and in turn determine sexual development. Mahler (Mahler and Furer 1968) subdivides normal development into the autistic phase (birth to three months), the symbiotic phase (to six months), and the separation-individuation phase (to three years).* Symbiosis is characterized as an omnipotent fusion by the infant with the men-tal representation of the mother, resulting in the delusion of a com-

---

* The infant's beginning ability to represent mentally its attachment figures is characterized by an intensity of separation anxiety around the eighth month of life (Bowlby 1960, Spitz 1945). Fraiberg (1969) explains this period in Piagetian terms as the infant's ability to use recognition memory when the object is perceived. Fraiberg states, however, that it is only at about 18 months of age that the infant achieves a stable mental representation of the mother and is able to evoke her im-age even when she is absent to perception.Bell (1969) found that a harmonious rela-tionship between mother and infant was a precondition for the development of ob-ject permanence, as defined by Piaget. Spitz (1965) similarly comments on the negative developmental effects of what he terms "derailment of nonverbal dialogue."

mon ego boundary. This fusion serves as a defense against the infant's helplessness by denying separateness; the infant attempts through intrapsychic maneuvers to magically control the mother, who is essential for survival. After the separation-individuation phase, the mother is no longer perceived as a part object but, rather, as a separate, whole person. Separation involves the gradual differentiation of the mental images of self and other and the establishment of stable introjects. Mahler (1964) found that normally the attainment of object permanence (in Piaget's sense) occurs after the first year, whereas object constancy (in Hartmann's sense) is achieved at approximately 25 to 36 months of age. Mahler (1952) also noted that certain psychotic infants, because of either an inborn defect or poor mother–child interaction, neither internalize the mother nor resolve the symbiotic phase. The child continues to require the mother to function as an auxiliary ego to organize its environment. Adult schizophrenics are considered by Jacobson (1954a, 1954b, 1967) and Cohen (Cohen, Baker, Cohen, Fromm-Reichmann, and Weigert 1954) to be similarly fixated at the symbiotic phase and as later tending to regress to an undifferentiated state in which self and object mental representations merge.

PSYCHOANALYTIC STUDIES OF THE FAMILY

In 1951 Lidz reported that the usual pattern he had found with schizophrenics was not overt rejection of the child by the mother during infancy, as had been reported by others, but the use of the child by the mother to complete her life, with rejection threatened otherwise (Lidz, Fleck, and Cornelison 1965). The child then became burdened with the continued responsibility for mother's existence, having to develop an "uncanny sensitivity" to her feelings and being unable to develop a separate identity. The classic study published three years later by Cohen, Baker, Cohen, Fromm-Reichmann, and Weigert (1954) noted that in manic-depressive psychosis the family of origin placed undue responsibility on the patient for the social prestige of the family. Gibson's follow-up study (1958) replicated these findings and found that by comparison the family of origin of schizophrenic patients assigned to the child a greater degree of responsibility for gratification of personality needs of both parents. The family's ongoing influence in preventing individuation and separation in the patient has been described in the literature in a variety of ways: as the "undifferentiated family ego mass" by Bowen (1960), as "intersubjective merger" and the "amorphous We experience" by Boszormenyi-Nagy (1965), and as "pseudomutuality" by Wynne (Wynne, Ryckoff, Day, and Hirsch 1958, Wynne 1965). Lidz et al. (1965) pointed to pathological coalitions, identity diffusion, and the breaching of generational boundaries. Burnham, Gladstone, and Gibson (1969) also noted problems in differentiation; mothers of schizophrenics, out of their own needs, imposed such definitions on their child as scapegoat, ego ideal, replacement of a lost object, and savior. Towne, Messinger, and Sampson (1962) carried out studies of symbiotic relations over two generations of married female schizophrenics and categorized the relations as representing one of three patterns: merger (the parental and marital families function as a single, three-generational unit); conversion (the marital family substitutes for the parental family); and oscillation (the wife alternates back and forth between the two families). The evidence is sufficient to conclude not only that there is an arrest of early ego development, but that the family system teaches the child maladaptive patterns during subsequent developmental phases.

THE SYMBIOTIC SURVIVAL PATTERN

Because the family teaches the child that each person's self-esteem and survival are determined by the behavior of other family members, it is hypothesized that the family reinforces the child's innate preoperational, magical thinking instead of providing the opposing reality necessary for the development of secondary thought processes in certain areas. Piaget (1954, 1963) noted that in preoperational thinking, the child uses the concept of magical participation in the existence of external objects. Objects are perceived as coming and going as a function of the child's own physical action, schema, or wishes (efficacy), or their temporal contiguity (phenomenalism). Because objects are not considered to be separate or to exist outside the infant's perception or action, the infant feels in magical control of and responsible for their existence. Thus, the child remains egocentric in these areas of relationships and does not learn to recognize that objects and individuals have a stable identity over time and despite contextual changes. The child's capacity for symbolic representation of reality remains limited and nonreversible; his or her thoughts are tied to action schema and are imagistic and concrete (metaphoric).

In attempting to understand the psychic factors contributing to the genesis of the symbiotic survival pattern, we became aware that the parents in our study seemed unable to be sensitive and to respond appropriately to the needs of their children as independent persons. The child was seen in terms of the parents' psychic needs and therefore did not receive validation of his or her own feelings and thoughts. This was also the most consistent finding in studies of families with a schizophrenic child by Jackson (1957), Wynne (1965), Lidz (Lidz, Fleck, and Cornelison 1965), and Laing (1964). Mishler and Waxler's study (1968) found a correlation between the degree of responsiveness of the parents and the degree of pathology and prognosis in the patient. Searles (1965) was perhaps the first to attempt to delineate specific processes underlying symbiosis, by extending Sullivan's concepts of personification. He noted that the child sensed the mother's great anxiety and feelings of worthlessness and subordinated his or her own personality needs to the maintenance of the mother's precarious narcissistic equilibrium. In turn, the mother related to the patient as a part object, as a personification of her own unacceptable self-images. Family interaction was based on projection and introjection. Because each member served as part object for each of the other, separation or individuation was felt as a threat to ego integration by all.

Although Searles's findings concerning the genesis of symbiosis bear many similarities to our own, there are distinct differences. Searles attributed the fluidity of ego boundaries in the patient to a constant shifting of these part object roles in the family. In contrast, the part object roles we were able to discern were constant. We hypothesized that the lack of ego boundaries was more related to the paradox of feeling controlled and helpless (having to be whatever the other member required) while at the same time feeling grandiose and omnipotent (responsible for the other's self-esteem and survival). In addition, Searles focused primarily on the mother-child dyad; fathers were found to be infantile and passive. Our findings focused on triadic relations, with either the father or the mother (or both) initiating the symbiosis and the other parent (as well as other sibs) also involved. Searles believed also that the child gradually learned to respond to forces coming from the mother because of his or her own security needs; we found the child to be an active participant, bringing into the field specific ways of perception and cognition. Our theory concerning the genesis of symbiosis is related to Melanie Klein's intrapsychic theories, but extended into the interpersonal sphere.

EXTENDING MELANIE KLEIN'S CONCEPTS INTO THE INTERPERSONAL SPHERE

Klein's studies of infantile development (1948) postulated a normal paranoid and depressive position that, if not traversed successfully, formed the prototype for later mental illness. She held that the infant's ego is formed by the projection of its own aggression, when frustrated, onto objects that are split, introjected, and incorporated as the good or bad mother and good or bad self. Because the ego is so identified with the good mother introject, preservation of this introject is as essential to the ego's survival as the preservation of the actual external object. Thus, the infant's ego needs to protect this introject from destruction by its own death wishes. During the paranoid position, the infant's ego is part object related and projects the bad introject back onto the object. During the depressive position, part of the ego is identified with the bad object and the id; by self-punishment there is preservation of the object and reunion with the good object internally. Although the depressive relates to others as whole objects, he or she has not been able to establish a permanent, good, introjected object and is still subject to intrapsychic loss and recapitulation by the magical, reparative mechanism we have discussed.

During normal infantile development, the good and bad split introjects of self and object are integrated into complex wholes, which in turn become differentiated from each other and from external objects. Mahler (1964), Spitz (1945), and others found that unification of these split good and bad introjects was essential for object constancy and ego identification processes. In our case material, we noted that not only was the identified patient developmentally fixated, but also that in most cases the parents had not achieved self and object constancy and thus perpetuated this problem for the child.* The parents had not accepted themselves as both good and bad, nor their parents as complex and separately motivated. Without a stable, integrated, and internalized system of introjects, the parents remained stimulus bound and needed external objects upon whom to project certain split introjects. In turn, other family members were required to introject, incorporate, and act out these split introjects.

In order to stabilize the internal narcissistic system of the parents, the entire family became locked into a rigid, mutually controlling external system of interaction in which each one's self-esteem and survival depended on the other member's participation. There was a demand that the spouse behave, feel, and think according to an introjected image, instead of a perception of the other as a separately motivated individual. This prevented differentiation, and the parents perceived their current interpersonal relations in egocentric terms. When their needs were not met, they felt rejected, worthless, and enraged and they perceived the other as depriving, controlling, or, in general, bad. The resulting anger was experienced as destructive to the marital relationship, upon which they felt dependent for their self-esteem and survival.

The parents used two mechanisms to diminish the strength of these destructive feelings. One was substitution of a family member for the

---

* According to Stolorow and Lachman (1980), in developmental arrest "the structuralization of the subjective world has been incomplete, uneven, or partially aborted so that the more advanced representational structures remain vulnerable to regressive dissolution."

absent stable, internalized, good introject (the good mother). This process was accomplished by projective identification into one family member and served to compensate for past or present deprivation, to counter destructive feelings, and to maintain cohesion of the self. The other was projective identification and displacement of destructive feelings into another member, who served as a scapegoat to reduce the overload of negative forces. Four introjects that the parents employed have been developed into a paradigm (Fig. 2). The good self (S+) is equated with conformity and security, the bad self (S−) with rebellion, lack of achievement, or other elements threatening security. The good maternal object (O+) is tied to gratification of needs by their parents' own parents (the child's grandparents), the bad maternal object (O−) to perceptions of overcontrol, deprivation, or abandonment. The family transactions involving these introjects were at least triadic, with one parent dominant and initiating this process. At times, however, both parents entered into an unconscious collusion and it was difficult to discern if one parent was more dominant than the other.

The scapegoat is always assigned one of the negative introjects, here O−. This role need not be filled by the child; it can also be filled by the spouse, as in the first case that will be presented. Even a positive part introject projected into the child (S+ or O+) was found to be damaging, however. Acceptance was so conditional on being hyperfunctional that there was no tolerance for failure or inadequacy. Thus, the child had no authentic base on which to develop legitimate self-esteem and needed to dissociate divergent negative feelings and thoughts. The child felt compelled to incorporate only the good introject and could not spontaneously identify and integrate aspects of the parents that he or she selected in order to achieve an authentic and autonomous self-identity. Thus, a false self evolved that remained dependent on compliance to others.

The symbiotic survival pattern provides an object relations, not a mechanistic, framework for understanding the phenomenon of family homeostasis. The child unconsciously senses that the parent(s) are dependent on his or her acting out their introject in order for them to sustain their self-esteem and to gain magical control over past and present relationships. Thus, submission to parental injunc-

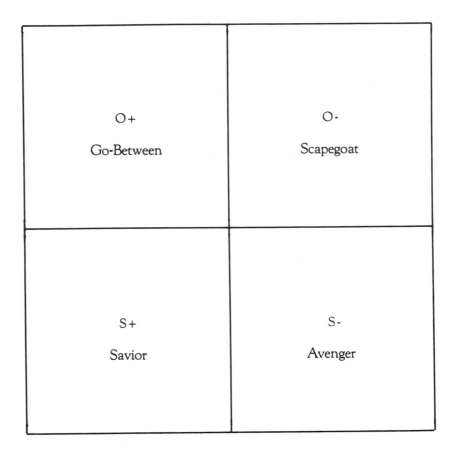

FIGURE 2. Paradigm of parents' internal system of split images of self and object and family role enacted by child. O+ represents the good maternal object, O— the bad maternal object, S+ the good self, and S— the bad self. In families of a schizophrenic, at least one parent employs splitting of the internalized maternal object. The spouse remains idealized as the good object (O+). Through projective identification, the child destined to become schizophrenic is induced into acting out the bad object (O—). Because anger is seen as dangerous and destructive, it is denied and displaced away from the spouse and onto the patient, who is scapegoated. This serves to reinforce primary process thinking, especially the patient's unconscious destructive fantasies. By retaining the spouse as the good mother in the external world, the parent(s) can sustain intrapsychic symbiotic fusion with the good maternal object (O+) to sustain their self-esteem and survival of the self.

tions also teaches the child that he or she has magical control over the parents. Symbiotic fusion is felt to be essential not only for the maintenance of his or her own identity and survival, but also for the preservation of the parents' narcissistic equilibrium. Jackson (1957) speculated that to preserve family homeostasis, the choice of the scapegoat was interchangeable.* We found, however, that the parents were quite selective in choosing the target for certain projections. The child having the constellation that most fit the requirements of the parents' introject, either good or bad, was chosen. Factors related to this choice were temperament, birth order, sex, degree of intellectual endowment, physical appearance, and disability of the child. This selectivity seemed to contribute to why within the same family one child became schizophrenic, whereas others did not.

THE SYMBIOTIC SURVIVAL PATTERN: CASE MATERIAL

Two examples will be presented to demonstrate several patterns of splitting and projective identification. In the first there was a dominant-submissive relationship between the parents; in the second an unconscious collusion existed. Each transaction is triadic, with projective identification of either good or bad self or object into the patient and the opposite split into another family member.

INDUCED COUNTERTRANSFERENCE IN BORDERLINE CONDITIONS

The patient was an attractive, intelligent young woman who came for psychoanalysis because of her inability to establish close relations and because of multiple phobias, compulsions, and depression. She

---

* In some instances, as in the second case to be presented here, we noted that when the system changed and the scapegoated child was freed, the child who had acted out a positive introject decompensated. Neither child, however, had an opportunity to develop independently an authentic and integrated self, but, rather, needed to preserve the self-esteem and survival of a parent.

was diagnosed by two psychiatrists as borderline.* These are the patient's verbatim comments taken from several sessions after two years of analysis:

> I never felt any good unless I was a reflection of what my parents wanted. They only cared for what I could give them; beyond that they were not interested. I felt there was nothing inside me. I felt both my parents kept me from being a separate person; I had to feel and think the way they did.... I don't think my mother was ever a separate person from my father. I felt my mother was trapped; she felt worthless and needed constant reassurance from my father. If I was too much of a person, mother would not talk to me, and she'd never back down.... With my father, I felt like a prostitute. I had to be untrue to what I really was. I didn't get rewarded like I hoped; I didn't get him to love me by not being myself, anyway. I intentionally did things he wanted me to do to make him love me and felt guilty I was taking him away from mother. I never really felt he loved my mother, and it made me feel that he'd stay around for me. I felt if he left, mother would lie down and die. I had to be good, to make him love me; it was important for me to keep everyone together. If I got angry with my father, I was afraid it would kill him; he was weak, and would fall apart and die. I felt tremendous power. I held everyone together, and if I got angry I could kill them. I kept them alive by being nice. I could cry, but not get angry; if I said I hate you, they would kill me.

This patient had remained symbiotically tied to her parents, and separation meant loss of her identity, an inability to survive psychologically, and destruction of her parents.* She defended herself by distancing maneuvers, because any close relationship threatened her

---

* Stone (1981) comments that the definition of borderline condition varies. As Stone points out, Kernberg describes the condition in terms of the level of psychic functioning (self and object are delineated, yet ambivalent aspects are poorly integrated and primitive defenses persist; reality testing is preserved). It is considered a distinct syndrome by Grinker and Gunderson, and an attenuated form of schizophrenic or manic-depressive psychosis by Kety and Rosenthal. Borderline conditions are subdivided into the schizotypal form (with obsessive-paranoid features) and the unstable-depressive form (with hysterical-impulsive features). The case described here fits into the latter subtype.

* The data in this case, obtained from individual psychoanalysis, have the limitation of not being derived from direct observation in family treatment. In addition, information concerning the grandparents was limited or unavailable.

again with being engulfed and dominated and with losing her autonomy. The father had formed a seductive relationship with the patient to compensate for a poor relationship with his wife. He was
described as a self-centered and fragile man who felt rejected whenever his wife contradicted him, failed to gratify his demands, or in
any way acted as a separate person. On an unconscious level, he
wanted his wife to behave toward him as the good maternal object
(O+), and, when she refused to submit to his coercive measures, he
saw her as the depriving, bad maternal object (O−) and turned to
the patient (Fig. 3). Thus, his acceptance of the patient was conditional, requiring her to gratify his demands by being the good, constantly nurturant maternal object (O+). The enactment of both the
O+ and O− was due to the father's use of splitting and projective
identification. The father expressed his hostility toward his wife by
openly degrading her and by comparing her to, and showing prefer-
ence for, his daughter.*

The mother, although having sufficient autonomy to resist submersion of her self and a loss of identity, was insufficiently assertive
to comment or to leave, remaining in a masochistic, scapegoated position. The patient felt guilty for defeating the mother and dysidentified with her for being so masochistic. The patient justified her own
submission to her father's wishes on the basis that she could magically control him by behaving as he wanted and so prevent his leaving. This in turn, she felt, preserved her mother's self-esteem and
survival.

The father's ego development seemed characteristic of a narcissistic
personality disorder in its lack of internalization of his mother and

---

* Lidz would classify this as a schismatic family, with disruption of the parental coalition and breaching of generational boundaries, because the father replaced his
spouse with his daughter. The father's domination and deprecation of the mother
deprived the patient of a model for feminine identification, interfered with resolution of the oedipal complex, and resulted in ego weakness. (This family also did
not teach the patient the instrumental techniques for social adaptation.) The symbiotic survival pattern, however, does not focus on shifting dyads but, rather, sees
the triadic relationship as essential to the father's use of splitting and projective identification and to his preventing the patient from achieving autonomy. As with other
borderline patients, the patient in this case both idealized and resented her father.

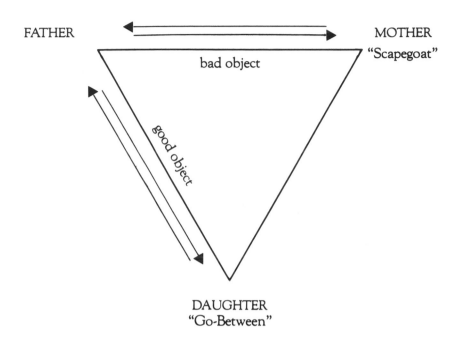

FIGURE 3. Symbiotic survival pattern in first case report, involving splitting, projective identification, and family role in borderline conditions.

poor differentiation of self from external objects. He felt entitled to dominate and use others as the good maternal object with whom he could symbiotically merge intrapsychically, to sustain his self-esteem. Interpersonally, this required that his wife behave as the good mother object. When she refused, the daughter was assigned this introject. Through the patient's introjection, incorporation, and acting out of the good mother object, she came to see herself in the omnipotent role of go-between. She felt that her behavior actually controlled her father's self-esteem, who, in turn, determined the mother's self-esteem. She did not see her parents as having a separate and independent existence apart from her; instead, there was a magical cause-and-effect relationship between her actions and their self-esteem and survival. Thus, primary process thinking was reinforced by the ongoing, symbiotic survival pattern in the family, which contributed to the patient's weak ego controls. During adolescence she felt blocked from further growth by the responsibility she felt for her parents, which resulted in an intense love-hate conflict. Because her feelings were poorly differentiated from action, she experienced her rage as a murderous, destructive power that she held over her parents. She feared loss of control and obsessively needed to protect her parents by behaving in a ritualized, constricted way. As she said, "I kept them alive by being nice."

INDUCED COUNTERTRANSFERENCE IN SCHIZOPHRENIA, WITH ACCOMPANYING DELINQUENT AND DEPRESSIVE FAMILY PATTERNS

An adolescent boy was seen in family therapy after making a serious suicide attempt while catatonic. At the initial interview he was grossly delusional, stating that his mother was present everywhere in the room. The patient was the youngest child and appeared less gifted intellectually than his older brother and sister. The patient was described as having had a stormy, pseudodelinquent personality prior to his breakdown. He had been disinterested in school, had no ambition to work, had been in frequent street fights, and had no close friends. There had been a constant oppositional relationship with his father. The father was so verbally and physically abusive toward the patient that the entire family blamed him for the patient's breakdown.

During the course of therapy, the father revealed that he had inflicted on his younger son exactly the same sadistic, humiliating punishment he had experienced with his mother. His own father had died when he was a small child, and his mother had become embittered, witholding, and jealous. She had turned to religion and had isolated herself socially. It is likely that she had displaced her rage at her husband, for dying and abandoning her, onto her son. She had also expected him to compensate her for her deprivation. There were no other siblings or close relatives. The father's mother had obstructed his independent strivings to go to college. She had not differentiated herself from her son and had rationalized that, because she was incapable of achieving middle-class status, her son would be unable to do so also. Instead, she had wanted him to work and support the family. Prior to the father's enrollment in college, she had

thrown out his books and secretly spent the money he had so pains-
takingly saved and entrusted to her care for his education. The father had then dropped out of college. Instead of feeling enraged at
his mother, he had continued to idealize her to preserve his dependent relationship. He had identified with the aggressor and turned
his aggression on himself, blaming himself for being too stupid and
lazy to continue college.

During his entire married life, he idealized his mother yet unconsciously acted out his anger at her by depriving his wife of economic
security (treating her as the bad maternal object). Thus, his wife was
forced to work and had become the breadwinner. The patient was
openly scapegoated as the bad object, which served to displace the
father's rage away from his wife (and mother), who consciously remained idealized as the good object (Fig. 4). The father also openly
accused the patient of being lazy, stupid, and a failure, all negative
images he felt about himself (the bad self). In contrast, the older son
was pressured into hyperfunctioning, in order to achieve the academic success of which the father had been deprived. He would be
father's savior and redeem him (as the good self). This protected the
father from depression, yet created a depressive pattern for the older
son.

Later in treatment it became apparent that the mother, who initially had seemed victimized and retiring, had the greatest influence
in defining family relationships. Although she did not overtly attempt
to usurp the father's legitimate authority, she did in fact exert actual control, through passive-aggressive means, so that all decisions
were made in her favor. The patient's delusional statement that his
mother's presence was pervasive was, indeed, a concrete description
of the extent of her influence. The mother had secretively formed
an alliance with the patient and subtly encouraged him to act out
her own rebellious, angry feelings against her husband. The patient
accepted and incorporated his mother's bad self (S−) into his self-
definition. He would provoke the father through oppositional behavior, thus acting out for mother as her "avenger."* In addition,
whenever the mother abdicated her parental authority and presented
herself as the helpless victim of her son's misbehavior to the father,
this served as a cue for the father to be punitive. In this way the

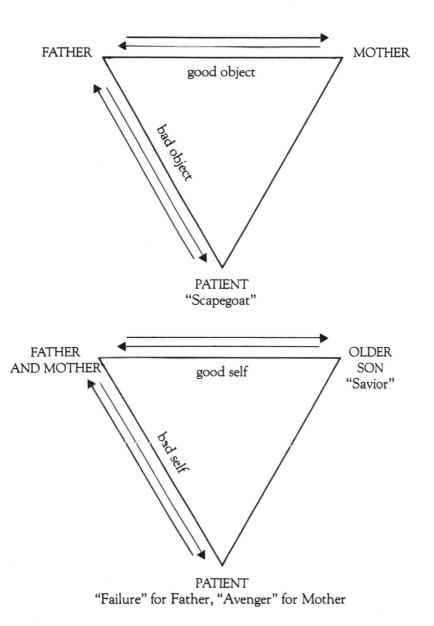

FIGURE 4. Symbiotic survival pattern in second case report, involving splitting, projective identification, and family roles in schizophrenia, as well as demonstrating the depressive and delinquent patterns.

mother provoked her husband into placing the patient into the scapegoated role, with the father playing the bad, punitive object (O−) and the son the bad, rebellious self (S−).

This pattern complemented the father's identification of himself with his own sadistic mother, and of the patient with his own bad self (S−). The father would then punish the patient harshly, and the mother would mildly reproach the father. In this way the mother's image of herself as the good self and the good parent, and as not responsible for her anger, was sustained. Through this maneuver the mother was also able to rally all the children around her to exclude the father and render him impotent. She had similarly formed a peer group alliance during her childhood to defeat her mother, whom she perceived as arbitrary, restrictive, and punitive.

Both parents had submitted to authoritarian control by their mothers in their families of origin. To preserve their security, they retained idealized images of their mothers by repressing their hostility and displacing it into the patient and onto the world in general, seeing it as a threatening place.* They also joined collusively to project their bad selves into the patient. In this way the mother could express her rage at her husband (and mother) through her son, and the father could project his angry feelings toward himself as a failure into the patient as the S−. In addition, the father could deny his rage at his wife (and mother), keeping her idealized as O+, and displace his rage onto the younger son, as the O−. Thus, the parents did not threaten their own relationship by openly expressing their anger, and they were able to sustain their intrapsychic identification with their own idealized mothers.

During the course of therapy the therapist served as a good grand-

---

* Johnson and Szurek (1954) were the first to observe that delinquents were subtly encouraged to act out unconscious rebellious wishes of their parents. The parents achieve vicarious gratification and appear blameless to authorities. Unlike the schizophrenic, the delinquent is rewarded and not double binded for acting out the narcissistic transference, and aggression is directed against an outside authority as well as a family member.

* (Wynne's "rubber fence" phenomenon of the family isolating itself from its environment is probably attributable to this process.)

father for both parents, enabling the father to identify with him, catharse his rage at his mother, differentiate, and develop better self-esteem. The mother became more able to assert herself directly and came to view men as supportive. The father became aware of responding to cues from his wife and acting out the bad parental role to please her. At the same time, he became aware of feeling alienated, impotent, frustrated, and enraged with his wife, just as with his mother. He then stopped acting out his rage—directly toward his son and indirectly through witholding behavior toward his wife. The father then accepted a steady job, becoming the breadwinner for the first time after 20 years of marriage.*

The identified patient had never learned to integrate and cope with his own angry feelings. Anger in the family was not openly expressed, because it was seen as destructive. This pattern only reinforced the patient's omnipotent destructive fantasies, prevented the integration of ambivalence, and interfered with his ability to control and verbally express anger. As the patient emerged from the roles of scapegoat and avenger, he became aware of his own murderous rage toward his father. He still needed external controls, but he transferred this need from the family system of mutual control to the therapist. He surrendered to the therapist for safekeeping a weapon he had hidden, lest he lose control and use it against his father. In the course of therapy, the patient learned to assert himself and express his anger in an integrated and effective way. The patient's emotional growth could be observed as he stopped playing with younger, delinquent children, resumed high school and was graduated, found a full-time job, and began dating girls his own age.

As the parents became close and the family system of interaction changed, the older son experienced an acute identity crisis, with severe depression nearly requiring hospitalization. He had never

---

* In treatment, as the father integrated his own ambivalent feelings and differentiated himself from his internalized mother, he developed greater self-esteem and independence and there was less need for him to project his O− and S− onto his son. The mother also differentiated herself and could express anger directly; thus, the son was free to move from his avenger and scapegoated role and to grow independently.

differentiated as a separate and authentic person, and he expressed a great deal of resentment toward his father for pressuring him to overachieve. He could never deal with his fears and limitations openly, and hence had never asked for nor received support and help in coping. In addition, he felt guilty at having submitted and "sold out" to his father for his approval. Many of the older son's previously hidden problems were now revealed and then worked through in individual therapy.

SUMMARY

The symbiotic survival pattern in the family is characterized as follows: Each person's self-esteem and psychological survival (ego identity) are felt to be dependent upon the behavior of the other family members. Each member, therefore, needs to control the other's behavior and feels controlled by his or her overwhelming sense of responsibility for the self-esteem and survival of the others. Because this system of interaction itself uses magical, infantile, omnipotent techniques to achieve control over past and present object relations, it reinforces the magical, primary process thinking that the child brings to the system innately. The child thus continues to use preoperational, primary process thinking to an abnormal degree in certain areas of personal relationships, because (1) the child's development is fixated at the symbiotic level of relationship; (2) the fixation makes the child pathologically dependent on the family relations for self-esteem and ego identity, and susceptible to continuing influence by this system (this gives the appearance that the pathology resides solely in the system); and (3) the fixation is reinforced by the ongoing, pathological family pattern of interaction.

The genesis of the symbiotic survival pattern appears to be based in the parents' lack of internalization of their mothers to regulate their own narcissistic equilibrium, and their failure to achieve self and object differentiation. Thus, there is a demand that the other think, feel, and behave in ways consistent with an introjected image of self or other so that the parent's self-esteem and cohesion remain intact. Because the parents use each other for narcissistic supplies and have not integrated their own ambivalence in order to individuate and separate, they cannot deal openly with hostility in the marriage. There is a reduced possibility for dialogue and problem solving. Thus, there is a need for a third person, the identified patient (or other family members), upon whom to project split good or bad, self or object introjects.

This triadic process has been illustrated through a paradigm of introjects and transactional systems. In schizophrenia the bad maternal object is projected into the patient, who is scapegoated. The identified patient is induced by one or both parents to incorporate and act out this O− introject. Because the parents cannot deal openly with aggression without fear of destroying their relationship, the schizophrenic patient's fear of his or her own omnipotent destructive fantasies is reinforced. Intrapsychic conflicts are acted out in the interpersonal sphere, and the parents depend on the patient to stabilize their own personalities continuously. Thus, the identified patient cannot achieve a separate identity with adequate ego controls. The patient requires a symbiotic relation to sustain his or her relational ego identity, and acts to perpetuate the system. Breaking from the symbiotic survival pattern is fraught with the fear of being destroyed, of not surviving intact alone, and of losing control and destroying the parents. When the individual's adaptational needs are dysjunctive with the family system, as a result of developmental growth or outside stress, he or she may be precipitated into an overt psychosis. This problem is especially acute during adolescence.

The two cases presented in this chapter demonstrate the four types of transactions within the symbiotic survival pattern that can be useful in understanding individual and systems dynamics and their role in the treatment process. The family patterns in depression will be discussed in the next chapter, those in hysteria and borderline conditions in chapter 8, and those in delinquency in chapter 10.

7

DEPRESSION:
THE DOUBLE BIND ON ACHIEVEMENT

Depression, even in the earliest psychoanalytic investigations, has always been related to disturbed object relations. Despite this connection, the main focus has been on intrapsychic factors and not on interpersonal processes. In Freud's later writings, however, he recognized that groups could determine individual functioning by exerting regressive and dedifferentiating forces.* This chapter will discuss certain forms of family group structure that tend to prevent individuation and separation, continue to be regressive, and contribute to the development of depressive phenomena. The underlying conceptual framework to be employed is an extension of the previously reported work on the symbiotic survival pattern of interaction found in families with a schizophrenic member (Slipp 1969, 1972, 1973b). A psychoanalytic theory of depression is proposed that includes both the intrapsychic and the interpersonal levels.

PSYCHODYNAMICS OF DEPRESSION

The first psychoanalytic theory differentiating depression from normal mourning was developed by Abraham (1911). In depression, unconscious hostility was believed to exist toward a lost love object. In "Mourning and Melancholia," Freud (1917) noted that the loss of the love object need not be real but can be imagined, and that the love object need not be a person but can be an ideal or money. Libidinal interest was withdrawn, and introjection and incorporation of the love object in the ego occurred. The rage toward the ob-

---

* In *Group Psychology and the Analysis of the Ego*, Freud (1921) discussed primitive societies and the military as prototypes of group functioning. We now know that these findings are not characteristic of all groups but, rather, are limited to those groups with autocratic leadership (Lippitt and White 1958), in which autonomy is surrendered for survival purposes.

ject was then retroflexed and expended on the ego. Abraham's clinical studies noted an infantile prototype of depression, which he termed "primal parathymia." The infant feels rejected and disappointed by both parents during the preoedipal period, resulting in feelings of abandonment, rage, a desire to bite, an inability to act, resignation, and hopelessness. Later in life, when the melancholic patient unconsciously reexperiences the loss of a love object, he or she regresses to this infantile fixation point between the early anal sadistic and late oral stages, resulting in anal destruction and total incorporation of the object. The superego then directs its sadistic impulses against the ego, causing depression.

Rado (1927) postulated a splitting of the lost love object into a good and a bad parent. The good parent (by whom the child wants to be loved) is incorporated in the superego and punishes the bad parent, who is incorporated in the ego. This serves to expiate guilt for rage toward the love object and is a plea for atonement and intrapsychic reconciliation with the good parent. Deutsch (1933) changed the object of the punishment and explained depression as the ego's devaluation of itself to gain forgiveness from the persecuting parent incorporated in the superego. Bibring (1953) viewed an ego state of helplessness to be the primary factor in depression. That state was believed to result from repeated early childhood experiences of helplessness. Similarly, Frank (1954) considered withdrawal and reduction of desires in depression to be a defense against the expectation of unavoidable frustration. Smith (1971) proposed that depression is a denial of differentiation so as not to acknowledge separateness and loss. During childhood the depressive feels coerced by a threatening love object into a more total, nondiscriminating identification, rather than spontaneously identifying with admired aspects of the object for growth purposes. The former style of identification serves defensive functions and thus is difficult to relinquish. In normal mourning there is acknowledgment of loss and separateness, resulting in enduring identification with aspects of, or relinquishing of, the lost love object.

Arieti (1959, 1962, 1965) was one of the first investigators to stress the cognitive factors of ego functioning as well as to focus on interpersonal relations. Arieti noted that the depressive remained psychologically dependent for the maintenance of his or her self-esteem upon a "dominant other," usually a withholding, depriving mother. Because the "dominant other" is the primary source of gratification, any direct expression of anger results in a fear of abandonment. Arieti considers failure to maintain this dependent relationship the cause of decompensation. The depressive feels unable to influence the environment alone and thus perceives his or her future as devoid of meaning and gratification. Bemporad (1971) noted that the depressive even fears autonomous gratification. The depressive establishes a bargaining relationship, hoping that performing for the "dominant other" will win love and acceptance. In Bemporad's observations, either parent could function as the "dominant other."

MELANIE KLEIN'S DEVELOPMENTAL TIMETABLE

Melanie Klein's theory of depression was built within a framework of the infant's developing human attachments. Klein (1932, 1948, 1950) found that infants were not simply autoerotic but, rather, were object related from birth. Because the mother is not under the infant's command, frustration of gratification results in rage and a desire to destroy her. The infant's ego is formed in part by projection of its own aggression onto the mother, who is then introjected and incorporated. This process is possible because of the lack of differentiation between self and object. Because the ego operates according to the all-or-none principle, the object is split and internalized as the all-good and all-bad mother images and corresponding self-images. Securing of the internalized all-good mother image is as essential to the ego's survival as preservation of the actual external object. Splitting serves to protect this positive mother introject from the bad mother introject, which contains the child's projected omnipotent death wishes and threatens the ego with destruction. Because the child re–projects these split introjects, the mother is perceived in these egocentric terms.

The child traverses normal paranoid and depressive developmental positions, which if not passed through successfully form the prototype for later mental illness. In the paranoid position, the ego is part-object related, cannot tolerate pain or displeasure, and automatically projects the all-bad self-object images. Through the mechanism of projective identification, "empathic" connection is maintained with this threatening all-bad external object, which thus must be controlled or attacked. The depressive position is whole-object related; therefore, the child recognizes the entire object as separate. When frustrated, the child experiences his or her aggression as omnipotent and feels "guilty anxiety" over destroying the object upon whom his or her survival depends. In order to restore the good external maternal object as a whole person, the infant attempts to undo this destruction magically by intrapsychically transforming the bad maternal introject into the good one through self-punishment. Because the depressive does not secure an internally consistent, permanent, and complex introjected image of the mother, he or she is subject to repeated loss and recapitulation of this infantile, magical maneuver. Klein postulates that in mania there is denial of dependency, of ambivalence, of guilt, and of loss. By omnipotently attempting externally to control, triumph over, and demean the love object, the patient defends against depression over the loss of a valued need-fulfilling object. During normal childhood development, there is unification of these split good and bad introjects, and they become differentiated from external objects. Mahler (1964) and Spitz (1945) viewed this developmental process as essential for self and object constancy.

THE SYMBIOTIC SURVIVAL PATTERN

In the parents of the families studied containing a schizophrenic or borderline patient, unification of split introjects, differentiation from external objects, and the internalization and securing of the good mother introject to regulate narcissism did not occur. As a result, their self-esteem and the integrity of the self were left vulnerable to external relations. The parents' acceptance of themselves as both good and bad, and of their own parents as complex and separately motivated, did not seem to have been accomplished developmentally. The self and other were either all good or all bad. These parents continued to idealize their own parents and displace negative feelings onto their current relations. Because of their egocentricity, when others did not gratify their needs, they experienced feelings of rejection, worthlessness, and rage. These parents did not perceive the other's behavior as independently motivated; instead, the other was seen as totally bad. They distrusted the other to be responsive to their needs and needed to control the other and to deny their own separateness. Other family members were thus induced into introjecting, incorporating, and acting out certain split introjects. These mechanisms usually involved at least three people, with one parent being more dominant and assigning a negative introject to one person and a positive introject to another.* In order to stabilize the intrapsychic system of one or both parents, the entire family of the schizophrenic or borderline patient became enmeshed in a rigid, mutually controlling system of interaction in which each member's self-esteem and survival were experienced as dependent on the other member's behavior. Thus, each member felt omnipotent and overly responsible for the other and, at the same time, helpless and externally controlled by others. This system of family interaction, although providing continuity and control of relationships, prevented differentiation of individual personalities. Thus, the child had great difficulty achieving an autonomous and separate identity, with adequate ego controls, apart from the family.† The child required this symbiotic family system to sustain self-definition, which remained reactive and relational to the system. In addition, the child felt responsible for the self-esteem and survival of the parents. To separate from this symbiotic pattern and be autonomous was experienced by the child as

---

* This process involves symbiotic fusion with the good maternal object intrapsychically to sustain self-esteem and self-cohesion.
† Freud (1921), in *Group Psychology and the Analysis of the Ego*, noted that members of a group give up their autonomous functioning and mutually identify with the leader, who functions temporarily as a superego for all. In the families we studied, the symbiotic interaction could be considered to be serving as a permanent external superego. Its origin is believed to lie in symbiotic fusion with the preoedipal good mother, which the group symbolically represents.

a loss of control over angry feelings and as destruction of the parents, and also activated the child's own fear of being destroyed and not surviving intact alone.

The family of the schizophrenic or borderline patient does not provide the appropriate reality context to test limits and work through omnipotent destructive fantasies; instead, the symbiotic pattern parallels and reinforces these fantasies by considering anger as dangerous and destructive. This process prevents the child from differentiating feelings from action and what is inside from what is outside (establishing ego boundaries), and prevents the transition from primary to secondary process thinking in areas of the ego related to interpersonal functioning and identity. The symbiotic family system initially contributes to the child's becoming developmentally fixated at what Mahler (1965) describes as the symbiotic level of infant-mother functioning. The ongoing symbiotic family system continues to reinforce this fixation through subsequent phases of development. In a circular fashion, such patients themselves actively perpetuate this system, because they are dependent on it to sustain their ego controls and identity.

Figure 5 illustrates the symbiotic pattern and the transactions involved in the family. A paradigm of four split introjects is shown for each individual. This paradigm includes the good maternal object (O+), which is tied to gratification of needs by the mother; the bad maternal object (O−), which is equated with perceptions of overcontrol, deprivation, or abandonment; the good self introject (S+), involving conformity and security; and the bad self introject (S−), which is connected with rebellion, lack of achievement, and other elements threatening security. Because the parents in those families with a schizophrenic or borderline patient have not integrated and differentiated their own internal sense of self from objects, the perception of the other remains egocentric. When the spouse does not gratify the needs of the dominant parent, he or she feels rejected, worthless, abandoned, and enraged. The spouse is considered to be the depriving and controlling all-bad mother. Direct expression of the resulting rage is experienced as destructive internally of the good mother and externally of the marital relationship, upon which the

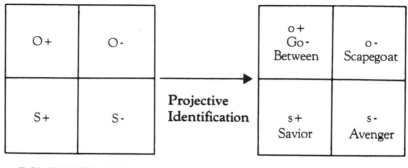

FIGURE 5. Paradigm of internal system of split, introjected images, family roles, and pathology. O+, good maternal object; O−, bad maternal object; S+, good self; S−, bad self; For the introject projected by a parent, large letters are used. For the introject internalized by a child, small letters are used. The latter include o+, go-between role—hysteria and borderline conditions; o−, scapegoat role—schizophrenia; s+, savior role—depression; s−, avenger role—delinquency and psychopathy (overinvolved type).

parent's own self-esteem and survival depend. The parent therefore feels unable to deal with the conflict openly.*

Two mechanisms of dealing with these destructive feelings have been noted, both of which preserve the dependent relationship and serve as an outlet for anger (see Fig. 5). One method is scapegoating, in which projective identification occurs and angry feelings are displaced from one member, who is idealized, to another, who is devalued and punished. When the O− introject is placed into another via projective identification, that person (who can be a child or an adult member) is seen as the depriving bad mother.

---

* Wynne's concept of pseudomutuality in the family relations of schizophrenics (Wynne, Ryckoff, Day, and Hirsch 1958) involves a retention of the illusion of symbiotic oneness with the spouse, who is seen as the good mother, by means of an absence of disagreement and fighting and by constant togetherness. The illusion is maintained at the expense of autonomy.

The other method of diminishing the strength of the "destructive" feelings is by substitution, in which another family member is induced to fill the lack of a stable good maternal introject. Projective identification also is the defense mechanism employed here. When O+ is projected, the other is expected to function as the good mother in order to identify with and make up for past deprivations. Usually the spouse or an oldest child is expected to take on this responsibility. When a child does, he or she often functions as a surrogate parent or *go-between* for the parents and is trapped into assuming the responsibility of preserving the marriage. In schizophrenia the child is induced into the *scapegoat* role (o-) and the spouse remains idealized as the good mother. In borderline conditions the child is idealized as the *go-between* (o+) and the spouse is demeaned and scapegoated as the bad mother. When S+ is projected, the recipient is expected to achieve or succeed socially, so that the parent will not feel a failure; the parent can identify with the success and live vicariously through the child. The child, destined to become depressive, functions as a *savior* for the parent's self-esteem by enhancing the family's social prestige. When S- is projected, the child is expected to act out unacceptable, angry feelings against society with which the parent can identify. The child, destined for psychopathy, thus serves as an *avenger* for the parent. These two last subtypes of the symbiotic survival pattern, however, have certain differences from those resulting in schizophrenia and borderline conditions. These differences will now be discussed; the differences between these subtypes and the pattern in the overinvolved form of delinquency will be described in Chapter 10.

OPPOSITIONAL SYMBIOTIC SURVIVAL PATTERN

We will now concentrate on the differences between families with a schizophrenic or borderline member and those with a depressed member. In schizophrenia the patient is induced by the parents, through projective identification, to incorporate and act out certain of their own split maternal introjects. This constitutes the bad mother (o-) *scapegoat* role in schizophrenia and the good mother (o+) *go-*

between role in borderline disorders. These roles determine not only how the patient will behave, but also how he or she will think and feel; they thereby control the patient's total self-image or identity. In depression the parental projective identification induces incorporation of the good self (s+), the *savior* role, with the threat of rejection of the bad self (s−), or scapegoat being held in the background for noncompliance. Clearly the incorporation of a split maternal introject, as in schizophrenia and borderline conditions, is more dedifferentiating for the child than identifying with an aspect of the parent's self, as in depression.* First, even though there is coercion in the latter, the child would normally identify with aspects of the parents' selves spontaneously. Second, control of the patient in depression has been found to be less encompassing of the personality, and emphasis is placed on behavior, or social performance (Gibson 1958). Third, the ego integrity of one or both parents and the survival of the family are not at stake, as they are in schizophrenia and borderline conditions. The parents of the depressive have achieved greater personality integration; cohesion of the self is not at stake, only self-esteem. The parents' narcissistic vulnerability is thus markedly less.

In comparing the pattern in the family and individual functioning, the construct of *family constancy* seems applicable. If there is family constancy, the parents' personalities and the cohesion of the family as a group are stable and do not have to be held together by the child's behavior. In depressive families the child is not burdened with such a life-or-death responsibility toward the parents or the family, and thus there is also greater freedom and range in the patient's response. This allows for a greater degree of autonomy, and the child's response tends to be oppositional. In the terms of Freud's theory of the psychosexual stages of development, the patient's reaction represents an anal conflict around control of the contents of the body, i.e., feces. The child either submits to parental pressure and control by performing, or retains control and autonomy by withold-

---

* Even here, incorporating the bad mother is probably more dedifferentiating than incorporating the good mother.

ing, that is, by being oppositional and not performing. The threat that is experienced is loss of love, which affects self-liking and self-disliking; it is not total annihilation of the self, as in schizophrenia and borderline conditions.

EARLIER STUDIES OF FAMILIES OF DEPRESSIVES

One of the first papers to study the familial context in manic-depressive illness was published in 1954 by Cohen, Baker, Cohen, Fromm-Reichmann, and Weigert. Gibson's follow-up studies (1958, 1959) replicated many of these findings. The work of Cohen and colleagues served as a beginning framework for our study of depressive phenomena in general. These investigators noted that, for a variety of reasons, these families felt set apart from the mainstream of society. Usually this feeling of separateness stemmed from social failure, for which the mother blamed the father. The mother was seen as the strong and reliable but cold and unloving moral authority whose approval the children desired. The father, who accepted himself as a failure, was perceived as weak but lovable. He conveyed a dysidentification message of "Don't be like me." One child, usually the most gifted, was selected and pressured by the mother into achievement to make up for the father's failure. Because the family adhered to a collateral group orientation, as seen in folk cultures, each individual was not differentiated but, rather, was seen as a reflection of the entire family. Thus, the family members were able to identify with, and live through, the accomplishments of this child, thus enhancing the family's social prestige, which defines their own self-esteem.

Cohen, Baker, Cohen, Fromm-Reichmann, and Weigert (1954) briefly mention that patients may do things that work against their own self-interests, or may minimize their accomplishments to avoid the envy of the family. We found this secondary factor extremely significant in our clinical study of manic-depressives and others with depressive conditions. In addition to the overt message to succeed socially, we found a simultaneous, covert, and contradictory message to fail. If the child becomes successful and autonomous, the parents lose control over the child. He or she is then viewed as a competitor and a threat to the self-esteem of one or both parents. If the child overshadows an insecure parent, there is the danger that he or she will be scapegoated and rejected. Such an event is particularly important if this parent is the sole source of nurturance and warmth, as the fathers were in the families described by Cohen and colleagues.

The form of family constellation described by Cohen and associates is found in situations in which the father does not perform his role function as breadwinner. Such a pattern is found in immigrant families, in which the father often does not have the language or technical skills to find employment, and also occurred during the Depression in the United States, when there was a lack of job opportunities. Currently, we find much the same family constellation among families at the lowest socioeconomic levels (Slipp 1973a, Slipp, Ellis, and Kressel 1974). The wife usually is able to sustain her self-esteem, because she can continue to function in her Familial role, but the husband cannot and feels a failure. In traditional families the wife submerges her own autonomous needs and aspirations to those of others in order to be a "good" mother and wife. She is rewarded by outside social approval for this self-sacrificing role performance, and her identity and self-esteem are also enhanced by the prestige of her husband's socioeconomic status. When the husband is unemployed, however, she is not compensated by him for her selfless, nurturant role; as a result she frequently feels angry and betrayed. Because of her husband's depression, the wife in this situation often feels coerced into assuming leadership. In these instances, the more the wife overfunctions (by taking over responsibility), the more the husband seems to underfunction. It appears that in families which generate a depressive, the husband uses passive-aggressive withdrawal and withholding to express his resentment toward the wife for usurping his authority. The result is a cold war between the parents.

THE DOUBLE BIND ON ACHIEVEMENT

Probably reflecting our currently more affluent society, the fathers in most of our cases were successful and overfunctioning, although they often felt insecure about their achievements. The wives were more often underfunctioning, seeing themselves as failures and frequently being phobic, depressed, or alcoholic. In these cases the father was the cold one, overtly pressuring the child for achievement, whereas the mother, who provided the warmth, gave the implicit message to fail. By blocking independent strivings and keeping the child dependent, the mother was able to sustain her selfless, nurturant role, which was the main source of her self-esteem. In other instances the conflict was not between the parents but, rather, arose when one or both of the parents individually imparted conflicting succeed and fail messages. The child was encouraged to achieve, yet when he or she did succeed, it was taken for granted; emotional reward came only with failure. Many parents pressured for achievement yet were so perfectionistic that whatever the child did, it was not enough. Other parents subtly transformed a victory into a defeat by ruminating about their concern that the child would not be able to win the next time.* The achievement could not be owned and serve to build confidence and security, because the negative was emphasized. In these ways the parental ambivalence concerning the child's achievement was communicated, independent strivings were inhibited, and control over the child was maintained.

The child's failure prevents invalidation of the parents, themselves leading a constricted, phobic existence. Risk taking is not reinforced; instead, the patient needs to be like the parents and embrace their unhappy, self-negating outlook to gain their acceptance. The patient constantly feels on the brink of disaster, fearing that the parents will suddenly change totally in their attitudes and become rejecting.

Thus, such children feel helpless and hopeless, because they are caught in a no-win dilemma, a *double bind*. If they win, they lose, and if they lose, they lose. They learn that compliance to the succeed message does not bring with it the hoped-for gratification. According to their perception, their social success only enhances the parents' prestige and narcissism; there is nothing in it for them. They feel exploited, deprived, enraged, and demeaned also by their own

---

* Variants of the technique of plucking defeat from the jaws of victory, which inhibits commitment to achievement, are "just in case you fail" (pseudoprotectiveness), and "anything you do is all right" (pseudopermissiveness).

compliance in giving up autonomy to assume a submissive false self. They identify with this exploited role and feel compelled to satisfy other's needs and guilty and unworthy concerning their own needs. For such patients success and strength bring the threat of independence from parental control, for which they risk rejection. Unless they gratify and feed their parents' self-esteem, they feel worthless and of no use to the parents. Because they have not been prepared to function as separate individuals, autonomy is equated with abandonment and with not surviving alone. The intrapsychic conflict is thus between domination and abandonment. In addition, the symbiosis functions as an interpersonal defense, providing external controls over feelings of omnipotent, destructive rage. Depressives evolve an oppositional form of symbiosis as a compromise solution to this double bind. By partial compliance to both succeed and fail messages, they avoid the risk of abandonment by either parent, yet by rebelling sufficiently against these injunctives, they preserve some autonomy. Through half-hearted compliance to their parents' wishes, they can play off both pressures and avoid being either too strong or totally helpless. By partially defeating themselves and losing, they can claim to be victims of external circumstances and thus avoid taking responsibility. They can thereby frustrate the parents' succeed message and disrupt parental exploitation of their success. They can passive-aggressively express their rage at the parents without being held accountable. Because they also comply to the fail message, they feel they can demand parental emotional support. In this process the controlled one becomes the controller; the patient can withhold gratification from the parents, thereby exploiting their dependency for narcissistic supplies as they did his or hers.

Bonime (1959) has noted a similar process with neurotic depressives. There is a constant need for dependency gratification, accompanied by an unwillingness to give gratification to others. Any expectation by the other is seen as an unjust demand. Bonime also found that depressives stimulate others to expect gratification and then frustrate them by withholding. The patient manipulates the other into expecting gratification, much like the patient's demanding parent in the paradigm presented here. In personal relations the exploitative, bad parental introject is projected and acted out in the transference. The other becomes dependent on the patient to satisfy his or her needs. The patient partially plays out being compliant (s +) in order to lead the other on, then rebels and acts out (s –) by withholding gratification, thereby indirectly expressing rage and sustaining an oppositional identity. These dynamics have also been found in underachieving individuals, as well as those suffering a work block who do not manifest overt depressive symptomatology.

DEVELOPMENTAL FIXATION AND FAMILY INTERACTION

On an intrapsychic level, the fixation point of the patient is seen as being at the resolution of the separation-individuation phase of development. It is proposed here, however, that the cause of this fixation is not simply the loss of the love object during infancy. The parent(s) do not relate to the patient as a separate person with his or her own needs, not only during infancy but also throughout subsequent phases of development. The patient feels isolated, alone, and under threat of abandonment continuously through childhood, because the parent(s) expose the child to conflicting messages about performance, threatening rejection and exploiting the child for their own self-esteem. This family interaction also intensifies and hinders the resolution of the oedipal conflict and identification with the parent of the opposite sex. When the father gives the fail message, he portrays himself as vulnerable and weak. Thus, the male patient has difficulty competing, winning, and asserting his independence. In addition, the son needs his father to be strong as an adequate model for identification. When the mother is the weak masochistic one, giving the fail message to subtly undermine the father's pressure, alliance of the son with the mother increases the threat of castration by the father, who is seen as a more threatening force. This latter pattern was noted with some male depressives who had homosexual conflicts. An oppositional adaptation allows for some autonomy, sustains the symbiotic dependency, indirectly releases anger without the patient's being held accountable, and keeps the patient externally controlled, as well as controlling the responses of the parents.

Because the parents of these patients are coercive, Smith (1971) states, identification with them is more total and more difficult to relinquish, because it serves defensive functions. We can further delineate the type of internalization that occurs. Because the parents have not allowed for separation and individuation and themselves employ splitting and projective identification as a major defense, the patient's identification with them remains undifferentiated. The patient is coerced into identifying with one aspect of the dominant parent's self, the good achieving self, through the threat of rejection for noncompliance. As we have discussed, this process is less dedifferentiating than that in which the parent's split maternal introject, either bad or good, is projected into the patient, as in schizophrenia and borderline conditions. Projection of an aspect of the parent's self is more limited and allows the patient a greater range of freedom for some separation of self from the object. Were it not for its coercive nature, this type of projection would be a natural process, initiated by the patient spontaneously. The patient's internalized self and object images are therefore experienced as more nearly whole and separate; they are not fused, as in schizophrenia or other narcissistic disorders. The patient's self, however, is still connected to the dominant parent and not fully separate and constant. The self that has evolved is a false, compliant self and remains linked to the parent, whose constancy depends on the patient's performance. Structurally, splitting persists in the patient; the good and bad maternal introjects are neither unified nor differentiated from external objects.

FAMILY INTERACTION AND SUPEREGO DEVELOPMENT

Because of the particular nature of the interaction in families with a depressive, we can postulate a unique pattern of superego development in the depressive patient. The patient is able to internalize and generally secure the bad maternal object, but not the good maternal object, into the superego, because the dominant parent pressures for achievement but does not gratify or provide mirroring responses when it occurs. As a result, a punitive, nongratifying, bad maternal introject (o−) is internalized in the superego. The actual family interaction parallels and reinforces the patient's intrapsychic process of splitting. Acceptance of the patient by the dominant parent is not stable; rather, it is conditional on submission by the patient to pressures for performance. The nondominant parent, who is often nurturant and soothing, is both devalued by the family and self-devaluing, and thus does not offer an effective good object who can provide meaningful comfort. The patient, unable to internalize and secure this good maternal object into the superego, cannot gratify and comfort himself or herself internally to sustain self-esteem and autonomy. Instead, he or she remains narcissistically vulnerable to loss of, and dependent on, the dominant parent (or a later trans-ferential object—the dominant other) to sustain self-esteem. By ei-ther submissively performing for the dominant parent or punishing his or her own bad self to atone for lack of performance, the patient hopes to avoid abandonment by the dominant other and to elicit nurturance and forgiveness. In this way, it is hoped, the bad mother introject in the superego will become the good mother, with which the self can fuse intrapsychically to sustain narcissistic equilibrium.

SELF-DIFFERENTIATION AND SYMBIOTIC RELATEDNESS

As we have stated, because of the greater degree of differentiation in the depressive, the internalized self and object images are ex-perienced as more nearly whole and more separate than in schizophrenia. Individuation is not complete, however, and splitting persists. Only the bad maternal introject is internalized and secured in the superego. In addition, the self and object remain linked to-gether in the form of a bad self–bad object gestalt. (These gestalts bear some similarity to the undifferentiated selfobjects that Heinz Ko-hut [1977]* describes in patients with narcissistic character disorders.) This partly fused gestalt of the introjected relationship is then projected and acted out interpersonally, forming the basis for sym-

---

* Kohut (1977) considers deficiencies in the self of narcissistic patients also to come from developmental arrest resulting from parental failings, and not simply from in-trapsychic conflict.

biotic relatedness. Splitting and projective identification then become the major defenses used interpersonally to sustain the patient's self-esteem. The other is induced into incorporating the bad maternal introject (o−), while the patient identifies with the bad self introject (s−). Arieti (1962) similarly describes the depressive as seeing himself or herself as the helpless, worthless, and dependent child who transfers the "dominant other" image onto others to sustain their self-esteem.

We also found that the spouse's personality characteristics frequently meshed to allow acceptance of this projected transferential relationship. The spouse of the depressive has often also experienced in his or her family of origin a dominant and nongratifying parent. By identifying with the aggressor in the superego and using projective identification, the spouse can employ a manic defense. He or she can play the role of the dominant parent and thereby displace the unacceptable, diminished, and dependent self onto the patient. Thus, the spouse does to the patient now what was done to the spouse during childhood by his or her own dominant parent.*

What becomes established is a subtle, unconscious collusion between the patient and the spouse. If the depressive gets better, the spouse often is greatly threatened by a potential reversal of the bad self–bad object gestalt. The spouse fears that if change occurs, he or she will become the helpless, dependent, and worthless child and the patient the dominant, punitive parent. In alcoholism and other sadomasochistic relationships, this gestalt does at times alternate back and forth. This fear of reversal of the collusion provides a psychological explanation for the phenomenon of family homeostasis. In addition, because the patient's identity remains relational in this symbiotic interaction, disruption of this externalized self-object gestalt

---

* An interesting form of countertransference, which we can term *dissociative*, is related to this mechanism. It involves the patient's identifying with the internalized bad object in the superego and projecting dissociated aspects of the self onto the analyst. The patient does to the analyst what was done to him or her as a child. Thus, the analyst's responses, if not contained and acted out, may be similar to those the patient experienced as a child. See also Racker (1953, 1957) on the "depressive-paranoid countertransference" which is similar.

is experienced as not surviving alone and is accompanied by fears of death, illness, accident, or going insane.

INTRAPSYCHIC UNDOING AS A MIRROR OF THE FAMILY DYNAMICS

Intrapsychically, during the depressive episode, the introjected, negatively perceived, dominant object (o−), incorporated and secured in the superego, punishes the rebellious, nonachieving bad self (s−), thereby expiating guilt for omnipotent destructive fantasies. This intrapsychic maneuver represents a submissive plea for atonement. It is hoped that the bad maternal object (o−) in the superego will be forgiving and become the good maternal object (o+), which will reunite with the good self (s+) to sustain the patient's self-esteem. This is an intrapsychically autoplastic, magical maneuver to undo hostility and sustain external relations with the parents.

This intrapsychic undoing often mirrors the undoing tactics in the relationship of the patient's parents. For example, when the father is the depressed, underfunctioning parent, he feels unworthy and guilty because of his lack of achievement as well as his passive-aggressive acting out of his underlying hostility. By accepting the wife's punishment, the father expiates his guilt and sustains his relationship with her. The depressive seems to identify the self primarily with the guilty and punished nonperforming parent. The parental sadomasochistic conflict thus seems repeated within the patient's ego, with o− punishing s−. This formulation bears some similarity to Rado's "good parent" or Deutsch's "persecutory parent," which we can redefine here as the dominant "bad" parent incorporated in the superego, intrapsychically punishing the depressed parent, with whom the patient's self is primarily identified. In the manic episode the patient appears to identify with the punitive, dominant "bad" parental introject, o− in the superego, while externalizing and acting out rage through projective identification by demeaning and punishing the other, s−. In bipolar conditions there appears to be alternation between these two identifications with split introjects.

CASE ILLUSTRATION

The patient was a talented writer who came for psychoanalysis because of symptoms of depression, work inhibition, and marital conflict. Despite a promising beginning to his career, he felt immobilized and unable to concentrate on his writing. This resulted in financial hardships, insecurity, and conflict with his wife. In this case the succeed-fail double bind not only came from the father, but also existed between the parents.

His father was depicted as overtly dominant, cold, and overfunctional. The father had wanted to become a physician but because of the Depression had settled for teaching. Despite his eventually becoming a school principal, the father felt dissatisfied with his achievement and saw himself as a failure. He had pressured his son (the patient) into academic and athletic achievement (Fig. 6a: $S+ \rightarrow s+$). This pressure had been particularly intense when his son was a student in his school. The patient felt his father was solely interested in "the appurtenances of success" for his own prestige and not genuinely interested in him. At the same time, the patient felt his father was competitive with him (Fig. 6b: $O- \rightarrow s-$). As he stated:

> I had to prove my inability to cope, to be inadequate, and I have to do something to pull myself down. Whenever I have a creative good idea, I have to pay dues first. To you, to my father. I was to have the rewards of society—be famous, rich, and successful—so he could show me off. But somewhere he didn't really want me to be truly potent [Fig. 6c: $s+ \rightarrow O+$]. He had to put me down. I would expose him if I were adequate, he had put himself down by settling for something he didn't want to do. He was always paying dues. I pay dues to be a little potent, play brinksmanship. I kill myself and him just a little bit—I never have a full heart on, only half a heart to preserve the relationship.

His failure thus enabled him to comply with his father's fail message as well as to express his rebellion at being exploited by his father for his own self-esteem needs. Thus, he could frustrate his father's pressure for achievement without being held accountable. He was fearful of directly asserting himself with his father because of considerable castration anxiety. He introjected his threatening fa-

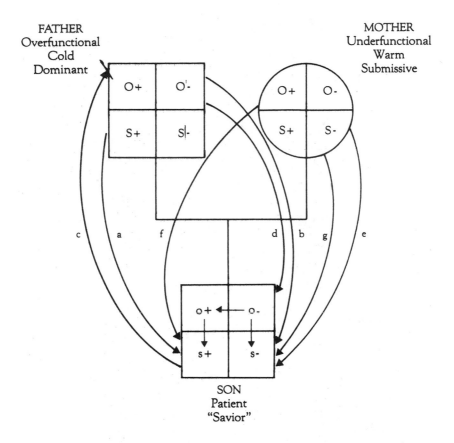

FIGURE 6. Genogram of case illustration. Interpersonal and intrapsychic factors.

  a. Father's "win for me" message (projective identification).
  b. Father's "lose for me" message (competitive).
  c. Patient's hoped-for narcissistic reward is frustrated.
  d. Patient introjects father into superego.
  e. Mother's "you cannot win—be a failure like me" message (projective-identification).
  f. Mother provides emotional warmth; noncompliance threatens disruption of narcissistic gratification and abandonment.
  g. Patient introjects mother into self.
  h. In depression, primary identification is with s−, and patient punishes self (o− →s−), hoping to change o− to o+, which would then reunite with s+. In mania, primary identification is with o−, with reexternalization of s− and projection onto another, who is punished (o− →s−).

(Adapted from Slipp [1976]. Used by permission.)

ther into his superego (Fig. 6d: $O- \to o-$). In his dreams he saw himself either as a wolf going for his father's jugular or as being killed by him. He was fearful of his father's power and of his own omnipotent rage, and wanted to be controlled. He identified himself with his submissive and depressed mother (Fig. 6g: $S- \to s-$). In one of his dreams he promised his father that he would behave like a good girl. "The only way I could assert myself with father was by being passive. It was the only weapon I had, the only way to express anger." When his father depended on him for performance, the patient felt protected against his power, although at the same time he felt deprived, trapped, and enraged. "There was an element of spite in my losing, but it was the only way I could get back." He felt guilty over letting his father down, and projected his guilt and self-hatred onto the analyst in the transference. He felt the analyst would be like his introjected father ($o-$), disappointed, judgmental, and angry. He thereby externalized his self-punishing intrapsychic maneuver ($o-$ punishing $s-$) to expiate his guilt and turn the bad parental introject into the good one, which could then reunite with the good self (Fig. 6h). He could thus sustain his oppositional symbiotic relationship, achieve some autonomy, control his own rage, control his father's responses, and express his anger indirectly without being held accountable.

The mother was described as submissive to the father, underfunctional, and warm to the patient (Fig. 6f: $O+ \to s+$). She had been her mother's favorite, had been infantilized, and remained dependently attached. When she married during the Depression, she and her husband had moved into her parents' home and lived with them for about nine years. She and her mother had formed an alliance against her husband, cynically putting down his education as useless because he could not earn a living. The patient's mother had not completed high school, because education and intellectuality were not valued in her home. The patient described his mother as neurasthenic and as suffering from headaches, insomnia, feelings of worthlessness and helplessness, and hypochondriasis. She instilled anxiety in the patient concerning his own bodily functions, as well as a constricted, negative world outlook. She had no confidence in her ability to achieve and saw her son as similar to herself (Fig. 6e:

S– →s–). She never expected anything from the patient and took no interest in his performance. When the family moved out of his grandparents' house, his mother formed a seductive alliance with him, treating him as an intimate and complaining about the father's stinginess with money. The patient felt "at the mercy of her ignorance" and controlled by her weakness. She was in a constant state of dysphoria but never did anything for herself. The patient felt his mother needed his reassurance, and he felt responsible for both his parents' sense of adequacy and happiness (s+, savior role).

The patient stated:

> I was in some way responsible for how both my parents felt. My station was making it up to them. I had no right to my independence or to good times if they were miserable. My parents were both weak and unable to function as separate people. I always took my cues from them also to define myself.... I always felt like a helpless child who couldn't cope; I remained dependent on others. I felt I had to perform to be loved; otherwise I'd be abandoned. My father would never say, "You're doing well," or, "I don't care how you do, I love you.".... It was always connected with making good for him. I don't want to give anything to anyone except my children.

The patient then worked through his relationship with his wife, who had been seen also as a bad, exploitative parent. Any expectation at all was interpreted as an unfair demand, and he resented it and withheld gratification just enough to avoid rejection.

In a dream, a turning point occurred concerning his giving up autonomy for acceptance, his rage, and his withholding behavior.

> I'm in a foreign car that I borrowed from a friend. It starts to roll without the motor. Cars begin coming in from the side roads. I reach for the key to start the car and control it, but I have forgotten the key. [He felt panicky, helpless, and inadequate.] I don't own my own talent or whatever powers I have. I was never doing things for myself— always to satisfy my parents—my father in particular. I never felt I could just do something for myself. When I first began to write, there was never complete satisfaction, it was tied in with other people's approval. I don't have the key to my motor, to me.... Having a need meant I didn't have any autonomy. I feel I have to give over, I'm not an equal. I feel guilty, angry, and deballed, and then I set it up as an adversary situation.... With doctors I look to be sick yet can't accept it if I am sick. I can give over, the weight drops off, I can be depen-

dent and it's sanctified. It's a powerful drive to regress. I have an excuse for not working, it's like being sick and not having to go to school. When I'd be in school my insides would twist, everything was a test situation. Recently I felt I could make my own life and despite being in certain situations, it doesn't mean I can't decide what I want. Psychologically I felt I had no choice, and I'd go on to prove it. In the dream, if I borrow the car then I assume there won't be a key. I have to borrow the car out of necessity, but I still can have control over myself and what I want.

As the patient worked through his conflicts over autonomy with his parents in the transference, he became productive and successful as a writer, as well as financially secure. The relationship with his wife improved temporarily but eventually ended in divorce.

EVIDENCE CONFIRMING A DOUBLE BIND ON ACHIEVEMENT

The work of Beck (1967) on the cognitive structure of depressives seems to reveal a personality style that confirms the existence of the no-win double bind in their families. On the basis of research findings, Beck postulated that the depressive's negative cognitive set precedes and determines affect and behavior, not vice versa. How an individual perceives an experience shapes his or her affective response. Beck found the thematic content of dreams to reveal that depressed patients portrayed themselves as losers to a greater degree than did a control group. Psychological tests, as well as content analysis of recorded psychotherapy interviews, also indicated that these patients saw themselves as losers. Beck describes the overall cognitive abnormalities of depressives as including low self-esteem, self-deprecation and blame (a bias against themselves), negative expectations (hopelessness), paralysis and fear in relation to decision making (avoidance tendencies), a sense of deprivation and aloneness, self-prodding and "should" thinking (often about mutually exclusive activities), perception of small tasks as overwhelming problems, and escapist or suicidal wishes. These cognitions are involuntary, automatic responses that seem highly plausible to the depressed patient. In summary, Beck postulates a cognitive triad consisting of a negative view of the self, the world, and the future as primary, and the depressed mood as secondary.

Certain experimental studies have demonstrated the sensitivity of performance to the mood of depressed patients. In a pilot study Beck noted that depressed patients showed an elevation of mood when they were given positive feedback on performance tasks.* Loeb, Feshback, Beck, and Wolf (1964) divided a group of depressed patients according to severity of depression. "High" and "low" depressed patients were exposed to tasks that would produce superior and inferior performance, and then shown their scores. The high-depressed group had a greater drop in mood following failure (self-rating) and greater increase after success. Loeb, Beck, Diggory, and Tuthill (unpublished study 1966) then used two card-sorting tasks with depressed and normal groups, interrupting their performance so that all subjects failed. Although the depressed patients actually performed as well as the controls, they reacted with greater pessimism and lowered aspirations.

PSYCHODYNAMIC ACTIVATION STUDIES

To investigate whether a double bind on achievement was present in depression, we operationalized the concept in 1979 using Silverman's laboratory technique of psychodynamic activation (1971, 1975) (Slipp and Nissenfeld 1981). Silverman noted that specific visual messages (verbal and pictorial) given subliminally through a two-channel tachistoscope activated specific unconscious fantasies. The cognitive and emotional responses that were triggered lasted sufficiently long to be measured accurately by psychological testing. This laboratory method is particularly useful in testing the validity of various psychoanalytic theories of psychopathology.

Our study group consisted of forty-eight nonschizophrenic neurotically depressed females, who were randomly assigned to experimental and control groups. The study employed a double-blind paradigm, with neither the experimenter nor the patient aware of the stimulus condition. After diagnostic screening (Beck Depression Inventory and Burdock and Hardesty's Structured Clinical Interview), each pa-

---

* "Psychopathology of Depression and Suicide," supported by Grant MH16616 from the National Institute of Mental Health.

tient was administered the Succeed-Fail Questionnaire. This instrument was devised by us to determine whether the patients had felt parental pressure for achievement, which parent had exerted the pressure, which was gratifying, and if the patients pressured or gratified themselves. In keeping with the theory of the double bind on achievement, four messages were employed: *maternal symbiosis*, as devised by Silverman ("Mommy and I are one"); *maternal aggression*, as used by Silverman ("Destroy Mother"); *exploitative success*, developed by Nissenfeld and myself ("Succeed for Mother or Father"); and *autonomous success*, developed by us ("Succeed for yourself"); as well as a *neutral control* message ("People are walking"). Before and after each tachistoscopic stimulation, each patient was given the Multiple Affect Adjective Checklist and the Thematic Apperception Test to measure depression, hostility, and feelings of well-being, and the Adjective Rating Scale developed by Silverman, which determines the level of self-object differentiation.

The maternal symbiosis message of "Mommy and I are one" was the only one that had a statistically significant effect in reducing depression. Correlational data showed that this message was especially effective if the mother was the nonpressuring, gratifying, and "good" parent, as shown by the Succeed-Fail Questionnaire. The maternal symbiosis message did not relieve depression, however, if the mother was experienced as pressuring and nongratifying (the "bad" mother). Thus, the findings indicate that internalized or ongoing relations with the mother have a pronounced effect on unconscious fantasies. This result is in keeping with Silverman's finding that only when the mother is perceived as the good, gratifying maternal object is the maternal symbiosis message ameliorative. The maternal aggressive message of "Destroy Mother" did not increase depression with this neurotic group, as it had in similar tachistoscopic studies done with psychotic depressives, indicating a higher level of aggressive fantasy toward the internalized mother in psychotic depressives.

The experimental laboratory finding here is in keeping with the formulations of one of Freud's earliest pupils, Karl Abraham. Abraham (1911) found from clinical case studies that the psychotic depressive regresses to the anal sadistic level and destroys the internalized love object (as well as the self). The neurotic depressive, in contrast, preserves the internalized love object. The effectiveness of the message activating the unconscious wish for fusion with the internalized good mother to preserve the self supports the theories of Jacobson (1971), Mahler and Furer (1968), and my own work (Slipp 1973b).

The exploitative succeed message of "Succeed for Mother" (or Father, depending on the patterns of parental dominance revealed by the Succeed-Fail Questionnaire) was found to cause increased feelings of well-being in more differentiated depressives. This message, however, caused increased depression in patients with a low level of self-object differentiation. This difference was explained on the basis of the bargaining relationship that more differentiated neurotic depressives establish, in which part of the self is given over to ensure the dependent relationship with the dominant parent. This is the primary form of adaptation described by Bemporad (1971) and myself (Slipp 1981). In the less differentiated depressive, however, complying and giving over to another raises the threat of total self-annihilation, because the self is already diminished and not sufficiently differentiated from the object. This corresponds to Silverman's general finding with other patients (1975) that if a message threatens the integrity of the self, it will not be ameliorative. The autonomous succeed message of "Succeed for yourself" also did not decrease depressive mood, as we had hypothesized it might. This verbal message was accompanied by a picture of a woman standing alone on a stage speaking before an audience. Probably the message and the picture triggered the core conflict around performance, that of compliance versus abandonment. Autonomous achievement is equated by these patients with loss, externally of the dominant parent and internally of symbiotic fusion with the good mother. This message probably resulted in feelings of aloneness and abandonment and a threat to the cohesion of the self. Such a result would be consistent with the formulation presented here: that the family prevents the resolution of symbiotic relatedness by not gratifying achievement, and thus an independent and separate self is hindered from evolving.

In another tachistoscopic study, conducted to validate the theory of a double bind on achievement with underachievers (Greenberg 1980), the autonomous succeed message was changed to "My success is OK." It was posited that this message would give permission for success while maintaining the needed dependent relationship with the parental object. The population was a group of 108 high school underachievers, with underachievement defined as a discrepancy between performance on tests of mental ability and grade point average. All students were given the Succeed-Fail Questionnaire, the Tennessee Self-Concept Scale, the Multiple Affect Adjective Check List, the Thematic Apperception Test, the Adjective Rating Scale for Self-Object Differentiation, and Cohen's Fear of Success Scale (1974). The students were randomly assigned to three groups, each group receiving one of three messages: a *maternal symbiosis* message of "Mommy and I are one"; a *sanctioned autonomous success* message, "My success is OK"; and a *neutral control* message, "People are walking." All subjects received subliminal stimulation of one of these messages four times a week for six weeks, and were then retested and their school performance noted. Again, double-blind procedures were employed.

The *maternal symbiosis* message significantly improved school performance for boys only; but for girls, only the *sanctioned autonomous success* message significantly improved their grade performance over that of the control group. Correlational studies showed the MOMMY message was most effective with boys who experienced their mothers as gratifying. The message also resulted in a significant reduction in anxiety, hostility, and depression in these boys, as well as increased need achievement. Those boys who perceived their mothers as conflictual toward achievement, however, did not respond beneficially to the MOMMY message. They had a high fear of success, a lower self-concept, and lower self-mother and self-father differentiation levels. The MOMMY message did not improve girls' performance and resulted in higher levels of anxiety, hostility, and depression, as well as lower need achievement, than were found in controls. The less gratifying and more conflictual the girl perceived her mother to be, the lower the need achievement and the lower the self-mother differentiation level resulting from the MOMMY message.

The MOMMY message may be less effective and less consistent in its effects with girls because even normally they experience differentiation from the mother as more difficult and conflictual than do boys. For boys the preoedipal mother remains the same love object during the oedipal period. For girls the preoedipal mother must be abandoned, and the mother made the competitor during the oedipal period, if femininity is to develop normally. Thus, the maternal relationship is more ambivalent, and symbiotic wishes for the mother tend to be experienced as more regressive and dedifferentiating. (Indeed, the MOMMY message was found to be least effective in both boys and girls who were least differentiated from their mothers.) Also, sicker female patients who have conflictual relationships with their mothers tend to turn to the fathers for nurturance. Nissenfeld (1979) found this to be true with female depressives, and Cohen (1977) found the symbiotic paternal message "Daddy and I are one" to be ameliorative with female schizophrenics. Both boys and girls who scored high on fear of success responded poorly to the MOMMY message, and they also showed a lower self-concept and further loss of self-mother differentiation. Fear of success has been attributed by Canovan-Gumpert, Garner, and Gumpert (1978), Cohen (1974), and Miller (1978) to negative reinforcement by one or both parents of the child's movement toward self-expression and mastery. Separation from the family and individuation is experienced by the child as threatening to the parent(s), and independent success is avoided to prevent retaliation or abandonment. Our findings confirm these theories concerning the effects of familial relationships on unconscious intrapsychic fantasy and overt performance.

The "My success is OK" message resulted in higher grade scores for girls than were found in controls, but these students showed higher levels of anxiety, hostility, and depression, as well as less self-father differentiation. This message was most effective when the mother was not gratifying and the father was less conflictual toward achievement. Thus, this message apparently operated as a gratifying message from the father, sanctioning success and enhancing these girls' self-concepts. This finding supports the conception that in depression one parent is the ungratifying, pressuring one who interferes with autonomy, whereas the other is the gratifying yet weak one. The SUCCESS message for these girls neutralized the fear of autonomy from the mother and increased the superego internalization of the good father, strengthening his sanctioning of success and their autonomy. The repressed affect was able to surface and be experienced, instead of being expressed behaviorally through passive-aggressive underachievement. Bolstering this identification with father apparently diminished the maintenance of dependency on the mother.

This sanctioned autonomous success message worked only with those boys having similar depressive dynamics, i.e., those having a high fear of success and autonomy. The SUCCESS message in these success-fearing boys, however, also resulted in a reduction of anxiety, hostility, and depression, an effect not found in the girls. As in the girls, the message reduced self-father differentiation. All these boys had nongratifying mothers, and therefore the father could function as a superego object, sanctioning autonomy and success. The SUCCESS message did not work with the rest of the boys; in them, underachievement probably had a different origin. The effectiveness of the SUCCESS message with girls corresponds to Miller's finding (1978) that mothers interfered with the differentiation of success-fearing girls very strongly but had this effect only moderately with boys, because independence and success were more congruent with the masculine cultural role. The conflict for the boys who did not fear success seemed to be rooted more at an oedipal level, involving the boy's rivalry with the father. Thus, because the SUCCESS message seemed to diminish self-father differentiation, it may have been threatening or may have increased guilt over defeating the father. This experimental evidence, although resting on correlational data, seems to validate many aspects of the theory of the double bind on achievement in depression. Clearly, more experimental and clinical evidence needs to be gathered. Chapter 9 will present a clinical study, also aimed at validating this theory, that investigated a group of children of Holocaust survivors, who in some cases received conflicted messages concerning achievement and autonomy from their parents.

SUMMARY

The symbiotic survival pattern provides a paradigm to explain specific intrapsychic and interpersonal dynamics occurring in the family

TABLE 2. Summary of Psychoanalytic Theories of Depression

Year	Theorist	Theory of Depression
1911	Abraham	Unconscious hostility exists toward the lost love object.
1917	Freud	Lost love object is introjected and incorporated into ego, and rage retroflexed.
1927	Rado	Lost love object is split. The good parent incorporated in superego punishes the bad parent incorporated in ego.
1933	Deutsch	Ego devalues itself to gain forgiveness from the persecuting parent incorporated in superego.
1944	Klein	Rage toward the frustrating mother is intrapsychically undone through self-punishment by the incorporated bad mother introject.
1953	Bibring	Ego state of helplessness results from repeated experiences of helplessness in childhood.
1954	Cohen, Baker, Cohen, Fromm-Reichmann, and Weigert	Success drive; parents pressure for achievement so family can gain social prestige.
1959	Bonime	Individual perceives others as demanding and unwilling to gratify them.
1959	Arieti	Individual is dependent for self-esteem on "dominant other" and cognitively feels helpless to influence environment alone.
1967	Beck	Failure expectation; negative cognitive set about self, world, and future determines the depressive affect.
1971	Bemporad	Individual fears autonomous gratification and establishes a bargaining relationship with "dominant other."
1971	Smith	Individual displays denial of differentiation, separation, and loss of love object.
1976	Slipp	Individual experiences succeed-fail double bind on achievement.
		Interpersonal-intrapsychic conflict
		a. If fails to achieve, loses love; if succeeds, loses love.
		b. Immobilized by conflicting pressures; feels helpless.
		c. Remains dependent on others for self-esteem and survival because of internalization and securing of only dominant bad maternal (paternal) object and not good maternal (paternal) object in superego.
		d. Submissive good maternal (paternal) object incorporated in self.
		e. *Intrapsychic conflict:* dominated versus abandoned if autonomous.
		f. Oppositional symbiosis provides an interpersonal

TABLE 2. (Continued)

Year	Theorist	Theory of Depression
		defense against omnipotent destructive rage and retains some autonomy.
		g. Compromise solution of partial compliance and rebellion, avoids commitment and withholds gratification from others.
		h. In depression, ego identifies with submissive parent, resulting in self-punishment to undo rage. In mania, ego identifies with dominant parent and punishes other.

in schizophrenia, depression, and other related conditions. This pattern is a mutually controlling system of interaction in which each person's self-esteem and survival are felt to depend on the other. Thus, each member feels overly responsible for the other, and too guilty to separate. Because of developmental fixation, autonomy is equated with abandonment and with not surviving alone. Symbiosis comes to serve as an interpersonal defense, providing external controls over omnipotent destructive feelings, and as a means for controlling one's environment. In schizophrenia the patient is induced by the parents, through double-binding communication, to incorporate and act out the bad maternal object (o−) (scapegoat role); in borderline conditions it is the good maternal object (o+) (go-between role) that is involved.

In depression the parental double bind induces incorporation of the s+ introject (savior role), with the threat of abandonment if the patient does not comply. This bind is also limited to social performance, with the conflicting messages concerned with success and failure. The depressive is immobilized by this no-win dilemma and is unable to commit to a course of action. To sustain ego functioning and prevent decompensation, the depressive attempts to cope with this dilemma. Through partial compliance with and rebellion against both parents, he or she establishes an oppositional symbiosis that binds separation and castration anxiety, expresses hostility, maintains external ego controls, controls and sustains dependent relations with the parents, and preserves some autonomy. When this oppositional symbiotic adaptation fails and the dependent relationship is disrupted, decompensation may result.

Intrapsychically, the primitive defense of splitting persists in the patient, with lack of unification of the good and bad maternal introjects and of their differentiation from external objects. The patient is generally able to internalize and secure the bad maternal object, but not the good maternal object, into the superego. This is because the dominant parent is nongratifying and the other parent, who may be gratifying, is perceived as weak and devalued. Not having secured a good maternal introject into the superego, the patient cannot gratify and comfort himself or herself to sustain self-esteem and autonomy.

In our tachistoscopic studies, strengthening the good maternal introject (by a "Mommy and I are one" message) lessened depression in a group of female neurotic depressives and increased school performance in underachieving boys who did not fear success. Both of these groups had relatively gratifying mothers. Strengthening the good paternal introject in the patient's superego (by a "My success is OK" message) increased school performance in underachieving girls and success-fearing boys, especially when the mother was nongratifying and pressuring. This experimental evidence seems to validate those aspects of the theory of a double bind on achievement in depression that concern the parents and the form of internalization of their relationships that occurs intrapsychically.

During the depressive episode, the patient's main ego identification appears to be with the underfunctioning, warm introjected parent (s−). Through self-punishment (o− punishing s−), the patient attempts to change the bad maternal introject in the superego into the good maternal object. This maintains the symbiotic fusion with the good maternal object, sustaining self-esteem. In the manic episode, the main identification appears to be with the pressuring, ungratifying, bad parental introject (o−), and hostility is externalized.

8

HYSTERIA AND BORDERLINE CONDITIONS: SEDUCTIVE BINDING

FROM ANCIENT MEDICAL THEORIES TO PSYCHOANALYSIS

From the earliest descriptions, almost 4,000 years ago, to the present conceptions, hysteria has always been closely tied to sexuality. The ancient Egyptians and Greeks considered hysteria to be a discrete medical disorder of women caused by the womb. The term *hysteria* itself is derived from the Greek word for womb, *hystera*. The womb was likened to an animal longing to create children; it was thought to wander about the woman's body, causing physical symptoms until appeased by sexual intercourse. Later, Galen proposed that hysteria resulted from the toxic effects of retained semen in men and uterine secretions in women (Veith 1965).

Freud's earliest writings mention that hysteria might be cured by sexual intercourse, and his theory of dammed-up libido bears some semblance to these ancient medical theories. Freud considered the hysteric to be fixated at the phallic phase of psychosexual development, not having resolved the oedipal complex and suffering from sexual conflicts. A reexamination by Reichard (1956) of Freud's cases of hysteria, however, which summarized the work of a number of psychoanalytic writers and used current diagnostic criteria as well as follow-up information, concluded that many of Freud's patients were either latent or overtly schizophrenic. Similarly, Marmor (1953) viewed the fixation in hysteria as occurring at an earlier, oral level, with the major conflict centering around dependency. Marmor noted a close relationship among hysteria, addiction, certain forms of depression, and schizophrenia. He also questioned correlating pathology with libidinal fixation without taking ego development into account.

Easser and Lesser (1965) attempted to reconcile these contradictions and to integrate ego psychology and the libido theory. They

147

formed a classification of hysterics based on the two extremes of the hysterical personality and the "hysteroid" (borderline) personality (see Table 3). Zetzel (1968) also divided these patients, into "good" hysterics, who function well and are fixated at the phallic level, and "bad" hysterics, who have weak egos and poor object relations and are fixated at the oral level. The latter cases seem indistinguishable from borderline conditions. Chodoff (1976) suggests that although the nucleus of hysteria appears to be the oedipal conflict, there is a range of fixation from phallic to oral, with the oral being more prevalent.

DIAGNOSIS OF HYSTERIA

Considerable controversy exists concerning not only the etiology, but also about the definition of hysteria. Slater (1965) recommends completely eliminating this vestige of prescientific nosology, because he doubts such a condition exists. In recent years this disorder has been delineated more precisely, a process based less on deductions from theory and more on empirical evidence. The symptom of conversion has been closely tied to hysteria since it was first described by Freud. On direct clinical examination of patients, Chodoff and Lyons (1958) found that conversion symptoms were not limited to hysteria but, rather, were found in a number of psychiatric disorders. This finding was replicated by Rangell (1959). Similarly, a clearer delineation of the behavioral characteristics of the hysterical personality, based on an extensive survey of the literature, has been provided by Chodoff and Lyons (1958). These characteristics are exemplified by the individual who is egocentric; displays labile and shallow affect; is dramatic, attention seeking, and histrionic (which may involve exaggeration, lying, and even pseudologia phantastica); is sexually provocative yet frigid; and is dependent and demanding. A more recent review of the literature by Alarcon (1973) closely replicated these findings.

One of the major problems with psychiatric diagnoses is that they are generally based not on demonstrable organic pathology but, rather, on descriptions of clinically manifest clusters of symptoms and

TABLE 3. Summary of Easser and Lesser's Differentiation of Hysteria

CHARACTERISTIC	HYSTERICAL PERSONALITY	HYSTEROID (BORDERLINE) PERSONALITY
Fixation	Phallic; oedipal conflict	Oral; basic distrust and dependency strivings
Symptoms	Sexual problems within relationships; need to seduce and conquer men, competitive with women	Sexuality used for pregenital aims
	Hysterical traits and symptoms less marked and circumscribed	More marked hysterical symptoms: aggressivity, exhibitionism, competitiveness, and egocentrism
Adaptation	Good academic and occupational performance; lively, energetic, ambitious	Poor, erratic performance; irresponsible; depressed, oppositional, with paranoid trends
Ego functions	Good integrative and synthetic; less primitive defenses; greater emotional control	Poorer, with difficulty tolerating tension; prone to action and depression
Object relations	Involved with outside world	Defends against engulfment by fantasy and detachment
	Good peer group involvement during childhood	Maladaptation and symptoms during childhood
	Long-term friendships, social and cultural interests as adult	Friendships start with idolatry and end in bitterness when expectations of rescue and nurturance not fulfilled
Family relations	Father seductive yet prohibitive and condemnatory of sexual activity when daughter reaches puberty	More disturbed, disorganized, and inconsistent
	Mother responsible but seen by daughter as sexually frigid and demeaned for housewife role	Maternal deprivation as a result of absence, death, passivity, depression, or disinterest of mother
	Fixated to father and envious of male attributes (penis envy)	
	Regarded by both parents as a pretty but inefficient little girl; self-image of child-woman	
Fantasies	Romantic; need to be loved and love	Masochistic, poor self-image
	Sees self as irresistible (femme fatale)	Sees self as disgusting and rejected
Dreams	Frequent and recalled	Frequent and recalled

TABLE 3. *(Continued)*

CHARACTERISTIC	HYSTERICAL PERSONALITY	HYSTEROID (BORDERLINE) PERSONALITY
	Symbolism simpler, universal, reflects trust and hope in relationships, frank wish fulfillment	Primitive imagery, filled with empty spaces, frequently surrealistic, scenes of desolation and destruction
Transference	Able to form therapeutic alliance and stable transference	Eroticizes transference and is prone to sexual acting out

Adapted from Slipp (1977). Used by permission.

behavior. Some writers (Reusch 1957, Rabkin 1964, Szasz 1961), question whether psychiatric diagnoses should be considered part of the medical model and suggest instead a communications model. The most immediate difficulty in diagnosis is that a single symptom, such as depression, may be both a normal mood and a major component of a wide variety of disorders. Similarly, clusters of symptoms may share a final common pathway but stem from a wide variety of conditions. Psychiatric diagnoses can be considered to be syndromes, which are constructs that have the same end state but may derive from different causes. This is generally now considered the case in schizophrenia, and is considered by Cleghorn (1969) to be true of hysteria as well. To arrive at a more meaningful diagnosis, we need to study other factors besides manifest symptomatology. The patient's level of ego functioning may be assessed by determining the degree of differentiation of internalized object relations clinically (Kernberg 1975, Slipp 1973b) or by psychological measurement (Silverman 1975). In schizophrenics the self and object internalized mental representations are fused. In depressive individuals the self and object representations are differentiated yet remain linked together (Slipp 1976), whereas in neurotics greater separation and individuation exist. It is important to examine the defensive structure; more primitive levels manifesting splitting, projective identification, denial, idealization, devaluation, and considerable acting out of conflict (Kernberg 1975). In addition, the integration and tolerance of ambivalence, the ability to sustain meaningful relationships, the level of functioning, the history, and the degree of precipitating stress provide some external indicators of personality organization.

RESEARCH FINDINGS IN HYSTERIA

The clinical course of hysteria has been studied by Ljungberg (1957), who reported a 60 percent recovery rate within a year. This rate is similar to that found in other neurotic disorders; 25 percent were still affected after five years, however. Ziegler and Paul (1954) found in a long-term follow-up study of 66 women hospitalized for hysteria that 22 were rehospitalized for psychosis (12 schizophrenic, seven manic depressive, two organic, and one psychotic with psychopathic personality). During the 19th century, hysteria was thought to be restricted to upper-class women; currently it is found predominantly among the lower socioeconomic classes and in rural settings. Transcultural studies (Carothers 1953, Vahia 1963, Gaitonde 1958) have found hysteria to be common in developing countries, whereas obsessive-compulsive neuroses are more common in industrialized nations. Some, but not all, of these differences may be attributed to different styles of diagnosis. Chodoff (1954) suggests that in our Western culture, an actual decrease in the prevalence of hysteria has occurred because of a lessening of authoritarianism in society, less belief in magic, and a decrease in sexual inhibition. Others believe that the form of expression, rather than the incidence, has changed. Today the major hysterical symptoms, involving loss of sensorimotor functioning or epileptiform seizures, have been replaced by more limited disorders, such as pain syndromes or simulated illnesses, as seen in compensation neuroses.

Other forms of investigation can provide valuable information to help in our understanding of hysteria. Guze's genetic studies (1975) showed a 20 percent incidence of hysteria among first-degree female relatives of hysterics, and an increased incidence of sociopathy and alcoholism in male relatives. Eysenck and Claridge (1962), studying cognitive styles, noted that patients with hysterical personalities tended to be extroverted, as measured by the Maudsley Personality Inventory, whereas those with conversion reactions did not differ from normals. This finding also substantiates Chodoff's differentiation of conversion and hysteria. Spiegel (1974) noted that individuals who became hysterical patients under stress tended to reach a grade 4 or 5 on the Hypnotic Induction Profile, indicating a high trance capacity, whereas schizophrenics attained a low grade. Another area helpful in establishing a diagnosis phenomenologically is the study of family interaction variables. Clinical and experimental studies have found particular patterns of family interaction, communication, power, and problem solving to be associated with families having a schizophrenic, delinquent, or depressive child (Lewis, Beavers, Gossett, and Phillips 1976, Mishler and Waxler 1968, Reiss 1971, Slipp 1976, Waxler 1974, Wynne, Ryckoff, Day, and Hirsch 1958).

FREUD'S SEDUCTION THEORY

In recent years family studies have become an area of rapidly expanding interest; it was Freud, however, who first explored pathogenic experiences occurring in the family and formulated an interactive explanation for hysteria. His original seduction theory combined interpersonal and intrapsychic factors.* The theory arose out of the histories of patients who recounted memories of sexual seduction by an adult during childhood. In hysteria the thought and associated feelings connected with the seduction were so morally unacceptable that they were not discharged but, rather, were repressed from consciousness and converted into somatic symptoms. Freud believed that the symptom symbolically represented the trauma and was used to coerce and manipulate significant others to obtain secondary gratification. Hysterics suffered from reminiscences that needed to be brought back into consciousness and relived, so that the affect would be discharged.

When Freud later found out that his patients' tales of childhood seduction were fantasy, he was confronted with a crisis in his professional life. Freud's solution was to concentrate on intrapsychic fac-

---

* In hysteria, Freud postulated, the patient was passive to the seduction, whereas in obsessive-compulsive neurosis, the patient was active. The data on borderline conditions support Freud's original theory. Stone (1981), in reviewing reports of actual incest in borderline women, found incidences of up to 33% in outpatients and 75% in inpatients. Incest included fondling and intercourse by fathers, close relatives, and friends.

tors. Fantasies in the patients' mind were considered to be as potent as actual happenings. The patients had repressed not an actual trauma, but their own infantile sexual fantasies.* From then on, Freud generally turned away from further explorations of interpersonal factors.

It is understandable but unfortunate that Freud abandoned the seduction theory. Seduction is often an interpersonal power game and need not go so far as to involve actual sexual intercourse. It is a way of emotionally controlling and manipulating another through sexuality. Seduction may not be seen as a single traumatic incident, as suggested by Freud, but as a continuing style of relationship. It is a prominent symptom of the coquettish hysteric, who persistently eroticizes nonsexual relationships as a way of manipulating and controlling others. The seduction theory also provided a more internally consistent explanation of why sexual fantasies in particular were aroused and why oedipal fixation occurred in these patients.

FAMILY INTERACTION FACTORS

In 1973 (Slipp 1973b) we reported on the symbiotic survival pattern found in families with a schizophrenic member, in which the patient played the role of scapegoat. When the patient was a young woman with a borderline condition, the "go-between" role was more common.† We also found that many hysterical women have this same symbiotic family pattern but are involved exclusively in the "go-between" role. The fathers in these families are narcissistic, demanding and exploitative, using others to maintain their self-esteem. When their demands are frustrated, splitting of the object occurs, and they

---

*Several psychoanalytic writers have commented that in paranoid ideation it is not simply the intrapsychic fantasies of the patient, but actual external interpersonal traumas as well, that are repressed and denied. Paranoid delusions may result from the unsuccessful denial of reality and the return of the repressed (Waelder 1951, Niederland 1974).

† Lidz, Cornelison, Fleck, and Terry (1957) describe a similar pattern, occurring especially in families of female schizophrenics, that they term "schismatic."

egocentrically perceive their wives as the bad mother and devalue them. The wives are too insecure to assert themselves or seek divorce, and they defend themselves by emotional detachment, abandoning their nurturant and protective maternal role. The fathers gratify their own dependency needs by turning to their daughters, who comply to the fathers' projective identification and function as the idealized good mother.

The daughters allow themselves to be parentified by the fathers, because they are deprived of maternal nurturance and a satisfactory female model for identification, and also because of their oedipal rivalry with their mothers. By fulfilling this "go-between" role, the daughters assume responsibility for holding the families together. Although these daughters gain some sense of importance and identity from being needed, their own needs for personal growth are not met and their autonomy is stifled. The mothers may be cold and permit this pattern to occur; it appears to be the fathers, however, who seductively bind their daughters into a symbiotic relationship that prevents differentiation. Experimental studies by Cohen (1977) with schizophrenic women, using Silverman's tachistoscopic technique, largely validated the hypothesis that symbiotic binding can occur with the father.What seems to differentiate the hysteric from the schizophrenic in this type of family is the method employed to establish symbiotic binding. The more these fathers employ seductiveness to control and exploit their daughters, the more the clinical outcome tends to present a hysterical picture. Probably when seductiveness is used to establish symbiotic binding, it is less devastating to ego functioning than the more encompassing disqualifications of perception and cognition that have been described in schizophrenics by Bateson, Jackson, Haley, and Weakland (1956), Lidz, Fleck, and Cornelison (1965), and Wynne, Ryckoff, Day, and Hirsch (1958).

Many hysterical women may be diagnosed as borderline, however. What other factors may militate against their becoming clearly schizophrenic? Don Jackson (1957) noted that a third figure was usually present, such as a grandmother or an older sibling, who served as a good-mother surrogate and counteracted the tendency toward psychosis. In addition, the real mothers in such cases do show concern for physical illness, although they cannot manifest tenderness generally. Blinder's study (1966) of 21 women diagnosed as hysterical, although limited by its small sample size and the fact that it was based on self-report and retrospective data, did find maternal deprivation and the use of mother surrogates. The description of the fathers was more favorable, but they also were unresponsive and often alcoholic or sociopathic. Hollender (1971) suggests that the fathers function also as a good-mother substitute and that men are seen as nurturant by these patients. One might speculate that the degree of ego growth and identity development of the hysteric depends on the nurturant supplies obtained from the father and other good-mother surrogates, and on the ability of the patient to identify with them.

Another factor that seems to differentiate the families of hysterics from those of schizophrenics is the power structure. In schizophrenia the family power structure is less clear, with each member being controlled and controlling the others. Lidz (Lidz, Fleck, and Cornelison 1965) discusses the lack of differentiation and oversensitivity of the family members. Reiss (1971) points to the consensus sensitivity, while Wynne and Singer (1972) note the concern for the relationship aspects and not the actual content of communication, which remains unclear and without a shared focus in these families. In families with a hysterical patient, the power structure is more clearly defined in a dominant-submissive pattern, as in depressive families (Lewis, Beavers, Gossett, and Phillips 1976, Slipp 1976). This structure provides the patient with an opportunity to establish boundaries and to identify with the dominant father as a way of mastering the environment. Instead of being overwhelmed by their powerlessness, these daughters can reverse the power relationship they had with their fathers, becoming the seductive, withholding, and exploitative ones with other men and thereby satisfying their own narcissistic needs. They can wreak vengeance on men, rendering them powerless, doing to men what was done to them by their fathers.

To employ these defenses successfully, the daughters must be feminine and attractive. Originally their attractiveness contributed to their being selected to be involved in seductive relationships with their fathers. Thus, the daughters' appearance becomes an essential factor in maintaining their self-esteem and a sense of self, as well as a major mechanism for mastering their environment. They feel able to compete with other women and become the center of men's attention through their appearance. They see and value themselves just as their father did, i.e., as a superficial sexual object. As a result, they expend considerable effort on their appearances and are concerned with how others see them, factors that in turn determine their self-esteem. These dynamics provide an explanation for the behavioral characteristics of the hysterical personality described by Chodoff (1976).

If identification with these narcissistic fathers occurs, why are these daughters not sociopathic like so many of their fathers? Indeed, Eysenck and Claridge (1962) found similarities between hysteria and sociopathy (both high on neuroticism and extroversion), and Cloninger and Guze (1970) found that these two conditions often coexist in the same patient. Frequently, these patients also marry alcoholic and sociopathic men like their fathers, and alternate back and forth between the manipulative, controlling and the victimized, helpless roles.

Chodoff (1976) views conversion symptoms generally as forms of nonverbal communication, transmitting both needs and emotional distress covertly through physical illness. Why do these patients' communications have to be covert and expressed physically? It is suggested that this necessity stems from the patient's compliance to the family's system of rules for behavior, which determines individual defensive structure. There is a pervasive collusion among family members to deny perception, thoughts, and feelings centered around certain circumscribed areas. In addition, there is a taboo against their direct verbal expression, which would necessitate that some action be taken.* The symptoms of hysterical blindness, deafness, and aphonia, as well as anesthesia, paralysis, denial, and dissociation, seem

---

* In schizophrenia this denial of perception, thought, and feeling is more pervasive, as has been noted by Lidz, Fleck, and Cornelison (1965), and Wynne, Ryckoff, Day, and Hirsch (1958).

to be concrete expressions of these family rules. Because the family does respond to physical illness, there is the hope that this form of plea for help and rescue will be heard.

We have noted five major conditions that appear to be correlated with the appearance of hysterical symptoms in women. These are (1) a symbiotic survival pattern of family relationships, with the patient in the role of "go-between"; (2) seductive binding by a narcissistic father; (3) maternal deprivation and underprotection, with the daughter finding good-mother surrogates; (4) a dominant-submissive family power structure; and (5) collusion among family members to comply to the rules of not recognizing or talking about certain occurrences, although physical illness is responded to with concern. The more the daughter is able to identify with the dominant father, the more a hysterical personality develops. The more the daughter identifies with the negatively perceived and victimized mother, the more a depressive and paranoid borderline personality evolves.

FAMILY INTERACTION IN THE CASE OF DORA

Freud's case of Dora is an excellent clinical example demonstrating the five conditions we have just discussed. Dora's family closely fits the symbiotic survival pattern, with Dora in the role of "go-between." When her father's narcissistic demands were frustrated, he used splitting and projective identification, with his wife demeaned as the bad mother (O−) and Dora idealized as the good mother (O+). The father had made Dora his confidante while she was still a child. He was proud of her intelligence, whereas he perceived his wife as uncultivated and inferior. He further demeaned his wife by openly preferring Dora to her to nurse him while he was ill. Dora saw herself as compensating for her mother's failings and complied with her father's demands for an "adoring" wife. She thus served to hold the family together, functioning as a good wife-mother to him to sustain his self-esteem.

Later in treatment, Dora commented on her father's narcissism: "He was insincere, he had a strain of falsehood in his character, he only thought of his own enjoyment, and he had a gift for seeing things in the light which suited him best." Freud agreed with Dora's assessment of her father. The father was a domineering, intelligent, charming, and promiscuous man who was seductive toward Dora in his behavior, so much so that she considered herself almost as his wife. Freud noted that Dora behaved more like a jealous wife than did her own mother. Freud also recognized the similarity of her father's and Herr K.'s relationship to Dora. Dora fantasized giving to her father and to Herr K. what both their wives withheld from them: sex. Indeed, Dora's tolerating Herr K.'s earlier seductive behavior and her guilt were seen by Freud as displacements from her relationship with her father.

When Herr K. actually attempted to seduce her physically, Dora noted a turning point in her feelings, because matters were getting out of control. Probably Dora's first reported dream, of her house catching on fire and her father rescuing her while her mother was preoccupied with saving her jewel case, is related. We can interpret as follows: Dora enjoyed the sensual hothouse in which she lived, but matters were becoming too hot and out of control; her fantasies were on the verge of being acted out in reality. She then wished her father to protect and rescue her. She recognized that her mother was too preoccupied with herself to help. The mother's withdrawal can be related to her being rejected, betrayed, and demeaned by her husband, as well as to her fear of being infected with his syphilis and tuberculosis. The mother was concerned with preserving her own ego, her genitals, and her health. (Indeed, she did eventually die of tuberculosis.) Dora's mother is described by Freud as being cold and compulsively clean. This behavior can be seen as a displacement of her fear of herself becoming infected physically or feeling dirty by prostituting herself psychologically, and also as a denial and undoing of her own rage. Mother did not provide Dora with nurturance but, rather, turned to her son as an ally, leaving Dora to the father. The father additionally bound Dora to him by involving her, like an accomplice, with his secret mistress, Frau K. Frau K. did, however, provide Dora with nurturance and an acceptable model for identification, as did Dora's governess, whom Freud described as "well read and of advanced views."

In terms of the family's power structure, the father was clearly the dominant one with whom Dora identified. She openly sided with her father's family, and because of this identification with her father, manifested homosexual inclinations toward Frau K. The family's conspiracy of silence and deception was threatened when Dora's governess openly mentioned the father's affair with Frau K.* This revelation was invalidated, however, because the governess also was secretly in love with the father and was considered only a jealous lover. The governess was dismissed, and thus there was no need to acknowledge openly the father's affair. Later, Dora herself revealed Herr K.'s attempted seduction of her to her mother. She thereby hoped her mother would be forced to tell her father, who would break off with the K.'s without herself having to confront her father directly. The father did then confront the K.'s, but he accepted their invalidating Dora's story as fantasy. Frau K. betrayed Dora, claiming that Dora must have been sexually aroused by stories they read together.

Insightfully, Dora told Freud she felt she had been handed over to Herr K. as the price for Herr K.'s tolerating the affair between her father and Frau K. Betrayed and abandoned by her parents and the K.'s, Dora was trapped in this web of denial and deceit. Dora turned to her paternal aunt for support, but the aunt died. Dora then attempted to communicate her distress through nonverbal body language, hoping that her father would hear and break off with Frau K. Physical illness had been used successfully in the family to manipulate others and to justify having one's needs fulfilled. Both her mother and Frau K. had used physical illness to deny their husbands sex, whereas her father's threats of suicide and his illnesses had justified compliance to his demands. Dora's suicidal threats, as well as the choice of her conversion symptoms of cough, dyspnea, confusion, and paralysis, were similar to her father's symptoms from tuberculosis and syphilis affecting the central nervous system. Unfortunately, these same interpersonal maneuvers that were successful for her par-

---

* Erikson (1968) relates Dora's pervasive distrust and illness also to her exploitation as a confidante by the adults around her as well as their dishonesty, deceit, and sexual infidelity.

ents did not work for Dora. In her second dream, Dora felt alienated from her family and dreamt her father was dead. This probably represented a fulfillment of her wishes that her father would die for his betrayal and collusion with the K.'s, as well as an unconscious mourning reaction and dysidentification with her father. Dora had been relegated by her father to the same humiliated and exploited position as her mother, and mother now fostered this identification with her by wanting Dora to help with the housework. In 1922 Dora was seen by Felix Deutsch and presented herself as a helpless, paranoid, and depressed victim who was sexually frigid, much like her mother. She complained about the faithlessness of her husband, and that men in general were selfish, demanding, and ungiving.

FAMILY INTERACTION IN HYSTERIA

In his paper "Libidinal Types," Freud (1931) attempted to differentiate the individuals prone to developing certain neuroses according to innate libidinal allocation within the mental apparatus. The erotic type, prone to developing hysteria, was under the supremacy of the id and concerned about loss of love. The obsessional type was controlled by the superego and was concerned with the anxiety of conscience; the narcissistic type, prone to psychosis and criminality, was under the control of the ego and was concerned with survival, tending to activity and aggressiveness. If we view these phenomena as stemming from interpersonal relations instead of as innate characteristics, Freud's insights assume new significance. We can postulate that the form of symbiotic binding within the family influences primarily one part of the patient's mental apparatus, i.e., the id in hysteria, the superego in obsessive-depressive disorders, and the ego in schizophrenia.

The symbiotic survival pattern was first described in families with a schizophrenic member (Slipp 1969). In such families each member feels responsible for the self-esteem and survival of the others. Thus, a pervasive system of control evolves that interferes with separation and individuation and causes each member to feel both omnipotent and helpless at the same time. The schizophrenic patient is placed into the role of scapegoat (o-) in the family. Because symbiotic binding here involves disqualifications and control of the patient's perception, thinking, feeling, and behavior, the greatest disruption of ego functioning occurs (Bateson, Jackson, Haley, and Weakland 1956, Lidz, Fleck, and Cornelison 1965, Slipp 1973b, and Wynne, Ryckoff, Day, and Hirsch 1958).* In families with a depressive patient, there is a more clearly authoritarian, dominant-submissive power structure (Lewis, Beavers, Gossett, and Phillips 1976, Slipp 1976). One parent is compulsive and overfunctional; the other is depressive and underfunctional. The symbiotic pattern of family relationships is oppositional and less pervasive. Double binding is focused on achievement, with one message pressuring the patient to be the "savior" (s+) by winning and elevating the family's social status. The contradictory message, given by the same or the other parent, is to fail. Here the binding of the patient appears to occur primarily in the superego, with the ego ideal incorporating the message to win and the punitive superego the message to fail. Ego identification occurs primarily with the depressed submissive parent, and the patient relates to significant individuals as if they were the "dominant other" (Arieti 1962).

In hysteria the family structure has elements of both these types of families. We have described on page 157 the five factors that appear correlated with hysteria. The binding with the father occurs primarily through the patient's id and is less disruptive to ego functioning.

Freud's case of Dora, as a clinical case demonstration, manifests all five factors. Dora originally dysidentified with her detached, masochistic mother and identified with her dominant, seductive father. Had Dora continued to be accepted by her father and been able to maintain her identification with his manipulative behavior, a hysterical personality structure probably would have evolved. Dora, however, was seduced, exploited, and then abandoned by her father. She was then thrown back onto her negative identification with her

---

* Stierlin (1976b) also views symbiotic binding as affecting primarily either the ego, the superego, or the id.

victimized, helpless mother. Thus, a more borderline picture resulted, with depressive and paranoid features.

FREUD'S ORIGINAL INSIGHT AS THE BASIS
FOR AN INTRAPSYCHIC-INTERPERSONAL THEORY

Psychoanalytic theory has changed considerably since Freud's original seduction theory. Freud considered the cause of hysteria to be a single physical seduction that was traumatic and repressed. Despite its limitations, the seduction theory was the first to provide insights into both interpersonal and intrapsychic factors in the evolution of a mental illness. When Freud abandoned this theory, the emphasis in psychoanalysis was then placed on intrapsychic fantasies stemming from the patient's infantile sexuality. With the introduction of ego psychology and, in more recent years, object relations theory, however, greater emphasis has been placed on adaptive functioning with regard to reality and human relationships. If we conceive of seduction as an interpersonal power maneuver and a style of relating directed toward manipulating and controlling others instead of as a single physical sexual event, Freud's original insights again become rich and meaningful.

9

INTERGENERATIONAL TRANSMISSION OF PSYCHIC TRAUMA

AWARENESS OF PSYCHOLOGICAL ISSUES IN CHILDREN OF HOLOCAUST SURVIVORS

The topic of the Holocaust has only very recently come to the conscious awareness of large numbers of people. Perhaps this interest arises out of our own concerns about the industrial and atomic age we live in, an age that threatens our health and very survival. Perhaps it comes from a search for roots and identity in a society that has lost many social structures and values that had contributed to the dignity and meaning of life. Perhaps it is simply that we have had to wait one generation to gain sufficient time and distance to look at this awesome period and try to master the trauma.

Our own attention was drawn to the Holocaust over the past five years after seeing a fairly large number of psychiatric patients coming to the clinic of Bellevue Hospital in New York whose parents were concentration camp survivors. These patients suffered from a variety of psychiatric disorders, most of which centered around depression and involved work and marital difficulties. Many of these young adults were experiencing conflict in trying to emancipate themselves from their parents, suffering guilt and showing self-defeating behavior. In contrast to this group, we were also acquainted with a number of children of survivors who were functioning very well, even at a superior level. They were socially adjusted, developing families, and growing in their careers. Some were psychiatric residents and psychology graduate students who were involved with us for training. Thus, we became interested in discovering whether there were different types of parent-child relationships at work in the two groups of children.

HISTORICAL BACKGROUND OF
HOLOCAUST SURVIVOR FAMILIES

We were aware that many of the marriages of the parents of these children contained innate problems from the time of their inception. When the survivors were released from the concentration camps, they were faced with the tragic shock of learning about the deaths of most of their parents and siblings, their spouses and children. During a time of mourning, most cultures provide rituals that surround the bereaved person with groups of people to diminish the sense of deprivation and loss and to provide emotional support. But the survivors were alone, naked in a strange world, deprived of social supports coming from friends, work, and community. Their world had been uprooted and destroyed. There was little opportunity to mourn and emotionally work through their losses. They could not go back to their old world, but had to face adjustment in new countries with different cultures and languages.

To achieve some semblance of stability, many of the survivors entered into hastily conceived marriages. Often the sole basis for the choice of a marital partner was some peripheral connection with the past. For example, the spouse knew someone from one's family or just came from the same country. This slim connection provided the survivors with some sense of continuity with their former lives and the world from which they had been torn away so mercilessly. Marriage was an attempt to master the traumatic loss of family over which they had had no control, providing a way to give and get emotional support at a time of great need and to reintegrate into culture and society. For those who had been married previously and who had lost a spouse and children, it was particularly difficult to enter a new marriage without being haunted by the specter of the past. To give to one's new family meant to be disloyal to one's former family, and to invest emotionally left one again painfully vulnerable to and impotent against the outrage of having one's loved ones wrenched away and lost. These marriages also had to bear the burden of a higher incidence of emotional and physical illness and a higher death rate, which stemmed from the severe degree and duration of stress the concentration camp survivors had had to cope with.

The systematic research into survivors conducted by both Eitinger (1964) and Matussek (1975) found a fairly high incidence of marital difficulties, often associated with downward social mobility. Only about one-third of the survivors studied in Norway, Germany, and Israel succeeded in attaining a stable socioeconomic level equivalent to the level they had enjoyed prior to their persecution. Matussek found that even those who were occupationally successful were emotionally constricted and closed off from themselves and others. They often denied and repressed their rage or defended against depression by compulsive work activity. Many were addicted to work, too busy to feel or to think. In most of the families we saw, stereotyped role performance dominated the self-definition of the parents. The man needed to be the satisfactory breadwinner, and the woman the good mother. This time they would be able to provide, care for, and protect their families; this time they would not be helplessly violated. But, as Niederland (1968) has pointed out, the parents' life was often dominated by the fear of impending catastrophe, the fear of ill health, financial insecurity, or renewed persecution. There was chronic anxiety, depression, and lack of joy. These attitudes often found expression in a fearful overprotectiveness of children, involving especially the fear that disaster would befall the children when they were out of sight. One could thus expect some of these children to become heirs to their parents' insecurity and to show phobic behavior and diminished expectations of success and pleasure.

PARENTAL TRANSMISSION OF PSYCHIC TRAUMA

There is now mounting evidence derived from clinical observations in Israel, Canada, and the United States that some of the children of these survivors have indeed become heirs to some of their parents' difficulties. Shami Davidson, director of the Shalvata Hospital in Tel Aviv, where a large number of children of survivors have been seen, stated, "The trauma of the Nazi concentration camp is reexperienced in the lives of the children and even the grandchildren of camp survivors. The effects of systematic dehumanization are being transmitted from one generation to the next through severe disturbances in the parent–child relationship" (Epstein 1977). Another group of investigators in Canada, Rakoff, Sigal, and Epstein (1967), studied a number of hyperactive and aggressive adolescent children of survivors. These investigators believed the children's problems stemmed from the emotional unavailability of the parents, who were closed off and still grieving for their lost families. Several psychiatrists from the Shalvata Hospital in Tel Aviv (personal communication 1978) stated that they felt that the most important dynamic in these families of survivors that produced problems in the children were the high expectations of these parents, combined with their envy over the advantages the child had that had been denied them. This belief is congruent with our own observations and with the theory of the intergenerational transmission of depressive disorders (Slipp 1976). The theory can be summarized as follows: At least one parent exerts pressure for achievement on a child and then lives vicariously through the child's success. Success is not reinforced, however, because praise and acknowledgment are withheld. This withholding occurs due to the parent's unconscious jealousy and competitive attitude and as an unconscious maneuver to prevent the child from separating by keeping him or her needy for gratification. A double bind on achievement thus results.

CASE ILLUSTRATION

The first contact with the S. family came in March 1977, when Linda, the 21-year-old daughter, was admitted to University Hospital following a suicide attempt. Linda's difficulties were only part of a larger history of suffering and anguish in her family that can be traced back to her father's experiences in Czechoslovakia. In 1938 her father, Saul, was imprisoned in Auschwitz with his family, where he lost his wife and seven-year-old son. After release, he emigrated to the United States. Alone, without family, friends, or position, and now over 40 years of age, he found himself a displaced person in a strange land, having to learn a new language and having to make a life for himself. He met and married Lilly, a teacher who was working with European immigrants. Lilly's first pregnancy ended in miscarriage, and Saul's anxiety for his wife's life was so great that Lilly felt compelled to protect Saul by minimizing the amount of information she told him. Two children were later born, Ben, now 27, and Linda, 21. Throughout the children's lives, Saul could not tolerate any problem or illness without severe anxiety, always dreading a catastrophe. In addition, Saul was paralyzed in decision making, always obsessively ruminating, always anguished over even minor decisions. Thus, Lilly felt compelled again to spare her husband by assuming the burden of family decisions.

Saul was a compulsive worker, constantly preoccupied with making his family "safe" and spending little time on relaxation or pleasure. He was a haunted and driven man. Ben also experienced pressure for good grades from his father. Ben felt that both his parents tried to live vicariously through him, compelling him to go to college and become a teacher, whereas they minimized his achievement in athletic and social areas important to him.

Both children experienced great resentment toward their parents for being overly protective and fearful, which they felt crippled their sense of competence and independence. Both children had difficulty emancipating themselves from the family. Both have been self-defeating and have failed in their careers, both failed in their marriages and were divorced, and both have had severe depressive episodes. When Ben's marriage failed, Saul accused his son's mother-in-law of having "taken a perfect boy and destroyed him." It was as if she were the Nazi who had killed his first son.

Shortly after Ben's divorce, Saul was diagnosed as having a serious heart condition. In addition, the neighborhood where Saul and Lilly lived in the Bronx had become dangerous. Lilly pleaded with her husband to move, but Saul flatly refused, stating, "I would rather die than leave my home." The situation became so unbearable that Lilly took it upon herself to find a new apartment. She then presented the lease for the new apartment to Saul, who reluctantly signed it. Saul was no longer in control of his life or world: he was again impotent and helpless to control his and his family's destiny. Two weeks later he hanged himself in the old apartment.

After Saul's death, several members of the family developed severe illnesses—Lilly breast cancer and her father metastatic colon cancer. All these illnesses were dealt with by the pervasive family style of denial and secrecy. Ben, in his fury, took it upon himself to confront the family members with the truth, which he did in a brutal fashion. In addition, he told his sister about their father's suicide, which had been kept a secret from her. At this time Linda was in the midst of her divorce, and the shock of this news from Ben precipitated a serious suicide attempt that led to her hospitalization.

Family therapy was commenced during Linda's hospitalization and continued on a weekly basis for six months after her discharge. Although a great deal more openness in communication and feelings developed in the family, everyone was always keenly aware of the presence of a ghost in the room. The specter of Saul's death pervaded the family, just as the death of Saul's wife and child had haunted him. Some of the guilt over Saul's death was worked through in the sessions. Ben dropped out of treatment and did not follow up on the suggestion for individual therapy. Linda improved with both medication and therapy. She was able to stabilize her work situation, began individual therapy, and was able to move into her own apartment.

This case dramatically demonstrates the transmission of survivor guilt from parent to child. (Although suicide of a parent who was a survivor was not common in the Krystal and Niederland study [1968], there was an increased risk of suicide among survivors studied in Holland by Meerloo [1968].) Saul's remarriage served to replace his lost family, to undo and master the loss of a wife and child murdered by the Nazis. This was a massive trauma in the face of which he was totally helpless and devastated. In the second marriage, however, he would be able to protect and provide for his family, to keep them "safe," as he termed it. Yet the very nature of his guilt resulted in Saul's becoming addicted to work and militated against the family's having pleasure and against a good marital adjustment. Ben felt that Saul's paralysis in decision making stemmed from Saul's gnawing self-reproach for being helpless to save his wife and child in Europe. Saul openly ruminated that if he had made different decisions then, perhaps his family would be alive today.

Saul was a constricted and emotionally isolated person who found it difficult to be open with his children. Many survivors feel that to give of themselves to their children in the second family means to be disloyal to the former, dead family. An emotional anesthesia or constriction also occurs, because to invest emotionally in the new family means to be open again and vulnerable to the trauma of losing one's loved ones. This fearful expectancy of loss results in a pervading sense of impending catastrophe and an overly protective attitude toward the children. In addition, separations are equated with death, and thus the normal process of separation and individuation of children is interfered with. Both children in the S. family were angry over this interference. Ben additionally felt anger over the pressure for achievement he experienced from his father, achievement that was then not praised or acknowledged.

Several possible factors in Saul's suicide were considered by the family and the therapists. These included: (1) An identity crisis arising from Saul's impending retirement. Saul's self-esteem and security rested on his role as breadwinner and provider. Retirement and the inability to continue to protect his family may have revived his old trauma and the associated guilt. (2) Saul's learning about his physical illness. In the concentration camps, illness and the inability to work were tantamount to a death warrant. Loss of health and the threat of death may have also brought back the fear of his and his family's dying. (3) The issue of uprooting, of being forced to move from the apartment because the neighborhood had become dangerous and people were being assaulted and robbed on the streets. In Europe, Jews were first harassed on the streets and then forcefully uprooted, arrested, and sent to concentration camps. Leaving one's home was the first in a long chain of events destructive to individual identity and dignity. Uprooting meant loss of social supports, loss of familiar surroundings, loss of family friends, home, and status. These traumas were followed by the massive degradation and dehumanization in the camps. Saul felt defeated and disappointed by life, and like the biblical King Saul who was defeated in battle, he could make one last act of defiance against his fate, to take his own life.

A STUDY OF CHILDREN OF HOLOCAUST SURVIVORS

The theory of the double bind on achievement in depression (Slipp 1976) was the basis for the selection of instruments with which to study the children of survivors. Certain aspects of the theory had been operationalized into a Succeed-Fail Questionnaire, composed of 30 attitude items that tap perceived pressure for achievement as well as gratification from father, mother, and self. We also selected Cohen's Fear of Success Scale (1974) to evaluate success phobias, the Beck Depression Inventory, and the California Personality Inventory. A structured clinical interview was also devised that investigated demographic and historical factors, both pre- and postwar, physical and emotional disorders, socioeconomic level, Jewish identity issues, self-other-world attitudes, family rules and styles of communication, achievement motivation, separation-individuation problems, and the degree to which the parents had revealed their war experiences. The results of this pilot study are preliminary, and no firm conclusions can be reached. Yet the results reveal very interesting trends.

Our original sample consisted of ten children of survivors, but one individual was excluded because her father had escaped from a concentration camp after a short time. The remaining nine all had at least one parent who had been an inmate of a camp for a significant period. All the subjects were in their mid- to late twenties; all except one had completed college, and five were in graduate programs. All reported having been moderately to severely depressed at some point as young adults.

They all reported having trouble reaching out for help and sharing intimate feelings. The world view communicated by their parents was that the world was dangerous and threatening, and there was a sense of impending catastrophe. Most reported considerable insecurity in their families about health and finances. All reported a great deal of difficulty and guilt involved in separating from their parents: they felt they were abandoning and hurting their parents by separating. They believed their parents lived through their achievements, and thus these children felt responsible for their parents' happiness or even for their lives. A few parents had overtly stated to their children, "If you leave, I will die." Separations remained equated with death more than 30 years after liberation from the camps. Even when the children did emancipate themselves, most of them stayed in the same neighborhood and communicated with their parents frequently.

This group of nine subjects was then broken down into two subgroups, those who were functioning well (five subjects) and those who were functioning less well (four subjects). This division was based on clinical judgment and history. The primary criteria were the extent of self-defeating behavior and the severity and number of depressive episodes. This judgment was corroborated by the subjects' self-evaluations in these two areas.

In the structured clinical interview one factor appeared to distinguish between the better-functioning and the more poorly functioning groups: the extent to which the parents had actively described to their children their experiences in the camps and their lives prior to World War II. There was no "veil of silence" in the better-functioning group. The father of one extremely well-functioning woman had made four hours of tapes concerning his war experiences for her to listen to and to keep. In the family of another woman who also functioned extremely well, the camp experiences had been discussed as dinner conversation, and the parents would not let her avoid confronting unpleasant events, which she herself tended to do. Thus, an active and confrontative approach to life was fostered in the healthy children, instead of one of fearful avoidance and denial.

On the Cohen Fear of Success Scale, all the subjects as a group scored substantially higher than large groups of college students tested in the past, suggesting the existence of ambivalent attitudes toward success.

The responses on the Succeed-Fail Questionnaire indicated that the better-functioning group perceived less pressure for achievement and greater gratification; the more poorly functioning group perceived greater pressure and less gratification for achievement. Fathers tended to pressure more than mothers, and mothers tended to gratify a little more than fathers. These subcategories, however, are confounded by sex, because in this limited sample all the women and only one of the men were in the better-functioning group, whereas those in the more poorly functioning group were all men. The structured clinical interview indicated that more achievement was expected from boys than from girls, whereas girls, especially oldest sisters, were more often privy to information about the parents' war experiences and about problems in the marriage. Even though we cannot report conclusive findings, there does appear to be conflict over achievement and problems around the issue of emancipation.

In addition, these families tend to teach their children a negative view of others and the world: One cannot trust others, and one must expect catastrophes. This negative self-other-world cognitive style has been described by Aaron Beck (1967) in depression. Those who functioned less well had parents who were overly protective and who tended to deny unpleasant realities. The combination of this negative world view and the use of denial and avoidance seems to create a maladaptive approach to life. The world is experienced as a threatening and hurtful place, but one is not supposed to look at the anticipated danger. This approach leaves the child insecure, vulnerable, and defensive, because he or she expects failure and not success, pain and not pleasure, helplessness and not competence to cope with and take charge of life. Another group of parents ruminated bitterly about their war experiences, creating an unhappy family atmosphere and a feeling in the child of having to compensate for the parents' deprivation.

Although the sample is small, this study provides some evidence of the importance of the double bind on achievement in depression. In addition, these families reinforced helplessness by denial and avoidance. It appears that those parents who were able to discuss their camp experiences with their children, not in a bitter or guilt-provoking manner but in a way that fostered mastery through an active approach to life, seemed to facilitate a better adaptation in their children.

The prophetic words of an unknown man whipped to death in the Dachau concentration camp were recorded by the Polish writer Jan

Domagala: "If a miracle should happen that you live to tell the tale, write it down and tell the world what they did to us." Remembering not only honors the martyred dead, but also recognizes the strength of the next generation to face and confront the problems of life actively and with confidence.

10

CLASSIFICATION OF FAMILY INTERACTIONAL PATTERNS

FAMILY PATTERNS IN FOUR TYPES OF PSYCHOPATHOLOGY

This chapter will summarize and bring together the studies of family interaction described in Chapters 6, 7, and 8, in which specific forms of projective identification were found to occur in relation to specific forms of pathology in the identified patient. These interactions form a typology of family patterns in schizophrenia, depression, and borderline and hysterical conditions that is related to general psychiatry and psychoanalysis. Although my own studies have not included delinquents, the clinical findings of Johnson and Szurek (1954) can be easily incorporated into this paradigm. Figure 7 brings together the various forms of family interactions, projective identifications, splitting, and the induced role of the patient in the family in schizophrenia, hysterical-borderline conditions, depression, and one form of delinquency.

In all these conditions, the family interferes with the child's integration of ambivalence, internalization of the mother, and self-regulation of narcissistic equilibrium, leaving self-esteem and identity excessively vulnerable to external relations.

In schizophrenia, the parents cannot deal with aggression openly, because they fear that direct expression of aggression will destroy their marital relationship. This is especially threatening, because loss of the marital relationship endangers their self-esteem and identity. Developmental arrest has occurred in the parents, with lack of internalization of the mother and an inability of the parents to self-regulate their narcissistic equilibrium. Each remains dependent on the other to function as a good symbiotic mother to stabilize his or her self-esteem and cohesion of the self. Therefore, the spouse is idealized as the good maternal object to preserve the marriage. Aggression is denied and displaced onto a child, who is induced through

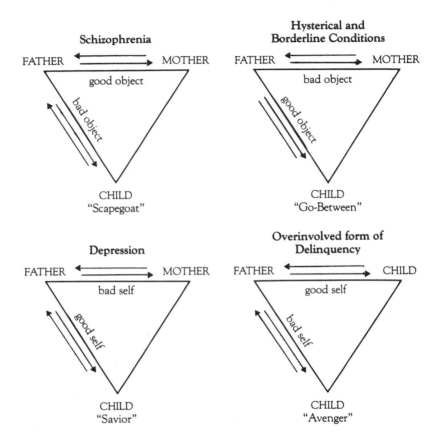

FIGURE 7. Categorization of family interaction. The father is indicated as the initiator of splitting and projective identification in all four patterns for purposes of
simplicity. The mother may just as well be the initiator, except in hysterical and
borderline conditions, in which the child is female. Projective identification is used
as the intrapsychic and interpersonal defense mechanism that induces others to act
out the internalized self or object image. The child serves as a container for the
parent's projective identification, and a negative feedback cycle is thus established
that (1) maintains the personality integrity of the parents, (2) maintains the family
homeostasis, or balance of defenses, and (3) sustains developmental fixation in the
patient. In all these instances the child is made responsible for the self-esteem and,
in schizophrenia and borderline conditions, the survival of the parent(s), thereby
establishing a symbiotic survival pattern. In one type of delinquency, splitting and
projective identification of the bad self into one child and the good self into another child occurs.

projective identification into the role of the bad maternal object, the family *scapegoat*. Besides preventing self-object differentiation, these families do not provide a holding environment. Aggression is not expressed, contained, and managed constructively but, rather, is treated as if hostility indeed were omnipotent, dangerous, and destructive to others. The family's actual behavior creates a negative feedback cycle that reinforces the child's fear of his or her own omnipotent destructive fantasies. This fear prevents the child from differentiating primary and secondary process thinking. Symbiotic binding and interference with self and object constancy occur in the child, because each member's self-esteem and survival are felt to be dependent on the others' thoughts, feelings, and behavior—"the symbiotic survival pattern." (Slipp 1969, 1973b, 1976, 1977). Thus, lack of gratification and prevention of resolution of symbiosis cause a lack of differentiation and fusion of self and object, which serve as a defense against omnipotent destructive wishes intrapsychically.

In families of women with hysterical and borderline personalities, the symbiotic binding is due to the emotional seduction by the father. This emotional, or id, binding tends to be less disruptive of ego functioning than the binding in schizophrenia, but it does have a profound effect on the identity of the self. These fathers are narcissistic characters who use the primitive defenses of splitting and projective identification. Because the wife is able to sustain some autonomy and does not simply gratify her husband's need for a good maternal object, she is demeaned by the father as the bad object. The daughter is idealized as the good object, especially because she tries to comply with the father's demands. The mother abandons her nurturant, protective role, often becoming depressed or obsessive. Because the mother cannot gratify the infant's symbiotic wishes, fusion with her as the idealized good preoedipal mother is prevented and displaced to the father to preserve cohesion of the good self. The daughter's siding with the father is facilitated by her attachment to him not only as a mother surrogate but also by her oedipal rivalry with the mother. Although the daughter's complaint behavior results in an oedipal victory over the mother, it also mollifies the father and prevents his leaving the mother for another woman. Thus, the daughter serves as a *go-between* for the parents. Just like the schizophrenic, the hysteric or borderline patient serves as a glue to hold together a fragile marriage. There is thus a lack of family constancy, and the patient attempts to heal the narcissistic vulnerability of the parents. The daughter's own dependency needs and strivings for autonomy are not met, however, and because they threaten the family integrity, they are subject to criticism. A hysterical condition is more likely to occur when the daughter's self-image remains identified with the dominant and seductive father. The daughter then becomes like the father, seductive and exploitative, using men for her own dependent and narcissistic needs just as she has been used. If the daughter is betrayed by the father, she is driven back onto her identification with the victimized, degraded mother, and a more borderline personality structure evolves.

An example of such a betrayal is exemplified in Freud's case of Dora (1905a). Initially the father involved Dora in his affair, encouraging her to identify with his mistress (almost as if Dora in fantasy were his mistress). Later, however, the father denounced and rejected Dora in favor of his mistress, leaving her desolate. Dora expressed her narcissistic needs in her dream of needing rescue, protection, and nurturance (mirroring) by the father.

In families with a depressive patient, the symbiotic survival pattern is limited to the area of social achievement, which is outside the family. The symbiotic binding also is not as widely encompassing of the personality as it is in schizophrenia; it is limited to the superego and does not affect the entire ego functioning. In depressive families one parent is generally overly powerful and dominant, whereas the other parent is weak, deflated, and depressed. The weak parent is viewed by the family (and also self-perceived) as a social failure. The actual power structure in the family, which is polarized into a strong and a weak parent, coincides with the child's intrapsychic splitting of the parent into a powerful object, incorporated in the superego, and a deflated, weak object, incorporated in the self. The dominant parent uses splitting and projective identification to dissociate the experience of oneself as a failure. Thus the bad self is put into the spouse, who is demeaned as the failure, and the good self is placed into the patient, who is pressured and compelled to achieve socially. The dominant parent then identifies with and lives vicariously through the child's social success to sustain his or her self-esteem. The child feels compelled to function as the *savior* who bolsters the prestige of the family and in particular the self-esteem of the dominant parent. If the patient does not comply, he or she fears being treated like the deflated parent, as the failure or the bad self who is demeaned and rejected.

Besides this conditional acceptance, the child cannot own his or her success and remains dependently bound to the family. This occurs because the dominant parent's overt message to succeed is accompanied by a covert and contradictory message to fail (the double bind on achievement). The child cannot win whether he or she succeeds or fails socially.* The dominant parent is competitive and jealous of the child's success and does not acknowledge and gratify the child's achievement. Using Kohut's terms, the child does not receive the needed "mirroring" responses acknowledging the achievement from the dominant parental selfobject and is therefore deprived of the positive feedback essential to confirm and encourage an independent self. Only the bad maternal (paternal) object, not the good maternal object, is internalized and secured in the superego. Thus, the child cannot regulate his or her own narcissistic equilibrium. In this way the child is kept insecure and hungry for gratification, does not separate and individuate, and can continue to be exploited to enhance the dominant parent's power and self-esteem. Feeling trapped and helpless by this double bind on achievement and remaining dependently bound, the child cannot directly and openly express anger. Instead, it is turned against the self, giving rise to depressive symptoms. The patient punishes himself or herself as the failed or rebellious bad self in order to master separation anxiety and to sustain the relationship with the dominant parent. (The dominant bad parental object in the superego punishes the bad self in the ego to sustain fusion of the good parent object with the good self.)

---

* This finding has similarities to the "learned helplessness" described by Seligman, Maier, and Gear (1967, 1968). In their studies, animals were placed in a situation in which they had no control over being shocked; the result was depression caused by this no-win dilemma.

When the patient is asymptomatic, the rage is acted out through unconscious passive-aggressive, oppositional behavior in which the patient preserves dependency on the dominant parental object as well
as some vestige of autonomy.

In a normal pattern of development, individuals evolve a relatively
stable core of identity and can regulate their self-esteem, yet this stability can be overwhelmed by massive psychic trauma and is affected
by intimate relations, support and reference groups, work, and losses
or victories in health and achievements. Even though symbiotic
wishes for fusion with the good preoedipal mother are gratified and
adequately resolved, they persist to some degree throughout life and
serve to shape or maintain the person's self-esteem and identity. This
persistence is demonstrated in the need to belong (to feel a part of
another or a reference group in society), in sex, in romantic love,
in empathy, and in artistic expression.

FAMILIES WITH AN OVERINVOLVED DELINQUENT
AND OTHER FAMILIES

The family structure in the symbiotic type of delinquency has clear
similarities to the structure in families with a depressive patient. In
both these types of families, the patient serves as a bound *delegate*
(Stierlin 1976a) of the family to perform in the outside world. Here
the patient does achieve something one parent cannot or failed to
do. In this way such families are unlike families with a schizophrenic
or borderline-hysterical patient, in which the induced countertransferential response of the patient is concentrated on functioning within
the family to preserve family constancy, due to at least one of the
parents having unmet dependency needs for a good maternal object.
In both schizophrenia and borderline-hysterical conditions, the patient's functioning (encompassing thoughts, feelings, and actions)
serves to sustain the very personality integrity of the parent(s) as well
as the survival of the family as a group. In families with a depressive or an overinvolved delinquent, the integrity of the family as a
group is essentially not at stake; there is family constancy, and the

child's performance affects only the self-esteem of one or more family members. The child here does not have to identify with the split introject of the good or bad maternal object but, rather, identifies only with the dissociated aspect of the self of the parent. This pattern is less disruptive to the child's identity and permits more autonomy than the pattern in schizophrenia or borderline conditions (Table 4).

In depression the pressure on the child is to perform and achieve in accordance with social mores, and thereby to prevent demoralization and to enhance the prestige and self-esteem of the family members. In the symbiotic type of delinquency, the child is induced to act out in the outside world *against* society's values. At least one of the parents feels rage against some social injustice, which usually involves displaced anger against a powerful authority figure within the family. One child is selected to contain this rage and to act it out against society. The child thus assumes the role of *avenger* for the parent against society, releasing the parent from having to own and assume responsibility for his or her own feelings and actions. This projective identification of the internalized bad self by a parent into one of the children is consistent with the findings of Johnson and Szurek (1954). Although these investigators did not use the term projective identification, their phenomenological description of the process involved corresponds to this mechanism. Unacceptable antisocial impulses of the parents are dissociated and are unconsciously projected into the child. The parents then identify with the child and can live vicariously through the child's acting out without taking responsibility for the antisocial impulses. In recent family studies Helm Stierlin (1976b) also noted that in adult sociopathic individuals, the sociopath serves as a delegate of one of the family members, acting out that member's antisocial impulses.

Although a number of delinquent and sociopathic patients have been clinically studied in the Family Therapy Unit of Bellevue Psychiatric Hospital, systematic research on this group of patients has not been performed. The findings just discussed and our own clinical work, however, form the basis for the inclusion of families with a symbiotically bound delinquent in our present discussion. This

TABLE 4. Patterns of Family Interaction

Condition	Parent Has Unmet Dependency Needs For Good Parental Object	Parent Failed To Achieve Success	Parent Cannot Avenge Abuse	Child Functions Inside Family To Preserve Family Constancy	Child Functions Outside Family To Preserve Self Esteem Of Parent(s)
Schizophrenia	+	−	−	+	−
Hysteria-borderline	+	−	−	+	−
Depression	−	+	−	−	+
Delinquency (overinvolved type)	−	−	+	−	+

fourth pattern serves to complete the paradigm in which good or bad aspects of the self or object are placed into a family member through projective identification by a parent.

VARIATIONS AND COMBINATIONS
OF THE FAMILY TYPOLOGY

Each of the four types of interaction in this paradigm does not always exist in its pure form. Variations within one form and combinations of several forms have been noted to occur. One variation within the depressive type of interaction seems to lead to an obsessive-compulsive neurosis instead of a depression. Here there seems to be less pressure to achieve socially outside the family, and more pressure to behave or perform within the family.* Another common combination is that of two patterns of interaction that can occur in schizophrenia. The patient may be pressured to achieve socially, thereby functioning as a family *savior*, as well as being the *scapegoat* to contain the family's aggression. Usually in these cases there is a strong depressive component to the psychosis, as seen in schizoaffective disorders.

The patient may also serve as both the *scapegoat* and the *avenger* in the family. Stierlin (1976a) describes this type of combination of the schizophrenic and delinquent patterns (schizopath) in the life of Adolph Hitler. Hitler's mother, Klara, at 15 years of age was sent as a maid to serve her uncle, Alois, who was 22 years her senior. Alois seduced and impregnated her while his second wife was dying of tuberculosis. Klara never extricated herself from this trapped, shameful, and guilt-laden position. Even though Alois later married her, her first three children died, which she probably experienced

---

* In an ongoing research project by Carol Hoover (1983) of obsessive-compulsive disorders at the National Institute of Mental Health, 174 family members have been studied. Relatives of obsessive-compulsive patients appear to place a high value on cleanliness and perfection within the family. Because of unfulfilled relationships and poor communication, the parents turned for intimacy to the patient as a child. In half the cases it was the father who developed the symbiotic tie.

as God's punishment. Alois was a brutal and tyrannical man who had numerous extramarital affairs and spent a good deal of his time away from home drinking with his male companions. Because of these events, Hitler was overindulged and overprotected by his mother, becoming symbiotically bound to her. As a child, Hitler served as his mother's bound delegate to express her angry feelings against her husband for his subjugation and humiliation. Thus, Hitler as a child served as an *avenger* (s−) for his mother to combat an abusive father within the family. Hitler then had to suffer the harsh consequence of his confrontative behavior by receiving daily physical beatings from his father, thereby serving as a lightning rod onto which all his father's rage was expended. The mother used Hitler to express her resentment toward her husband without assuming responsibility, and the father used him as a *scapegoat* (o−) to funnel his anger away from his wife. Thus, Hitler avenged his mother's degradation and protected her from retaliation, thereby preserving the family.

Later in life Hitler served as his mother's avenger in the outside world. He identified himself with Germany, as with his mother, and his mission was to avenge Germany's shame and humiliation by others, thereby restoring the people's self-esteem and pride. Hitler openly identified himself *as* Germany, stating, "Hitler is Germany, and Germany is Hitler" (Mommy and I are one). Through this message he encouraged others to relinquish their individual identities and to merge with him in his mission of vengeance. Here, Hitler did to others what was done to him by his mother, and enlisted them symbiotically as avengers. History has recorded the disastrous results of massive brutality, the degradation and murder of many millions of innocent people. Obviously the disaster was not due simply to Hitler alone. His vengeful mission, bequeathed by his mother, came at a crucial time in history.* He was able to harness the existing German Volk movement with its rabid anti-Semitism, as well as to exploit the economic and political chaos and the resultant anomie.

It is clear that not all forms of delinquency are simply a result of

---

* Hitler lived in Vienna during the time the anti-Semitic Karl Lueger was mayor.

the child's acting out the antisocial impulses stemming from a parent. The other form of delinquent is the deprived psychopath who even lacks the capacity for attachment to others. This pattern is seen in institutionalized children and in unattached, alienated families. Also, if the family authority structure is inadequate to cope, if it collapses, or if it is excessively punitive and inconsistent in its boundaries, the child may identify with a deviant peer group culture. Such a mechanism was also operant in the Nazi German culture and currently is seen particularly in some poverty-level families, in which the parents are overwhelmed by their circumstances. Because the authority structure of the family is inconsistent or inadequate, the child identifies with the street gang as the reference group. Such identification seems to have occurred at a massive level in Germany, where almost an entire nation identified with the S. A., a gang of street brawlers that formed Hitler's private army. In this instance a delinquent culture became elevated to national policy.

USING THE FAMILY TYPOLOGY IN INDIVIDUAL THERAPY

The diagnosis of the type of family interaction we have described can be extremely helpful in individual therapy in determining the particular form of projective identification these sicker patients are most likely to employ in treatment. Specific forms of pathology in these more disturbed patients generate specific forms of projective identification that influence the transference-countertransference matrix. In treatment these patients attempt to recapitulate the interaction that occurred in their family of origin. They may either try to induce the therapist to be like one of their parents or do to the therapist what one or both of their parents did to them. This mechanism involves projective identification of the internalized good or bad object or self, which even during the same session may alternate from self to object and back again. These patients attempt to repeat and recreate their pattern of parent–child interaction in the transference and countertransference to reaffirm their past experiences as a way of mastering and/or perpetuating their pathology. Originally, in the patient's family, external reality corresponded to the patient's intrapsychic inner world. In treatment the patient again attempts to distort, shape, or control external reality to parallel, and provide negative feedback to reinforce, his or her internal reality. The patient thus attempts to manipulate and shape the therapist to be like the parental object(s). When the patient attempts to do to the therapist what was done to him or her by the parent, the patient is engaged in a repetition compulsion. By identifying with the aggressor, the parent, the patient takes an active stance instead of being the helpless victim, which was the case in childhood. Thus by doing to another what was done to one, one achieves a sense of mastery and control over the environment.

To provide an example of this process, we can present the typical case of the help-rejecting complainer, who is usually a masochistic, self-defeating, depressive individual. The patient at first attempts to induce the therapist to be like the domineering and exploitative parent, who pressured the patient to perform and then, without gratification of the patient, vicariously fed off the patient's success. To accomplish this induction of the therapist, the patient may behave in a submissive and helpless manner, asking the therapist repeatedly for all sorts of advice. If the therapist, by offering advice, accepts being put in this directive position, the patient immediately finds something wrong with the counsel offered. No matter what the therapist suggests, the patient says, "Yes, but..." and goes on to indicate that it won't work. The therapist may increase his or her efforts to perform for the patient, but none of these efforts is ever rewarded as being sufficiently helpful. The patient has subtly and cleverly turned the tables. The patient initially set up the therapist by projecting the powerful parental object into the therapist, and then switched position by projecting the helpless, angry, and frustrated self into the therapist. The therapist thus becomes the victim of the double bind on achievement and cannot win, regardless of how hard he or she tries to perform. Thus, the entire childhood drama that the patient experienced with a parent is reenacted in the treatment, with the therapist induced to play first the dominant parental object and then the helpless and frustrated self. This is the same no-win dilemma that the patient experienced passively as a child. By the patient's identification with the aggressor (the parental object) and use of a manic defense, he or she can actively try to manipulate the therapist into becoming the trapped victim.

If the therapist is open to experiencing the "objective" countertransference, important clues can be obtained that concern the transference and are useful in reconstructing psychogenetic material. If the therapist acts out the countertransference feelings by punitive behavior, this will reconfirm the patient's mistrust of authority figures and reinforce a sadomasochistic interaction. The patient may respond by becoming masochistically compliant and attempting to please the therapist with more material, or may become withholding and oppositional. In optimal treatment it is important that the therapist not deny the induced feelings but, rather, be open to experiencing and containing them. In doing so, the therapist can gain a genuinely empathic understanding of the patient's early family relations that can serve to enrich the therapeutic alliance if handled properly.

With the help-rejecting depressive patient, for example, treatment often reaches an impasse. The therapist, after carefully considering the patient's internal processes operative in the here-and-now interaction of therapy, can openly discuss the induced countertransference reactions experienced as a result of this double bind. He or she might state, "I recognize your need, but I feel in a no-win dilemma. If I say nothing you feel rejected, and if I offer help no matter what I seem to say, it's never good enough." The therapist can then continue by saying, "I wonder if you also felt in such a no-win dilemma during childhood when you were expected to do something. If you didn't do something that was expected, you would be considered bad, yet whatever you did do was never good enough."

Through the careful use of the countertransference, an added tool is made available to the therapist to unravel the transference-countertransference block, and to the patient to own and then cognitively and emotionally deal with the past traumatic events. Instead of the therapist's being induced into acting out the countertransference by becoming aggressive or defensive, which would only provide negative feedback and reinforcement for the patient's pathology, the therapist openly reveals the countertransference and connects it to past object relations. This technique provides the empathic understanding that will encourage the therapeutic alliance and foster a safe condition for growth. The therapist metabolizes the induced feelings, retains autonomy, carefully scrutinizes the feelings, and brings them out into the open for discussion. The therapist thereby changes the frame of communication from one that is outside conscious awareness and based on action to one that is in consciousness and is expressed symbolically through words. Instead of projection, self-observation can occur. Thus the therapist and the patient can join together in exploring and understanding the helpless and frustrated child within the patient. This is a form of metacommunication that serves as a cognitive model for the patient to talk about the here-and-now therapeutic relationship, which is shaped by internal objects that have arisen from past relations. Such communication permits emotional catharsis, intellectual understanding, differentiation of self from object, and working through of pathological interactions from the past. The transference-countertransference relationship is not simply a repetition of the past, and the patient's internal world of fantasy can be differentiated from external reality. According to general systems theory, the therapist is part of and affected by the system yet can use this very influence as a lever to change the communication mode from action to symbolic verbal expression. The negative feedback cycle is broken, and change and growth can occur.

USING THE FAMILY TYPOLOGY IN FAMILY THERAPY

In individual therapy, once the patient overcomes the fear and resistance to change, problems may develop as others in the patient's family openly manifest resistance to this change. Because the patient served as the container for the projective identifications of other family members, permitting them to disown their own conflict by placing it into the patient, the homeostatic balance of the family tends now to become disrupted. Thus, at the point at which the patient is starting to undergo personality change, the therapist performing individual therapy may need to recommend treatment for a spouse or other members of the family. Such treatment will prevent disruption of the patient's therapy or the development of pathology in another family member. The family member may be referred to another therapist or may be brought in for conjoint family therapy, depending on the training of the therapist and the particular characteristics of the case.

Very often, however, more seriously disturbed individuals first come for treatment requesting family or marital therapy. They would be resistant to individual therapy, because they have difficulty observing themselves and their effect on others as a result of their low level of self-differentiation. Because of the tendencies of these patients to externalize, and their excessive need to control and manipulate others, serious marital problems often arise. Aspects of their own conflicted internal object relations are put into others, and these patients tend to act out their pathology interpersonally in the family. For example, a narcissistic husband who felt conflict and ambivalence in his relationship with his mother may demean his wife as the bad mother and idealize the child as the good mother. This pattern, as we have noted, may lead to hysterical behavior in the child. If the husband entered into individual therapy, he might self-righteously complain of his nongratifying, bad wife and her damaging effect on their child. He would tend to draw the therapist into an alliance with him through the skewed picture he presents. If the therapist was not drawn in and confronted the patient to look at his share of the responsibility, the patient might simply experience the therapist also as a critical, rejecting bad parent and drop out of treatment.

More seriously disturbed patients have difficulty sustaining a stable transference, because their self-esteem is unstable and requires extensive mirroring or positive responses from the therapist. Anything hinting of criticism is seen as a blow to their self-esteem, thus making the transference too fragile and intense. If the therapist is drawn into an alliance that is restricted to only the provision of support and is unable to question the limited and egocentric perspective of the patient, movement in individual therapy is halted, at least until the patient has grown and is better engaged. Individual therapy thus is slower and may not even be beneficial. Family therapy, in contrast, can be suitable and can bring about fairly rapid change in narcissistic individuals. Through the involvement of other family members in treatment, the transference is diluted, as it is in group therapy. Thus, the pressure on the therapist to join in an alliance with the patient to blame the spouse is less subtle and intense. Also, these patients have difficulty establishing a therapeutic alliance because their level of self-object differentiation is too low. Their observing ego cannot join with the therapist to examine problems from an objective perspective. In family therapy the therapeutic alliance is established not with an individual but with the family. All the family is encouraged to join the therapist in looking at their interaction in a parallel, nonjudgmental fashion. Observations by other family members may be less threatening than those coming from the therapist. The very diversity of perspectives among family members is beneficial to the patient's and the other family members' narrow, egocentric perspectives. They can hear about others' needs and motivations as well as the effect they have on others. In addition, the symptomatic child has a vested interest in curing the parents. Therefore, the child or other family members may come forth as allies to the therapist, offering information, and particularly bringing family secrets out in the open, to help the therapeutic process along.

TECHNIQUES IN FAMILY THERAPY
DERIVED FROM OBJECT RELATIONS THEORY

In the beginning phase of work with these sicker families, it is useful to focus on interpersonal relations rather than on individual pathology. An impartial and empathic approach will encourage trust and the development of a therapeutic alliance with all the family members. After this alliance is consolidated, the family members can be helped to perceive one another as separately motivated individuals. Various family members may be questioned about their feelings, reactions, or motivations. Each should speak for himself or herself instead of using "we" language, which blurs individual differences and boundaries. The other is not simply an aspect of oneself, or only an object to gratify one's needs. The family should be helped to recognize and give up primitive defenses. For example, in splitting, others are seen as either all good or all bad; we can therefore encourage the family to look at each member's share of responsibility for the problems in the family. Here the use of "I" language instead of "you" language is encouraged, so that the individuals will express their own feelings without blaming or condemning others. The goal is to help them become aware of their own feeling, their effect on the other, and the other's effect on them. Some people are totally unaware of this interaction as a result of their low self-esteem and egocentricity. After the family is firmly engaged in treatment, the underlying conflict between the parents is brought to the surface. The parents must be made aware of the connection between this conflict and their own past experiences in a nonjudgmental and empathic fashion that sustains the therapeutic alliance. In this way the child will not be continually drawn into their interaction or made to feel responsible for holding the family together. Once family constancy is achieved, the child is released from the role of scapegoat, savior, go-between, or avenger. Autonomous functioning should be encouraged in all members, and they should be helped to deal with their fears of destruction as they continue to work through conflictual areas centered around aggression and dependency. Once the parent's self-esteem is not preserved by the child's performance, the child is released from the role of savior or avenger. As they become more aware of their individual psychopathology and have less need to act it out interpersonally, individual therapy may be suggested for one or more members to consolidate their gains further. Individual therapy can be most effective when inner and outer reality are differentiated, so that one's own conflicts are not placed into another individual.

11

FAMILY EVALUATION AND TREATMENT

DEVELOPING A TREATMENT PLAN

When a patient first comes for psychiatric help suffering from an emotional disorder, the therapist needs to evaluate the patient and develop a treatment plan. Usually the choice of the particular treatment prescribed by a psychotherapist, whether it be individual, family, or group therapy, is based on the orientation of the therapist. As a result, one type of therapy is often applied to all problems. The decision concerning the form of psychotherapy that is most applicable should be based on a careful evaluation and diagnosis of the patient and, when indicated, a diagnosis of the family as well.

The treatment plan that is formulated should reflect the needs of the patient and, when appropriate, those of other family members. Ideally the therapist will have the training and competence to offer a wide spectrum of treatment modalities, or else will be flexible enough to work collaboratively with another therapist who can provide a second type of treatment that may also be necessary. For example, when an individual is in psychoanalysis, problems with the spouse may come out of repression and to the forefront as the patient changes. Couples therapy would be indicated here, and yet the analyst will not wish to distort the transference by providing it. In such instances, one can work collaboratively with another therapist who provides couples therapy for the patient and spouse. In this way the analysand's transference toward the analyst is not disturbed, and couples can express and work through problems in their relationship that may have been damaging to the patient, the spouse, or their children. Collaborative therapy with another therapist can also be used to provide individual therapy or psychoanalysis for the spouse to enhance that person's growth as the initial patient changes.*

---

* Collaborative therapy in which a patient is referred by an individual therapist for group therapy, however, can be fraught with difficulty. The referral to group frequently is precipitated by a transference-countertransference impasse in individual treatment, and the patient tends to feel rejected. In addition, having two therapists for one patient encourages splitting and manipulation of one therapist against the other.

Involving the family is not necessary and is even contraindicated when starting treatment with neurotic patients. These patients are not suffering from preoedipal developmental arrest. They have separated and individuated adequately and tend to function fairly autonomously. Neurotic patients have internalized the mother and can maintain their own narcissistic equilibrium, thus being relatively independent of others in sustaining their self-esteem and identity. As a result, such patients are less influenced by current interpersonal relations, such as those stemming from the family. In turn, they do not use the primitive defenses of splitting and projective identification in order to control and manipulate others. More mature defenses are employed, such as repression, denial, displacement, and perceptual distortion due to projection. Symptoms stem from internalized conflicts during childhood and result in intrapsychic structural conflicts currently. This is the area best treated by individual dynamic psychotherapy or psychoanalysis to bring unconscious drives, perceptual distortions, and defenses associated with the conflict into consciousness and to work them through. Family therapy would not accomplish this purpose and would only tend to divert such patients from working introspectively on their intrapsychic conflicts.

When the patient is still living with and/or deeply involved with the family and the family appears to play a major role in causing and perpetuating the patient's problems, then it is imperative to involve all or part of the family in conjoint family therapy. This is particularly true if the patient has a preoedipal developmental arrest, as in schizophrenia or borderline and narcissistic conditions, because there is insufficient self-object differentiation. These patients cannot maintain their own narcissistic equilibrium and are excessively vulnerable to the influence of others, particularly family members. In addition, they themselves use primitive defenses in an attempt to control and use others to sustain their identity and self esteem. Intrapsychic conflict becomes externalized and acted out in the interpersonal sphere. Thus, the *level of differentiation* and the *diagnosis* is most significant and should be used in determining the choice of treatment.

During the course of family therapy or after it has been completed, individual (concurrent or collaborative) treatment may be indicated. Simply releasing the patient from a symbiotic bind in the family is not enough; it is only the beginning of psychological growth for the patient. Individuals who are not psychologically oriented and who need to be provided with an opportunity to learn from others how to define, verbally express, and resolve problems can benefit greatly from couples, group therapy, or multiple family therapy. These groups also dilute symbiotic dependency within the family, open up the family boundary to input from others, and provide a social support network. Members of a family may overcome their shame or guilt through finding out that they are not alone with a particular problem, and can offer one another empathy, encouragement, and alternate ways of coping themselves by taking on the role of helpers.

THE PRESENTING PROBLEM:
INDIVIDUAL AND FAMILY DIAGNOSES

Making an individual and family diagnosis is the next step after establishment of rapport with the patient and the family. The presenting problem of the patient must be defined according to its onset, background, and effects on others in the family. What do the patient and the family consider the cause of the problem, and how have they tried to remedy it so far? At this point it is useful to take a developmental history of the patient as well as the family. Each phase of the family life cycle has its own developmental tasks and stresses on its members. The courtship and early stages of the marriage in particular are significant, since this knowledge of the family is as critical as that of the early childhood of the individual patient in understanding current functioning. Another important family life cycle phase is launching, when children separate from the family. Once an individual diagnosis is made of the patient, the family typology presented in the previous chapter can be extremely helpful in the search for the particular forms of family interaction associated with the diagnosis. The typology provides meaning and direction to the data that are collected.

The questions that the therapist needs to explore include: What is the patient's level of differentiation? Are the primitive defenses of splitting and projective identification used? Is the patient able to sustain narcissistic equilibrium, or is he or she excessively vulnerable to the influence of others? Is the patient involved in preserving the family homeostasis or defensive equilibrium by functioning as the scapegoat or go-between, or in sustaining the self-esteem of any of the family members by being the savior or avenger? In turn, does the family system of interaction require that the patient remain bound to one of these roles, thereby perpetuating the patient's pathology unconsciously? If the patient is functioning at a neurotic level, is the problem essentially internalized and not significantly influenced or perpetuated by current relationships? If this is the case, the symptomatology may be largely a result of intrapsychic conflict from childhood and, although compulsively repeated during adulthood, must be traced back and worked through in individual therapy. Another area that needs to be explored is the ethnic differences of the parents, which may or may not produce conflict in the family.

EVALUATING FAMILY CONSTANCY AND BOUNDARIES

A careful assessment of family structure and function is necessary if the family does seem to be involved significantly in creating and perpetuating the patient's pathology. It is important especially to ascertain the level of family constancy and the intactness of the boundaries for both the individual members and the family as a whole. When family constancy is adequate, the patient does not have to assume responsibility for maintaining the survival and self-esteem of the parents and can separate without guilt. To evaluate family constancy, the stability or vulnerability of the parents' personalities as well as the degree of cohesion in the marriage must be explored. Have there been previous marriages, divorces, or separations? Are there any sexual conflicts, and is there a history of extramarital affairs? Are there any serious physical or emotional illnesses in the parents or another sibling? What is the work history of the father and mother? Is there satisfaction with their socioeconomic level, or has it declined and the major breadwinner or the other spouse come to be seen as a failure?

In addition, how the parents resolve differences or disagreements also must be investigated. Does one of the parents demean the other, attempting to intimidate and dominate? Is there a constant state of uproar and chaos, with each parent inflicting narcissistic wounds on the other? Has there been loss of control and physical violence? Or is there a massive denial of conflict, as in pseudomutual families, and displacement of aggression onto a scapegoat inside or outside the family? Is there splitting of parental functioning, with one parent being the good, indulgent one while the other is the bad one, responsible for discipline? Does one parent inhibit himself or herself or feel suppressed by the spouse, and therefore feel no entitlement to make demands or set limits with the children?

Besides maladaptive behavior, the therapist needs to evaluate the loving and caring feelings that exist within the family, the feelings that serve as a buffer or stabilizing force to sustain cohesion of the members in the face of conflict. Can the members communicate well? Do they have enough self-awareness and honesty, as well as empathic connection with others, to own their share of the responsibility for problems? Is there a sense of humor and some objectivity, i.e., an observing ego that can form a therapeutic alliance to explore issues together? Are the members individuated and secure enough to engage in cooperative behavior with one another, instead of falling into coercive and controlling power struggles? These questions and others that are appropriate in evaluating the strengths and the narcissistic vulnerability of the parents will provide some estimate of the level of family constancy.

The intactness of the boundaries of individual members in the family must be measured as well. Are the boundaries too rigid and closed, so that family members are distant and alienated from one another, as in delinquent families? Or are the boundaries too permeable and open, so that symbiotic merging occurs, as in schizophrenic families? Is this boundary disturbance pervasive throughout the family or limited to certain subgroups? The degree of autonomous behavior permitted in the family can be evaluated by noting how free members feel to express divergent opinions or angry feelings. (Indeed, in some families even the expression of loving feelings is suppressed.) Does the expression of angry feelings simply turn into a shouting match that leads nowhere? Or do people not become too defensive;

can they listen to one another and attempt to work through and resolve conflict without retaliation or rejection? Do members assume individual responsibility and not project blame onto others constantly? Is there an attempt to manipulate others through projective identification, thereby impinging on the other's separate identity? Are there unconscious collusions that determine the members' thoughts, feelings, or behavior patterns? Are there alliances between a parent and a child that breach generational boundaries, as in families with a borderline patient?

The boundary of the family as a group also must be evaluated. Often families whose members are symbiotically overinvolved with one another internally are closed off and isolated from relatives and others in the community. This is the rubber fence described by Wynne, Ryckoff, Day, and Hirsch (1958), which often exists in schizophrenic families. The family boundary is too rigid and encompassing, so that an outside support system is lacking and the child's separation from the family becomes difficult. In other families the boundary is too open, as when one parent remains overly involved with his or her own parents. This transgenerational alliance generally proves detrimental or even destructive to the marital dyad, because it undermines authority and responsibility. Towne, Messinger, and Sampson (1962) found that these symbiotic relationships can exist among women over several generations, and they noted three varieties: the merger type, in which the parental and marital families function as a single unit; the oscillation type, in which one parent alternates back and forth between the two families; and the conversion type, in which the marital family substitutes for the symbiotic parental family. The last of these represents the closed and isolated family boundary type we have discussed.

My clinical work indicates that the transgenerational symbiotic involvement is not limited to women but, rather, exists also with some men and their mothers or even their fathers. For example, in one very wealthy family, the father was overly involved with his own father. His life choices and identity revolved around pleasing his father, who was very powerful and successful. He had married a woman from the right family whom his father essentially had chosen for him, and had pursued an education and a career that his father had dictated. He eventually entered his father's business firm and threw himself into his work. His marriage suffered from his lack of involvement with his wife and children, even though a stereotyped facade of a happy marriage was maintained for the world to view. His wife's feelings of deprivation of love, and of jealousy of her husband's greater loyalty to his father, resulted in her becoming inwardly angry and withholding. The anger was displaced onto and openly expressed toward the children, who both later became emotionally disturbed. When the father's father died, however, he suffered a severe identity crisis and a revolution occurred. He divorced his wife and even changed the direction of his career. The pieces of this marriage needed to be picked up in family therapy so that each member of the family could develop a separate identity and work through and integrate his or her feelings. Family therapy was successful in resolving many of the conflicts so that each person could lead a productive life.

DIRECT OBSERVATION OF
FAMILY STRUCTURE AND FUNCTION*

Another way of evaluating the structure and functioning of the family is to observe directly the members' spoken and nonverbal behavior during the interview. One can make tentative assumptions concerning the order of dominance from a number of observations. Frequently, the first person to come into the office and the one who

---

* A variety of psychological tests can also be used to evaluate family functioning. These tests have not been standardized, but do approach the family from different perspectives. They include (1) Self report tests which evaluate the subjective perception and experience of members within the family concerning current problems and how they might ideally like to see the family change in the future. (2) Family behavioral self reports, where members are asked to keep track of and write down their own and other's behavior in the family during the week. (3) Family projective techniques, such as the Family T.A.T. or story telling technique, which reveal shared themes and fantasies. (4) Interactional tasks which are assigned the family to work out, and the process and outcome measured by trained observers from outside the family. Another variation, introduced by Reiss (1971), uses the data itself and does not call for outside observers for measurement, yet requires complicated laboratory apparatus.

sits down and speaks first is the most dominant. This person may do most of the talking, especially if a question is directed generally at the family. In addition, others may tend to look at the spokesman. This individual may take the most comfortable or imposing chair, sitting either directly opposite the therapist or at the extreme side of the family. Dominant individuals often sit at the ends of the family, like bookends. (This is similar to the behavior of baboons, in which the dominant male takes a peripheral position, guarding the central troop of mothers and infants.) Dominant individuals often have a more erect posture and generally dress better or more colorfully than those who are depressed or submissive.

Spatial seating arrangements can also offer some clues concerning alliances, triangles, and subgroup formations. Notice who sits closer to whom and who is physically distant, because these positionings often are equivalent to emotional closeness or distance. Frequently, if a child is scapegoated, he or she will occupy the distant position, whereas a child who functions as a go-between usually sits between the parents. Members who are more compliant or seeking support often sit closer to the therapist.

Individuals who are overly dependent symbiotically on one another often sit in postures that parallel or mirror one another. Members who are more defensive and guarded may cross their arms or legs, whereas those who are more open and less vulnerable will not cover up their bodies and genitals. Defensiveness is also indicated by a member's averting his or her eyes or turning the body away from the therapist. In addition, Scheflen (1963, 1964) has described certain nonverbal cues that regulate the degree of distance or closeness and the interactions in families. These behaviors include preening (which are seductive and inviting movements) and leg blocking (which creates barriers and distance). There are also cues that indicate deviance from family rules, such as nose-wiping movements or brush-off motions with the hand, which express disapproval of the preceding verbal or nonverbal communication. (For a more thorough review of kinesic regulation, it is recommended that the reader look at the two articles by Scheflen just cited.)

Careful observation of verbal interaction is also extremely valuable in understanding relationships. Do people listen to each other and respond appropriately? Or do they demean others who differ, blame or rigidly categorize others, or in general prevent a meaningful dialogue from developing? Is there communication deviance: an unshared focus of attention, vagueness, and ambiguity concerning what is being spoken about, which serve to obfuscate and avoid hostile or divergent feelings? Is the topic of conversation arbitrarily shifted, or does someone monopolize the family time by telling long-winded, tangential stories as a cover-up? Do people interrupt one another, speak for one another as if they were merged, or impinge on the autonomy of others by telling them what to think, feel, or do? Are the family members so tuned in to one another that they can almost read one anothers' minds without having to speak? Or does one member demand that his or her thoughts be magically read without speaking, and otherwise feel rejected? In addition, are the child's grooming, dress, and behavior, as well as the way the parents relate to him or her, appropriate to the child's age and sex? These surface indicators may point to deeper manifestations that concern whether the child is being acccepted for who he or she is and whether the child is being infantilized or parentified. The direct observations of verbal and nonverbal communications in the family may be added to the historical information obtained to provide an additional dimension revealing the individual and family dynamics.

THE EFFECT OF PRECIPITATING STRESS ON INDIVIDUAL AND FAMILY HOMEOSTASIS

It is essential to identify the precipitating stress that led to regression of the patient, and possibly the family as well. This may be a seemingly minor event or a massive psychic trauma following a natural or man-made catastrophe that permanently changed the total functioning of the family. For example, in some families of Holocaust survivors, there occurred a closing off of the boundary of the family against the outside world, which is perceived as threatening, and a persistent fear of separations, which are associated with death. In the majority of other families, the precipitating event usually occurs at a transitional point in the family life cycle. The most profound stress comes from the addition or loss of a family member, because such an event requires a major realignment of interpersonal relations. Addition of a family member may come about through birth, adoption, remarriage of a parent, or the moving into the house of a relative, such as an elderly parent. The loss of a family member may be due to the death or emancipation of a child or separation, divorce, or the death of a parent.

Certain other life event stresses, such as retirement or the loss of health, money, employment, or prestige, may strongly affect the existing family homeostatis. Paradoxically, a return of physical health, coming into more money, an advancement at a job, or a gain in prestige may also strain a marriage. For example, if the breadwinner feels like a failure and the spouse has a dominant position in the family, advancement at work may add to the self-esteem of the breadwinner and disrupt the existing power relationship in the family. Alternately, some individuals with a profound fear of success may fall into a deep depression or act out self-destructively following an advancement at work. Psychological growth of one partner may drastically alter the marital relationship, because this partner's way of relating, interests, and even his or her underlying basis for the relationship may change. For example, a newly liberated woman may revolt against simply being the traditional home-oriented wife who selflessly supports and lives through her husband's career. She may come out of his shadow, disrupt the existing dominant-submissive power structure, and actively pursue her own career and independent identity.

Changes in the family homeostatic balance do not occur only as a result of psychotherapy; they can also be due to the effect of medication, as one report will illustrate. About ten years ago, a rash of family crises occurred at the New York University Medical Center in patients stabilized on a regimen of lithium (Samuel Gershon, personal communication, 1975). Manic-depressive patients, as a result of lithium medication, were functioning better than they ever had in the past. Their marriages had survived the trauma of repeated bouts of severe acting out by these patients, which had occurred during manic episodes. They had spent large sums of money or behaved destructively toward the marriage in other ways. Yet now that these patients were self-assured and more assertive, their marriages were in jeopardy. During the course of family therapy with many of these couples, it became clear that the projective identification of dependency by the spouse onto the patient was disrupted, just as with the recovered alcoholic. With this shift in defensive equilibrium came a shift in the power structure as well. The patient was no longer the sick one, no longer in the one-down position. In treatment the patients openly acknowledged that they thought their spouses preferred them to continue in the role of the needy, sick one. Indeed, some of these patients, fearing abandonment by their spouses, had discontinued their lithium medication and regressed into being the sick one. Thus, the stress even of positive, growth-enhancing experiences may profoundly alter the power relationship and may prove to be disruptive to the marital interaction. By understanding the precipitating stress, one becomes able to work with its effects on the individual and the family. Through careful questioning one can also trace back an especially high degree of vulnerability in a current transition point to a similar situation in one or both of the parent's childhoods, or even through several generations of families.

ESTABLISHING A THERAPEUTIC CONTRACT

A therapeutic contract with the family ensures that the goals of treatment set by the family members and those of the therapist are generally congruent. With time these goals may change, but at the starting point there should be agreement. The methods of achieving these goals must be spelled out so that the frame or the boundaries of the treatment are established. These boundaries include the time, place, and length of visits, the fee, who shall attend, procedures for cancellation, and what is expected of the participants. The aim is to establish an atmosphere of safety and mutual helpfulness in resolving problems. One can present certain rules, suggesting that these will facilitate treatment. Members should be encouraged to try to avoid premature closure and to listen to others' opinions, rather than judging, condemning, or blaming, especially if they disagree; to try to communicate as openly and honestly as they can; to try to be helpful to one another; not to interrupt or speak for one another; and, whenever possible, to speak directly to the individual they are talking about. One can propose a rule that issues brought up during the session not be used as ammunition against one another after the session. Participants should be made to realize that simply looking to blame and demean the other results only in an impasse or stalemate; it tends to escalate conflict as each party defends himself or herself, and is counterproductive.

FAMILY DIAGNOSIS AND TREATMENT PLAN: A REVIEW

1. *Presenting problem* of patient and its background are explored.
   (a) See if it seems related to overall family functioning, and/or to stress from a family life cycle stage.
   (b) What has been done so far to remedy the problem.
2. *Individual diagnosis* for each family member is established, including a judgment concerning the level of differentiation, and the use of primitive or mature defenses.
   (a) Gather data on the patient and family development.
   (b) Note any ethnic differences or conflicts.
3. *Family Constancy* is determined if parents can maintain their own narcissistic equilibrium, or if patient is needed to sustain their self esteem and survival (the symbiotic survival pattern).
   (a) Note if a rigid homeostasis or defensive equilibrium exists that binds and prevents the patient from individuating and separating.
   (b) Is there pressure for personality compliance within the family, or social achievement outside the family?
   (c) Determine whether one or a combination of the *Family Typology* seems appropriate by evaluating affiliative, oppositional, and alienated attitudes.
4. *Precipitating Stress* is explored, and its relation to a loss or other traumatic event (negative or positive) or a transitional point in the family life cycle that has disrupted homeostasis.
5. *Individual Boundaries* for members are defined next. These may be rigidly too open (a symbiotically close relationship) or too

closed (an emotionally divorced and distant relationship).

    (a) Are *Generational Boundaries* intact, or are there parent–child coalitions?

    (b) Are the parental coalition, the subsystems, and authority hierarchy intact?

6. *Family Boundary* is defined to see if too open (symbiotic relations persist with family of origin) or too closed (family is isolated from community without social support system).

7. *Ability to negotiate differences* and problem solve through verbal dialogue is determined, involving respect for one's own and other's views, opinions, and motivations versus an egocentric controlling viewpoint resulting in coercion and manipulation.

8. *Observe* communication patterns and kinesic regulation to determine if spontaneous versus rigid-stereotyped, distancing, or obfuscating (Communication Deviance); level of initiative versus passivity; rigidity of family rules; and the *power-role structure.*

9. *Loving and caring feelings* amongst members are evaluated, which allow for separateness rather than acceptance only by conformity; provide warmth, support, and comfort.

10. *Treatment goals* are defined in terms of difficulties that have been uncovered, and the *frame* or boundaries of the treatment process are presented.

FACILITATING A THERAPEUTIC ALLIANCE

A number of techniques can be used to facilitate a therapeutic alliance. For example, it is sometimes appropriate in the treatment process to inject some humor to help a couple gain distance and objectivity on their problem of constant blaming. In a light-hearted tone, one might ask, "You both have been blaming each other now for a number of years and it has led nowhere, and I was wondering how many more years you both wished to lose by continuing to blame each other—let's say another 10, 20, or 30 years?" This technique attempts to delimit projection of blame in such a way that no one is scapegoated and each individual is encouraged to assume some degree of personal responsibility for outcomes. Once this technique is successful, each member can be asked to engage in an experiment: to assign a percentage to their share of responsibility, and one to their spouse's share. This procedure stimulates self-examination instead of externalization, and it diminishes the demand that the other person change first. It reduces the splitting process, in which one sees the other as the bad villain and the self as an innocent good victim, and redefines a dominant-submissive competitive battle into a framework that encourages mutual cooperation.

Once one member assumes some responsibility, the other may feel less defensive and be more willing to reveal and openly share the problems in the relationship. Here the therapist can review the sequence of interactions, suggesting in a nonjudgmental and informative fashion why each may react to the other in a particular way, so that each member can perceive his or her own contribution to negative outcomes. These suggestions about motivation can then be assessed for validity. Even if they are not accurate, the member can explain the correct motivation, which will diminish the other's taking remarks as a personal assault and encourage clearer communication and introspection. Different ways of dealing with conflict can be suggested by the therapist, such as sticking to issues and avoiding personal attacks, which do not inflict narcissistic injury. Different ways of responding also can be explored, to increase the members' interpersonal coping repertoires. For example, instead of saying "you are wrong," the person can state, "I disagree." In this way a rigidly defensive and egocentric stance is diminished, and the members come to feel less narcissistically vulnerable and can deal with substantive issues. Ideally they can give up splitting (seeing issues in black and white terms and projecting blame) and can recognize the separate and complex motivations and needs of others.

With repeated success at conflict resolution comes a greater sense of self-mastery and trust. The family members are less likely to feel hopeless and to lose self-esteem, and have less need to respond defensively by emotional or physical withdrawal, violence, or frustrating the other by passive-aggressive games. With many of these families, lack of control is more a problem than are inhibition and restriction of affect. Here one might suggest learning control by counting to ten, cooling off the anger before verbally responding to the other. It is also useful to suggest that when they note that conflict is escalating, one of them "blow the whistle," much like a referee in a sporting match. They can then calm down in their separate corners, rather than responding with aggression and accusations defensively. They can try to become aware of and discuss their own hurt and angry feelings and try to recognize those of their spouse. "I" language needs to be substituted here for "you" language. In this way personal blows below the belt that inflict narcissistic injury may be prevented, and conflict is not escalated. The partners learn how to fight clean, sticking to the issues, avoiding personal attack, listening to the other, and negotiating differences more effectively.

SAFEGUARDING THE THERAPEUTIC ALLIANCE

The establishment of a firm therapeutic alliance with all the family members must be encouraged and protected in order to foster their becoming engaged in treatment and continuing to work on their problems. It is essential that the therapist assume a neutral and impartial stance in the treatment and not be drawn into a collusion with the parents against the child, the child against the parents, or one parent against the other. Indeed, the optimal position in working with a family is that everyone in the family is a full partner in the treatment process. Each member is affected by and influenced by the others; thus, each member has a unique contribution to make and needs to be heard. In this way the mature, growth-seeking aspect of each person is enlisted. The goal of this therapeutic partnership is to provide sufficient trust and safety for the family members to decrease their defensiveness and reveal their vulnerabilities to one another. The therapist needs to inspire confidence in his or her ability to understand and to help the entire family.

In addition, the therapist must provide a safe holding environment to contain conflict when it erupts, without scapegoating. Indeed, it may help to preserve the therapeutic alliance to forewarn the members that at times they may feel misunderstood or angry at the ther-

apist or at one another. At that time they may be tempted to withdraw in silence, not to come, or to discontinue treatment. These
moments are very important, however, and actually provide a unique
opportunity for the participants to learn how to explore and express
uncomfortable feelings in a different way. Acting out these feelings
through disruptive behavior may only perpetuate tension and difficulties within the family and ultimately may prove to be self-defeating.
The therapeutic goal is for the mature and observing part of the ego
of each of the family members to identify with the therapist, and with
one another, in order to permit exploration of the relationship. It
is hoped that there will be enough mutual, empathic understanding
to contain conflict, to avoid the use of splitting and projective identification, and to foster acknowledgment of individual responsibili-
ties. The participants can then honestly work toward enhancing each
family member's autonomy and becoming aware of and meeting one
anothers' needs.

THE BEGINNING PHASE OF TREATMENT:
CASE MATERIAL

A family therapy case recently presented for consultation began
with a dilemma for the therapist. A young man was admitted to the
hospital because of a drug overdose and problems with legal authorities. His father contacted the therapist and immediately described
his own power and importance. He had considerable wealth and influential friends in high political positions. These connections, he indirectly indicated, could be used to help or harm the hospital. He
knew exactly what the hospital had been negotiating for with outside authorities. He dropped names and particulars to confirm his
claims. Having attempted to intimidate the therapist, he then
proceeded to attempt to dictate the treatment, and asked the therapist to lie to his son about a certain issue. Without any subtlety,
the father asked the therapist to abdicate his position of medical
authority and to compromise his integrity or else risk inflicting serious
economic loss to the hospital.

The therapist, a junior staff member, felt insecure and conflicted by this dilemma. It was suggested that he get more information from the patient concerning the family structure, to see if a similar dilemma existed there; often the way in which a family presents itself provides a great deal of information concerning its structure and function.

Indeed, this was the father's typical intrusive and manipulative mode of operation. It had proven extremely successful in the business world as well as in the home. The father was described as a controlling, grandiose, and authoritarian person who became violent or punitive if his will was opposed. The patient's mother had abdicated her parental authority and compromised herself in order to retain economic security. Her son, the patient, however, became the "avenger" for her humiliation at the hands of her husband. The son acted out the mother's unconscious anger by constantly opposing and provoking the father into rage. The patient later engaged in the same sort of behavior toward authorities in society, which resulted in his legal difficulties. On a conscious level, the mother preached compliance with the father's demands. She told her son that if he were not nice to his father, he would have to sell his body on the street like a prostitute to live. Implicitly, the mother's conscious message was that if the son did not prostitute himself symbolically to his father as she had, he would be forced to prostitute himself physically. Unconsciously, however, the mother communicated her anger at her husband's impingement on her autonomy and self-respect, and subtly encouraged her son to be her champion.

The following family diagnosis and treatment plan was formulated: The presenting problem of this patient was an overdose of drugs that required hospitalization. The individual diagnoses were for the patient, an overinvolved sociopathic character disorder with drug addiction; for the father, a narcissistic character disorder; and for the mother, a dysthymic disorder with masochistic features. Family constancy was stable, and the patient was involved in a symbiotic survival pattern of sustaining the mother's self-esteem. The family fits the fourth form of the family typology, the delinquent-sociopath type of structure, with the patient functioning in the role of his mother's "avenger." The son introjected his mother's angry, bad self (S−) and acted out her rage against the father. The precipitating stress was the drug overdose of the patient following legal difficulties.

Individual boundaries of the family members were too closed between the parents, who were alienated from each other, and too open and symbiotically fused between mother and son, representing a transgenerational alliance. The family boundary was not disturbed. The parents were unable to negotiate differences, and a dominant-submissive power relationship existed. The father used coercive threats to manipulate and dominate others, and the mother on the surface complied masochistically. It was never possible to see all the family together to observe kinesic regulation as a group, but clearly the parents' level of positive feeling for each other was minimal. If the parents had been accepting of family treatment, some of the goals would have been (1) to foster family stability, so that the patient was released from the symbiotic bind of having to sustain his mother's self-esteem; (2) to resolve the transgenerational alliance between mother and son; (3) to reestablish the parental coalition; (4) to repair the emotional divorce between the parents; and (5) to help the parents negotiate their differences on a more equal, verbal level without threats or manipulation, which would in turn release the patient from having to act out his mother's humiliation and anger as her avenger. Unfortunately, the parents rejected any treatment, and there existed as well a potentially damaging situation for the hospital. Thus, individual therapy was prescribed, with the goal of providing the patient with insight into the family dynamics, which he acted out in the social sphere.

The information gathered from the members, as well as the way in which the family presented itself for treatment, provided the therapist with an immediate and profound understanding concerning the dilemma faced by the mother and the patient. This understanding helped direct the therapist's exploration and delineation of the family problem with the patient. When the therapist asked the patient pointed questions, the patient felt understood, which facilitated the development of a therapeutic alliance. The therapist in his actual dealings with the father did not compromise himself (as the patient's mother did), nor did he become provoked into a hostile battle with him (as the patient did), despite the father's manipulation. He was firm and assertively held his ground with the father concerning the best medical treatment for the patient. The father acquiesced and accepted this judgment. Thus, the therapist did not act out his own countertransference reaction, nor did he avoid dealing with it, and he did not set the patient up to act out for him. Instead, the therapist served as an adaptive model for the patient of how to deal with the father openly and verbally without compromising one's autonomy and integrity. In individual treatment, the therapist helped the patient verbally define the dilemma he faced with both parents and start to work through his feelings associated with it.

PITFALLS DURING THE INITIAL PHASE OF TREATMENT

Another problem that frequently disrupts family therapy at its very inception is the therapist's being manipulated into siding with one person, or a part of the family, against another. This error is most common among trainees and inexperienced family therapists and accounts for a high percentage of the early dropout rate (Slipp, Ellis, and Kressel 1974). When a couple or a family comes for treatment, sometimes one spouse or a child assumes the role of the bad, sick, or irresponsible one, with the other spouse being the good, healthy, or responsible one. This phenomenon is generally the result of splitting and projective identification. Inexperienced therapists generally fall into the obvious trap of siding with the apparently healthy, responsible spouse and form an alliance against the sick, irresponsible family member.

Therapists who are a bit more experienced usually can avoid this initial trap but may fall into the next one, which is more subtle. Such a situation occurred with a therapist who was familiar with the concept of family homeostasis and had read about projective identification. He began working in couples therapy with an alcoholic husband and wife. The wife recounted her long list of complaints against her husband and portrayed herself as an innocent victim of his drinking. At this point the therapist turned to the wife and asked, "What do you think it is that *you* do to make your husband drink?" Here the therapist joined in an alliance with the sick member against the healthy member, which was disruptive to the development of a therapeutic alliance with all the family members. The wife experienced this question as personal criticism and blame for her husband's condition and refused to return to treatment. In supervision, the therapist revealed that he felt he was being manipulated and controlled by the wife and was annoyed at her. Unfortunately, he had misused his knowledge concerning projective identification to act out his own negative countertransference, which was destructive to the therapy. The potential for misuse of the concepts of family homeostasis and projective identification must be recognized. The therapist here, by his particular intervention, reinforced the denial of autonomy and individual responsibility of the husband and simply painted the wife as the villain. Like an alliance with the healthy spouse against the sick one, this opposite type of alliance consolidates the process of splitting and projective identification. One spouse is seen as all good and the other as all bad, instead of the two being perceived as sharing the responsibility.

Even though individuals with more serious personality disorders come to therapy seeking change in their spouse, there is a strong unconscious resistance to change. Because internal aspects of each person are placed into the other through projective identification, an unconscious collusion results that stabilizes each personality. Change in one partner results in drastic intrapsychic change in the other, and a profound shift in the relationship then takes place. When such a shift does occur during the course of therapy, it represents one of the crisis points in treatment. If it cannot be worked through, the couple or the family frequently drops out of therapy.

CRISES DURING THE COURSE OF THERAPY: CASE MATERIAL

The following case illustrates the type of crisis that can develop during the course of couples or family therapy when one spouse changes, thereby endangering the continuation of treatment. The M.'s entered marital therapy ostensibly because of a conflict in deciding whether to have a child at that particular time. Both were successful in their careers as academicians in colleges. The wife had completed a psychoanalysis several years ago, and the husband was currently in analysis with another analyst. When they first met, Mrs. M. had been attracted to her future husband because she felt he had a great deal of potential and she would make something of him. At the time they were both graduate students in the same department of a prestigious eastern college. He was shy, insecure, and introverted, which she found attractive. Mrs. M. was more socially adept and took the more aggressive role during their courtship. After their marriage she developed a block while writing her doctoral dissertation. In her analysis she had discovered that she unconsciously felt inhibited in competing professionally with her husband and feared abandonment if she surpassed him. To protect her husband's self-esteem, which she felt was vulnerable, she inhibited herself and suffered a profound fear of success. As a result of her own suppression of her autonomy, she built up unconscious resentment toward her husband, and their sexual life declined. Her husband had actually encouraged her a great deal, and she did complete her dissertation. She obtained a position in industry and became quite successful. Again, however, she feared that the demands of the job would wreck her marriage, so she quit and obtained a part-time teaching position; she could be more of a housewife and become pregnant. Again their sexual life declined, and they avoided each other not only sexually but also socially. At this point they decided to enter marital therapy.

Diagnostically both could be labeled as depressive neurotics who seemed moderately well differentiated. The husband had been the only child of a mother who was described as dependent, manipulative, and possessive. Never having potentiated herself as a person, the mother had pressured her son for achievement and lived through his achievements to sustain her self-esteem. When her husband died, she was totally unprepared to run their business, and the son felt forced to drop out of college for a year to help. Shortly after he married, the mother again had a business crisis, and he had to return to help her. He had felt dominated by his mother's demands all his life, and if he did not comply to them, she would withdraw and pout or become punitive. Whereas earlier he had served in the role of his mother's savior (s+) through his achievements, after his father's death he felt coerced to become a substitute good husband-parent (o+) to his mother.

The wife also came from a traditional family, with the father being the competent businessman and dominant and the mother being a childlike and submissive housewife. Mrs. M., an excellent student, had been encouraged to achieve by her father. Although he bragged about her accomplishments, he did not gratify her. Like her mother, she felt she always had to play a subservient role to the father to build him up; she would risk rejection if she were autonomous. She played the savior role (s+) for her father and was always the "good girl" who never challenged him or asserted her own demands. Thus, her identity remained reactive and false, based originally on compliance to her father's, and now to her husband's, demands. She felt she was worthless unless she performed, yet she was perpetually preoccupied by the fear of object loss if she became too successful or independent. When she became the housewife herself, she felt trapped into giving up her autonomy and becoming subservient to her husband's needs, as her masochistic mother had done.

The husband's self-esteem seemed vulnerable, and the wife felt responsible for maintaining it. Family constancy was good however, since the personality integrity of its members was not threatened. During their childhoods, both Mr. and Mrs. M. had been part of families displaying the depressive interaction pattern. The precipitating stress was the conflict in identity for the wife, centered around limiting her career and being a housewife and mother. The individual boundaries between the couple were too open, but the family boundary was essentially normal. Both partners were unable to negotiate differences, and both acted out their hostility indirectly by passive-aggressive means. There was mutual respect for the other's intellectual ability and considerable underlying caring, which made the prognosis seem favorable. The therapist's goals were to help Mr. and Mrs. M. to deal with conflict in an open and direct way verbally, and to diminish narcissistic vulnerability so that each could function autonomously. Achieving these goals would involve dealing with and interpreting the transferential reactions each had established by reconstructing past genetic material from their families of origin.

In therapy the husband related that he felt dominated by his wife and also deprived of her attention. He had felt the same way with his mother when he was a child. The wife felt intimidated by this accusation of being like his mother. Whenever they disagreed, he repeatedly accused her of being just like his selfish, demanding, and domineering mother. During the fifth therapy session, however, the wife paused, reflected, and insightfully commented, "It is not me; it is you who were behaving much like your mother." When she did not comply to his demands for attention, he would withdraw, sulk, and become guilt provoking or behave punitively, exactly as his mother had. She said, "We really have this situation reversed. If I don't do exactly what you want, you become the manipulative, bad mother, not me." This was a breakthrough for the wife; she openly and directly asserted herself and gave factual evidence concerning their relationship. The husband had identified with his mother and now behaved toward his wife the way his mother had toward him. At this point, the husband felt he had lost control over his wife and threatened to terminate treatment.

In the following session, the wife initiated and took over the conversation, totally avoiding what had been discussed previously. She talked blithely about their plans for the summer, when they would be going on a trip. At this point the husband complained that they were dealing only with superficial items and again questioned the validity of continuing treatment. The therapist commented that indeed he could understand his frustration and also wondered about the relevance of discussing summer plans here, but that he thought that the reason the wife had changed the discussion to a lighter topic was that she had felt threatened by his angry comment in the last session about their discontinuing therapy. The wife validated this interpretation, stating that she felt frightened of abandonment if she was assertive and that, by switching to a light, noncontroversial topic, she was being protective of his personality. Indeed, she was overly sensitive to his reactions and responded this way automatically. This was the old problem she had had with her father, whom she saw as both vulnerable and volatile. By being compliant and responsible for her husband's behavior, she felt more secure. He was aware, however, of her not being genuine; he sensed it and felt alienated and cut off from her.

In the next session Mr. M. related a dream he had had repeatedly over several years. He dreamed he saw himself as a wild and destructive man, similar to one student they had both known in college. This man was like an uncivilized animal; he had a great deal of body hair and was hostile, intrusive, and uncouth. On further exploration, it became clear that this was also how he experienced his father, especially because he was seductively overinvolved with his mother. In his analysis he was currently working on resolving his oedipal conflict. His father was experienced by him as a dangerous, castrating animal. Mrs. M.'s own fear of her father then emerged. Her father had been coerced into working in the family business, and he felt dominated and compromised by his own father. When he was at home with the family, however, he overcompensated and became overbearing and tyrannical.

The therapist interpreted that Mr. and Mrs. M. seemed to share the unconscious fantasy that men were controlling and destructive animals. For their own sense of security, they both needed to control the beast they felt existed in men. Previously this fantasy had developed with their fathers, and now it surfaced in their marital relationship. The wife admitted that as a result of her experience with her father, she had been fearful of being dominated and destroyed by men. She felt controlled not only by her father's anger, but also by his weakness, which deprived her of autonomy. She had felt safe in picking her husband, who seemed shy and insecure. By entertaining a Pygmalion fantasy of developing and shaping her husband into a success, she came to feel in control of her fear of men. As this shared unconscious fantasy about men was worked through in treatment, the couple's relationship improved markedly. They could be more assertive without fear of hurting or being hurt by the other, and they could negotiate their differences. They became more understanding and genuine with each other. Because the therapist was sensitive to, and helped the couple deal with, the change in their relationship, therapy was not disrupted. Their defensive equilibrium and their power relationships were reestablished at a more equal and healthy level. After completion of the marital therapy, Mrs. M. felt that she still had some unresolved issues concerning her father that she wished to deal with, and she entered individual therapy.

12

INDIVIDUAL TREATMENT

In this chapter clinical material from individual therapy will be reported to show how an understanding of the family dynamics presented in this book can be useful in individual treatment.

USING FAMILY DYNAMICS IN INDIVIDUAL THERAPY: CASE MATERIAL

A writer who had an excellent education and showed talent had not potentiated himself in his career. He was overly constricted, polite, and formal, almost like a caricature of a 19th-century gentleman. He was also unable to find pleasure in his work, was excessively self-critical, and was unable to commit himself to a permanent relationship with a woman. He had always been viewed by everyone as a promising young man, but, now in his early forties, he had never lived up to his potential. He entered individual therapy complaining of depression. He had been brought up with his younger sister in a wealthy family in the Midwest. His father, who was the chief executive officer in one of the Fortune 500 industries, was a hard-driving, self-made man. He had married late in life, and he ran his family as the chief executive officer at home as well. Each week, as if it were a ritual, the father called the patient into his office at home, sat behind his desk, and sternly gave him a comprehensive performance report. Ostensibly for the good of the patient, the father unearthed and discussed the patient's imperfections of the preceding week, so that he could work on them and correct them.

The mother came from an upper-class southern family and had been overprotected from the practical and seamy sides of life. She was like a Tennessee Williams heroine, ethereal, refined, and cultured but too weak to stand up to life. She was totally dominated in the home by her husband and gradually withdrew emotionally to become a solitary drinker. The mother's alcoholism was never openly discussed; there was always a polite and glossy façade presented within the family and to the world. The family, the patient said, was very much like that depicted by Eugene O'Neill in *Long Day's Journey into Night*, with its domineering, withholding father and its weak and addicted mother. "But there was one difference," the patient said. "In my family there was never the denouement as in the O'Neill play, where everyone breaks that polite façade and vomits out the truth from their guts onto the floor."

The patient was expected to perform, yet he was not gratified. Also, whatever he did do was never good enough for his exacting father. His mother became a pathetic and powerless individual who could not provide strength or comfort. Instead, she only compromised herself further and supported the legitimacy of the father's pressure for performance. The patient himself bought into this depressive pattern of family interaction, viewed his father's demands as beneficent, and justified them to himself. The father tried to relive his life through the patient, but this time he would coach the patient, so the mistakes he had made would not be repeated. Therefore, the patient served as "savior" for the father (s+). Everything his father did was for the patient's benefit, and he hoped that eventually his performance would be good enough and he would be gratified by his father. He thus internalized and secured in his superego the pressuring and ungratifying bad father (o−) but no comforting good parent (o+), because no effective one was available. Instead of becoming independent and autonomous, he remained dependently attached to his father to sustain his self-esteem and developed a reactive, false compliant self. He learned all the details about what makes a person successful from his father, yet he wound up feeling passive, empty, and inadequate. As he described this, "It was like I learned to be the icing on the cake, but there was no cake inside."

The patient then went on to discuss the identification of his self with his mother. He stated:

> I've integrated a great deal of my mother into my psyche; I'm a lot like her—tolerant, forgiving, and understanding of my father. It was the way she adapted to being with my father as his wife. When a decision came along as to the children's discipline or school problems, she com-

plied to his wishes and became submissive. Now I know there is a lot of suppressed anger in her toward him, yet she was brought up to be acquiescent to her husband. She had been disciplined and treated in her own family as if she were a child. My father not only ran the traffic court but the appellate court as well—he was the law—there was no appeal or a second opinion. Mother only supported him. To object was useless; you just accepted my father's rules.

Compliance to the father's perfectionistic demands was buttressed by his mother, who stated, "If you rebelled against your father's wishes, it would give him a heart attack. You know your father is older, and he will not always be around." In turn, the mother was portrayed by the father as a figure of refined gentility and sensitivity. The father's sentimentalizing of the mother, however, served only to demean her as a vulnerable and helpless child. The mother's feelings were easily hurt, and the father warned the patient about this, saying that the mother was not cut out for "grown-ups' work" and needed to be protected. She did not have the qualities of self that were needed to be an adult. Thus, both parents were portrayed by the other as vulnerable to the patient's aggression.

The patient noted:

My sister didn't get the weekly lectures and the discipline imposed on me. Her school performance wasn't pushed, or her homework judged like mine, since she was a girl. My father felt men were put into the world to run things. Women were assigned a role of submission or noninterference. It was the price women paid for being protected; he was the captain of the ship. If I went to Mother to complain, she just supported him. She herself accepted what he said and never said a thing in opposition.

Father was such a stern figure, she wasn't willing to be my defense lawyer and take up my case. I never even got any validation of my position; she just justified my father. She drowned herself in her loyalty to him. I recall she disagreed with him several times, and father wrote her off as being too sensitive and not able to deal with serious problems. There were never any dramatics; everything was handled in a contained and low-key manner—he was managerially effective. When I felt hurt or beaten down, father would say, "Oh, you are so sensitive, you're just like your mother"—or "You are too passive, feminine, undisciplined," or "You're not tough enough to face what life calls for." I wasn't supposed to be like my mother—compassionate—yet my role as a writer is feminine.

The therapist commented that he needn't be ashamed of the traits of compassion and sensitivity he took in from his mother, and that being a writer or being a sensitive human being had little to do with being either masculine or feminine, strong or weak. To categorize these qualities rigidly, as his father did, represented rather old-fashioned sexual stereotyping. He continued, "Our home was like a Victorian novel out of Henry James. The irony is that the masculine, macho, take-charge person my father wanted to fill my blood with resulted in a person cowed by that. I couldn't discriminate and take the good values and discard the rest that he presented. I bought the whole textbook, instead of the lesson. I wound up not feeling in control, not assertive or self-confident, and even questioning my masculinity."

Gradually he accepted, and became no longer ashamed or critical of, the sensitive side of his nature, as he modified the values in his superego that he had learned from his father. He then began to question the weekly performance reports his father had subjected him to, supposedly for the patient's own benefit. In a subsequent session he commented, "There is an echo constantly ringing in my ears that I'll never get things done. If the smallest thing goes wrong, a light goes on: You're wrong again. I hear my father saying, 'Bad person; see, I told you, you are a failure.' Instead of dealing with it as a problem, I get overly discouraged. I was told by him that flaws in me would hold me back, so when a failure does come along it's proof he was right. My mind starts going—it's like a computer search—which of the things my father saw in me needs working on." The therapist noted how hard he was on himself when he stumbled, instead of being able to comfort and soothe himself (an attempt to modify his harsh superego). He continued, "Well, in my family there existed the 'Yes, but...' syndrome. Even when things went well, I didn't get comfort or rewarded; whatever I did there was always something lacking. It undercut any joy. Life was a serious business, and whatever I did was never as perfect as it should have been. There is a stern little martinet in me now that still looks at pleasure as playing hooky. Let's get back to business and not putter." The therapist interpreted, "It sounds like your father talking." The patient responded, "Yes, and now it's me talking like him, he's with me all the day long and till the end of the world it seems. It's hard to get rid of that dybbuk. My father himself was ascetic and always wondered if he really should have been a priest or a monk instead of going into business. When I'm hardest on myself, I feel it's for my own good—I find a grim kind of pleasure in keeping up that stern supervision over myself."

As treatment progressed, the patient was able to modify the austere and critical father internalized in his superego and to accept the more gentle qualities of his mother in himself without self-castigation. As he became less perfectionistic and critical of himself, he was able to comfort himself when he was not totally successful. He developed insight into his performing the role of his father's "savior," and into his father's need to relive his own life through the patient to correct past mistakes. He gradually became aware of his father's double-bind message concerning success; i.e., he was pressured for achievement, yet no matter what he did, it was never good enough. He developed insight into his father's need to sustain a dominant role over him, as well as into his father's ambivalence toward and jealousy of the patient's successes.

For example, in college the patient had written and directed a play that was considered by his teachers and fellow students to be very successful. When his father came to a performance, however, he was critical of a number of points in the play (the patient's treatment of religion and the conflictual parent–child relationship). The father felt that the patient's mother should not see it; because she was so sensitive, it would be hurtful to her. The patient felt totally deflated by his father's responses. Instead of sharing his success, his father had turned victory into defeat.

The patient then in treatment became aware of his own anger and resentment toward his father, which had been repressed. Consciously he had continued to idealize his father, yet unconsciously he had sabotaged his father and himself by acting out his anger in ways that prevented him from becoming successful. The patient developed insight into the lack of family constancy, into each parent's portrayal of the other as vulnerable. He felt compelled, therefore, to comply to both parents' wishes to sustain their self-esteem and even his father's continued existence (the symbiotic survival pattern). These were the family myths and overt messages he had received concerning the narcissistic and physical vulnerability of the parents. His aggression if expressed could wound or kill; thus, it had to be suppressed and he had to develop a false, compliant self.

The patient developed a keen sensitivity to cues coming from his parents and from others, which determined his behavior. His alertness to the responses of the therapist were also evident in treatment in his attempts to be the "good," compliant patient. The transference was interpreted as it developed, which allowed him to examine his constricted and rigid response pattern. With patients who have a false compliant or oppositional type of personality, but a sufficiently differentiated and cohesive sense of self, use of the couch can be extremely helpful. Because the patient cannot see the therapist, the therapist's nonverbal responses are cut off as cues for the patient to react to. The interaction is limited to the verbal sphere. In this way transferences that develop are more open to exploration and interpretation, instead of being acted out in submission to or rebellion against the therapist.

During treatment the patient began to write and directed several successful productions, and also became engaged to marry. As the false self, which had warded off anger, was diminished, he began to struggle to give up his identity as savior and to find another. He stated:

I am in an amateurish way trying to be like you, to listen to people, to understand and comfort them. But I can't remain objective and become drawn into becoming a player in the drama. So many people depend on me that I feel exhausted. I have Good Samaritan burnout; my altruism gets drained away. But if I try to be objective, I start lecturing like my father. I have all the disadvantages of your profession but none of the income. There is my old girlfriend, my new one, and my sister; and I take on a good, passive, understanding role with them all. My sister was treated by my father as a china doll, my old girlfriend's father ignored her and preferred her brother, while my new girlfriend lost her father through death when she was an infant. I have an intuitive sensitivity to their problems; I know it's a good quality. I read an article in the *Times* about dependent people and altruistic people finding each other and becoming attached. My new girlfriend is fearful I won't make a commitment and I will just disappear like other men in her life. My old girlfriend recently called in a panic after everything went wrong, and I went and helped her out. I equate saying no as if it's a dread disease. I can't solve their problems, yet I still try. I'm starting to want to say no without hurting them. I'd like to be able to say, "I hope you can figure out a way to solve this yourself, but right now even though I'd like to help, I'm exhausted."

The therapist commented that this pattern was similar to his needing to help his mother because he saw her as sensitive and vulnerable.* He replied:

Yes, I respond at the first sniff of vulnerability, and I come charging to the rescue. My father was also protective of my mother; he kept the world at bay and provided her with everything, including deciding all issues, with the stipulation you played by his rules. I absorb everything; it all makes an impression on me; it's why I became a writer. With my mother I sensed her potential was dampened; like a good blade that is dulled, her personality was sanded down and contoured. Even if a person is not born submissive, in the face of a dominant person, she became that way in order to exist. Even though my mother was overprotected as a child, when she was a young adult, she went to college, graduate school, and then worked and lived alone. But the independence, the play, the fun in her were leached out; her qualities of curiosity, outrageousness, and wit were dissolved. I did feel sorry for her; these traits were not permitted by my father. She became a lonely, detached, and resigned woman. When I go home now, I try to bring back some color in her cheeks and inspire her to become interested in things, especially since my father's death. Not long ago I went to a family funeral and got glimpses of her as a young adult. She had wanted to become a writer; she was a rebel and questioned everything. Living with my father, she gave up fighting, and then gradually her curiosity also died. She accepted his set of rules for the sake of harmony. I was aware we were both caught in the same net and felt a kinship with her. We were comrades in servitude; we tip-toed around, lest we wake up the giant. I never felt qualified to save her. In fact, any kind of aggressive, dominant role turns me off; the paternal leadership image was so offensive, I'd rather abdicate.

---

* Patient also seems to have played the role of go-between (o+) for his mother, and showed some borderline features.

The therapist commented that the patient had an aversion to being at all like his father. He replied, "Yet I know there were positive qualities in him, steadfastness and decency. My father's love was tinged with depression; it was a dark love; it carried with it the weight of responsibility. It was a conditional love, built on performance; acceptance was qualified. I myself go around being kind and without any conditions." The therapist acknowledged his yearning for unconditional love and acceptance from his father and asked if he was being the good father to others, as he would have liked his own father to have been with him. He replied, "Yes, I know I serve as a good father figure to my sister and my girlfriends; I don't want to be the bad, stern taskmaster. But I go from one extreme to the other and generally fall back on this soft, understanding, nurselike role." The therapist commented that he did not have to go to these good and bad extremes, that one can combine understanding with discipline. Fathers can be tender, supportive, and understanding and, when appropriate, can set rules and limits. This was also true of mothers. The therapist stated that he understood that in the patient's family, the parents were polarized, with father the stern, demanding disciplinarian and mother the tender, selfless, understanding one. In addition, the mother's qualities were downgraded, and, as the patient had stated, he felt her support was less important than his father's. The patient said, "I know my mother could have been different. In an effort to be loved, she made a pact with herself. The marriage was not perfect, but the positives outweighed the negatives, so she settled. By turning away from that overly disciplinary role, I become more like my mother. I know I need to integrate both their qualities. Now I swing from one pole to the other."

In this and subsequent sessions, the patient worked on the intrapsychic process of splitting, which the family structure had reinforced by the discrete and opposite roles of mother and father. Mother was the understanding yet weak and submissive one, whereas Father was experienced as the disciplining, strong, and controlling parent. Father had been totally incorporated and secured in the patient's superego, whereas the patient had identified his ego with the mother. He had dysidentified himself from his paternalistic father as a result of his own unconscious rage toward him, as well as because he had formed an alliance with his mother. This dysidentification had only made it more difficult for him to function aggressively or assertively. As he achieved insight, he no longer needed to merge with his parents symbiotically as a defense against his anger and disappointment. He started to resolve his magical sense of responsibility for their self-esteem and survival, and gradually differentiated himself from them.

In the following sessions, he continued to work through the exaggerated sense of responsibility for others he had learned from his parents. He had been taught by each parent to be sensitive to the other parent's vulnerabilities, yet by doing so, he wound up being criticized for being too sensitive. He became aware of his anger and felt betrayed by his parents. His upbringing had resulted in his experiencing his family as inconstant and in his feeling that others' self-esteem and survival were dependent on his behavior, and this had necessitated denial and constriction of himself as a person.

With a sigh, he started a session as follows:

> I still feel responsible for keeping everybody sane. If I am not paying enough, they will shatter. I thought of the huge figure of Atlas holding the world at Rockefeller Center. I really know how he feels; I know the weight on his shoulders. If I disappoint somebody I feel it's rude and something major may happen. I will start a series of events that will bring them to ruin. In my family, not to be obliging was an aggressive act. I hold reality at bay by being nice; I control reality by trivia, by being considerate. Not to do so gives pain, upsets others' lives. I feel I should pass through life without making a ripple; I need to be invisible without making a wave. I'm not supposed to make waves.

At this point the therapist interpreted the double bind he was experiencing, commenting that this must be a dilemma for him, because either he upsets others by being assertive and making waves, or he wipes himself out as a person. He replied:

> I have to anticipate the effects I have on others before I do anything, so I tailor my actions. I bought my parents' whole act. As a child I saw them as powerful people, and if they got angry they would withhold things. I recall several birthday presents being taken back and held for years as punishment for my insolence or disobedience. If I was a good little boy, I would get presents, vacations, allowances, and fine schools. It seems that this arrangement would have been more appropriate for

a business, like Beneficial Finance, than in a family. I've felt submerged all my life. Now I'm like a fish swimming to the surface, and I feel such anger. There were other alternatives possible. When I'm annoyed or frustrated, I've always walked away instead of dealing with it directly.

The therapist noted that in his family, as he had said, there was never that denouement as in the Eugene O'Neill play. There was never direct confrontation; people did not vomit out the truth. He replied:

I know my mother was an escapist who taught me avoidance. I keep submerged and only let out my anger when the pressure cooker gets too hot and needs to let off steam. Then I make an irrational, angry outburst or quit impulsively. The way I was brought up was that a marriage was OK if people respected each other, a child was OK if he was not rude. If one were a well-reared person, one let the annoyances of life pass without making a remark or rebelling. But it was emotionally castrating. It closed off a lot of possibilities. I couldn't take risks. I minimized implementing my talents by not even making a start. I also wind up being taken advantage of, since I can't show irritation. It dulled the sense of my own feelings and thoughts; it anesthetized me to things that should realistically piss you off. I always followed the path of the middle of the road, yet you know all the accidents happen in the middle of the road. It's not a safety zone, and I feel angry. I only got myself into pickles by not sticking up for myself. I'm so good at adapting; I've been a reactor and always walked away from opportunities to be assertive, to be involved, to be me.

After having experienced and worked through some of his anger toward his father, he then mourned the loss of his mother's and his own spontaneity and vitality, a result of their submission to the father. Both his mother and he had compromised themselves and had lost touch with their own wellspring of creativity. Because a symbiotic survival pattern had been established in his family, a lack of family constancy had developed, which in turn contributed to a deficiency in self and object constancy for the patient. This form of binding to the family prevented the patient's separation and individuation and resulted in developmental arrest. His own growth was hindered, because he experienced his parents as not having integrated, separate, and stable identities over time. Instead, he felt that his parents' self-esteem and survival, as well as his own, depended on how each family member behaved toward the others.

Gradually he developed insight into this family constellation that prevented self-object differentiation and perpetuated magical, omnipotent thinking. People were not as sensitive and vulnerable as his family had portrayed them to be, and his anger was not omnipotently destructive. Thus he could relieve himself of the burden of his grandiose sense of responsibility for keeping the world intact, and could function more autonomously. With the help of individual treatment that dealt with these familial issues, the patient was able to understand and realistically order his experiences. He was then able to develop for himself a more intact and identity-sustaining self-representation. His ego was able to integrate and handle aggression, so he could verbally express his rage against his father and his disappointment in his mother without excessive guilt. He then worked on shedding the constricting and self-critical superego values he had internalized from his family, in order to make a greater commitment to his work and to his fiancée.

ADDITIONAL CASE ILLUSTRATIONS

Two other case studies of individual therapy will be presented to demonstrate the usefulness of an understanding of family dynamics in working with intrapsychic processes. In these two cases a great deal of the family structure is similar; the pathology that each patient developed is markedly different, however. Superficially, these facts might be viewed as minimizing the importance of familial factors. The different end results might be seen as simply a result of genetic loading, or of the fact that each of the patients had been born with diverse temperamental traits to which the parents responded differently. Although these factors undoubtedly are always operative, they seem of minimal importance here. It is the actual functioning of the family in these two cases that will be demonstrated to be most significant. Although the structures of the families are similar in terms of power and role functioning, the actual parent–child interactions are quite different.

Both patients were women who had pursued careers in the arts, and both had difficulty using their talents. Both came from families in which the father was a narcissistic character who needed to be the center of attention, an insecure, controlling, jealous, and competitive individual. Both fathers had poor impulse control. They flew into rages if they were frustrated, and bullied their wives through threats of leaving if their demands were not met. Both mothers were childlike and submissive, assuming little if any parental authority. Each portrayed herself to her children as an innocent victim of the father and as vulnerable to his aggressive behavior. More like a peer than a parent, each formed an alliance with her children to placate the father. Each mother would tell her children not to speak up or not to behave in a manner that might upset the father. Each mother also saw herself as a sublime martyr, superior to her husband. The husband was viewed as an uncontrolled and insecure infant who needed to be indulged. A symbiotic survival pattern was set up that prevented the development of family stability, with both parents being depicted as vulnerable.

In each family the children felt responsible for their parents' self-esteem and for preserving the marriage. In the first case, however, the patient developed a hysterical-borderline character, whereas in the second instance the patient clearly had a depressive disorder. It will become apparent as we discuss these cases that the family interaction was more important than the clinical diagnoses of the parents or the power-role structure of the family. One significant factor that did influence each of these family interactions, however, was the birth order and the different experiences that resulted.

The first patient was the younger of two siblings, having an older sister who constantly confronted and battled the father. The patient felt frightened of the shouting battles that she observed, in which the father was on the verge of losing control. She turned to her mother for protection against the father. In therapy she stated:

> My mother was the only one who could comfort me, and I was afraid to give her up. She made me feel better if I was frightened, and protected me from my father. I was afraid to give her up, since she saved me from my father, who was hateful, mean, and angry. She saved me from a world that was terrifying and violent—a world that was like my father. If I couldn't sleep and needed my mother to stay up and be with me, she wouldn't go to sleep. If I was afraid of going to the doctor, to

the dentist, or to school, she didn't make me go. No one is like that, not my husband, and not even you, even though I pay you. But I felt if I didn't see her, she wasn't going to love me. She might choose father; I thought she'd forget me if she were with my father. I feel the same with you; if I don't see you, you'd forget me.

The patient here questions her mother's and the therapist's evocative memory, i.e., our object constancy. This uncertainty is a projection of her own lack of self and object constancy, which developed in the wake of a lack of family constancy. She also demonstrates here fluid ego boundaries.

She continued:

But my mother wasn't fickle—the world began and ended with me— but I thought she was fragile. It was as if when I didn't see her and she was with my father, she might die, she was so vulnerable. I felt that she would die and abandon me if I weren't constantly with her and made her feel better. My father was mean; I had to be the good little girl.

The therapist commented on her feeling as if her being the good little girl kept her mother alive. She replied:

But my mother always did say, I only live for my kids. [The patient here comments on the confluence of fantasy and reality in the family.] I brought her the only happiness she had; otherwise she'd be depressed. She didn't get any happiness from my father. I was afraid to be angry: she was fragile; she might die. I hid my feelings. I was afraid my father would kill her and me; I hated him and wished he would die. He tortured her, and I hated him for being so mean to her. But she took it, and let him get away with it. She was a doormat. He is a selfish, narcissistic person who was never there for me; he was mean and made me miserable. I can't look at you; you remind me of my father; I don't care about anybody—I myself am like my father, narcissistic. When I don't see my husband, I don't feel connected; I even forget what he looks like. My father felt that when he was not with my mother, she wouldn't care if he cheated with other women. He wasn't connected. My being separate is scary. I see a circus with lions in it, and I'm one of the lions looking out of the cage. I want to be angry, but I'm afraid I'll kill unless I'm kept behind bars. I'm afraid to be separate from my mother; being with my father alone, I'm afraid of violence and death. I know at one level I won't kill him and he won't kill me, but I'm afraid to check it out. Asserting myself could kill someone or me. [Her observing ego is weak here.] Separation is not having my mother in the cage with me; she could talk me into not killing him or protect them from killing me.

The therapist pointed out the slip of the tongue; she had said "them" instead of "him." She replied, "Mother would calm father down. I'm not ready to be a mother. I'm the baby; how can a baby be the mother?" In this session she denied her rage at her mother and did not explore the slip of the tongue any further. The patient's oedipal conflict was reinforced by her earlier developmental arrest, which made her anger at her mother be experienced as more dangerous. She was jealous of her father's preferring her mother and had unconscious death wishes for her, which she feared might magically come true. Her defense of being the good little baby and her symbiotic attachment to her mother defended her against her competition and murderous rage at her mother. Essentially, she was saying, how could a dependent baby be a threat to mother?

In a later session, the patient acknowledged her anger at both her parents and went on to discuss her oedipal rivalry with her mother. She stated:

I was angry at both my parents and wanted to kill them. They infantilized me; then they wanted me to break away. I'm furious they gave me such a lousy beginning. I feel guilty for wanting to hurt them. I play crazy or helpless; I'm afraid if I don't and I stand up for myself, it would feel like I killed them, and I'd be left alone. They were my world. I know I won't hurt anybody even though I am mad at everyone. [Here the patient's observing ego and reality testing are shown to be intact.] I had a dream the other night of a swimmer being followed by a shark. The shark is my mother, preventing me from making it. I'll pass her by. I was afraid to excel or move on without her, or she'd be hurt. She also stood in the way of my father. I was attracted to him, but because of my feelings for her, I felt it was dangerous. I needed her and was afraid to make her angry at me. I felt I could not make it alone, yet I was angry at her for keeping me dependent. The shark in the dream could also be my father, and I needed my mother to protect me. But instead she pulled me down, and I had to worry about her and keep her afloat and happy. I had to protect her; she was like a weight on my legs; I felt suffocated by her, couldn't breathe. But on the other hand, I couldn't break loose; my father was like a land mine; we were fearful he would explode, yell and scream, or attack.

In subsequent sessions she dealt with her ambivalence toward her mother. The symbiotic attachment, which had served as a defense against her aggression, was gradually resolved. She stated:

> To cut my mother off is violent and bloody. We're like Siamese twins; something terrible will happen. It's like cutting off an arm or removing a heart. I know we are separate physically, but emotionally we are one. It's like a cancer; she's in me to take care of me. Yet I've been taking care of myself for years; I lie to myself. I want to keep her alive somewhere in me. It's the part that makes me kind and loving. Taking that cancer out is a 17-hour operation to take out only the parts that are not good for me and leave the good parts of my mother. I would have liked to stay a baby all my life; she really was fun and loving. She didn't make me go to school, cancelled doctors' appointments, took me to the movies and shopping instead. I didn't want to be separate, I wanted to make her happy. I was too sensitive for her; she was mistreated and hurt by my father; I was upset for her. I wanted to separate from the family, but I felt bad for her. Had they been happily married, I would have felt less guilty going out and being independent.

The therapist asked whether she resented her mother's not being stronger and standing up for herself. She replied:

> Yes; she didn't speak up to my father and took a lot of shit from him. She shushed me and let me know she was in pain. Her suffering became my suffering. I felt what she felt, empathically. Her suffering made me depressed and angry. If I took care of myself only, I'd feel disloyal. She needed the job of taking care of me; it gave her an identity, and I was an ally against my father. I now resent that I have to pay for what my parents didn't give me, the basic tools to deal with life. I know I don't have to kill my mother off totally; I did take in also lovely parts from her—my creativity, humor, and a theatrical sense. When I was a child, I remember wanting to kill myself, to get the unhappiness and suffering over. If I didn't take care of myself and remained a dependent child, it gave her joy, and it felt good being taken care of. I was also too scared to be independent; my mother was always afraid I'd get killed or hurt, and I was afraid always that Father would get mad and kill me if I did anything wrong.

In this family a variant of the hysterical-borderline form of family interaction occurred, with the child playing the role of go-between since there was a lack of family constancy. A seductive alliance was formed between the mother and daughter. The mother set no limits and was totally indulgent and infantilizing of the patient. The mother established a mutual protection pact with her daughter: Each would serve as the protective, comforting good mother for the other against the bad father. This alienated the patient from the father and interfered with resolution of her oedipal rivalry with the mother. The patient felt it would show disloyalty to Mother if she preferred Father. She felt a responsibility to make her mother happy, to preserve her personality, and she felt she needed to remain an infant to provide her mother with an identity. To do otherwise, the patient felt, would destroy her mother. The patient remained dependently bound to her family, and when she did eventually separate from the family as a young adult, she experienced considerable guilt and difficulty functioning independently. In treatment she worked through these conflicts and was able to function autonomously. She was able to date and to marry a fine man and to pursue her career more actively.

The second patient was the older of two siblings, having a younger sister who was the father's favorite. Unlike the patient just discussed, who had remained infantile and sought protection and refuge, this patient took on a protective role devoted to helping others. She tolerated considerable self-deprivation and frustration, because she never felt entitled to give to herself. Her father had been an immigrant to this country who had escaped his fatherland as a young boy, without his family, to avoid persecution. The father was never able to obtain the education he wanted, and he worked in a blue-collar occupation. He would come home from work exhausted and yell at his wife to feed him and take care of his needs. The mother had been born in this country but had not married until late in life because of her deafness. She also had not been able to obtain the education she had wanted.

The patient proved to be an excellent student, to the delight of her mother, who attempted to live vicariously through her academic achievements. Because of her father's difficulty in speaking English and her mother's deafness, the patient often had to negotiate matters for her parents with neighbors, shopkeepers, and the landlord. This placed her into a parentified role, in which she achieved a sense of her identity and importance by doing for her parents. When she married, she again selflessly devoted her life to her husband's business and to her children. When her children left home and she was no longer needed in her husband's business, she attempted to resume writing. She had written a number of short stories in the past and had received acclaim for them. Now she was suffering a severe work block in her writing, which brought her into individual therapy.

In treatment she described a family dynamic in which she felt responsible for the self-esteem of both her parents (the symbiotic survival pattern). She stated, "My mother always wanted something from me. There was an image I was expected to fulfill, and I'm still not sure who I am. I'm not going to write just because I'm supposed to." She then went on to discuss how she was expected to perform for her parents scholastically and socially but was never gratified for her achievement. For instance, both she and her sister would sing for guests, but her sister always sang the lead and the patient the supporting part. She was unhappy but could not express her disatisfaction, because her mother would say, "My girls don't say things like that." The patient inferred from her mother's statement that

If I weren't what she wanted, I wasn't one of her girls. If I spoke up for myself, she felt hurt. I saw she was vulnerable; she was deaf and easily felt hurt. She'd get quiet and look hurt or say, "How can you say that? You're hurting my feelings." But she never fought for herself, and I felt like a bully if I asserted myself. I'd apologize or say I really didn't mean it. I wasn't given the right to express myself; I had to make nice, and never had the satisfaction of standing up for my rights at home. If I stood up for myself, it meant I was attacking my mother, she was so vulnerable. I felt superior to her and took care of her in every way. Poor thing; she was so sweet and wanted the best for me. I was ungrateful. I couldn't demand what was mine; it was greedy or wrong. In fact, I never even knew what I was entitled to. It was never spelled out, what rights a human being was entitled to.

In subsequent sessions she discussed her identification with her mother's selfless and victimized role.

I was not supposed to satisfy myself, like my mother. She sacrificed herself, and she didn't expect she had the right to be happy. Her husband was a bastard, he put her down always, and she learned to live with it. I feel I should also sacrifice myself for my children as she did. I should chop off my fingers if it could help my kids. But I know I should write, because I need to, and there would be enough for my kids too.

I can visualize my mother sitting in a dimly lit room in a corner, sad and empty, having given everything to us. Her life was futile. Why don't I see how wasteful it is not to satisfy yourself? Why don't I say, "Me first"? Why don't I take mine first?

The therapist interpreted that perhaps she would then see herself at the other extreme, like her father, whom she described as a "me-first" person. She replied:

We all viewed him as a selfish man. You are right: I am sacrificing my own talent like my mother did, and if I didn't do that I'd be like my father—a me-first person. He thought nothing of demanding all the attention; he was self-indulgent. I feel that being a writer is self-indulgent. People who work have job jobs—it's like meat and potatoes—it's concrete—I can sit in the wilderness for two hours just thinking and the work doesn't always emerge as it should—it's not a real job. I doubt my own authority and power. I write the way I talk, full of self-doubts. I don't have a sense of my own worth; who am I to write a complicated book?

The therapist asked where this self-doubt and negative judgment of herself came from. She replied:

My father was critical of my singing; it was never good enough. My sister sang the solo and I was the yes person. My father never commented on my report cards. I had all A's, but he said nothing. He probably was jealous; in fact, I remember him saying that if he had had an opportunity to go to school, he'd get all A's too. He never said, "Wow, my wonderful girl. I'm so proud of you." With my mother you weren't supposed to boast. It was vulgar to boast; only common people boasted of their children. So she withheld and didn't say anything either. I didn't get the validation I wanted from them and lived in my fantasies. I would fantasize winning and receiving prizes and acclaim. If I had gotten real feedback, I wouldn't need to satisfy myself in fantasy. Because whatever I did wasn't recognized sufficiently, I can't do that for myself; I can't give to myself and feel confident. I don't know if I'm afraid to try. Maybe I'll be proven to be inadequate, so let me live in my dreams. Maybe I'm afraid the novel *will* be successful. If it's not successful, I'll have fallen on my face, but I'm also afraid of success. It's the old Cinderella complex: Men won't like me if I'm successful. But I know that is not the case; on the contrary, if I'm successful it's more likely that I will be liked.

As she continued to discuss her fear of success, she began to reveal to herself what she subconsciously knew concerning the underlying interaction between her parents.

> If I was successful, my mother used it as an implicit accusation against my father. She would imply, "So why weren't you successful, you failure?" He would then become angry at me and defensive. He'd complain he didn't have an education or the opportunities I had. I felt my success was used by my mother to demean my father, and then I became the object of his anger. To be successful was fraught with complexity; I have a sense of danger about taking risks. I also felt that with my husband, I was never certain if he wanted me to be successful or not. I felt immobilized; what he thought had a great influence on what I did. Now I think he wants me to be a success; it would enhance his narcissism. I always thought I would lose my children and husband if I were a successful writer. How I don't know. What would happen to them if I weren't there to take care of them? I chose to be a housewife and mother over being a writer. I felt I had to make the choice; I felt it was being selfish. I couldn't divide my loyalties between myself and my family. Yet I have a friend who is a successful writer—her writing comes first—and she is also supported in this by her husband.

The therapist asked if she put herself second to protect her husband and avoid his anger and rejection, as she had felt she needed to do with her father. She replied, "Yes, I was sure if I went off into a successful career, he would turn to someone else for comfort and companionship. Now I know it would not have weakened but strengthened the marriage. If I thought of myself, took care of my creativity and pursued my career, he would have preferred it. I was always there for my husband; it was too all consuming, and he just couldn't tolerate all that self-sacrifice."

This patient's family showed the typical depressive type of family interaction, with the patient playing the role of savior. The father was portrayed as the failure, and the mother was seen as vulnerable because of her deafness. Although the parents pressured for achievement, it was not rewarded. Father was the dominant parent who was jealous of the patient's success. The patient internalized and secured her father into her superego and was self-critical and unable to give to herself. Her main ego identity was with her selfless and martyred mother. She was not able to pursue her talents as a writer and devoted herself to her husband and family. In individual therapy she worked through the resentment she felt toward her parents for being out of touch with her needs. She expressed her angry feelings about her mother's using her successes to demean the father, and at the father for exploiting her to inflate his own narcissism. She was no longer depressed and started writing her novel. She could become successful for herself and would not be exploited or abandoned. She now was entitled.

These examples demonstrate how the family typology and the other family constructs developed in this book can be useful in individual therapy. They provide a richer understanding of the reasons for developmental arrest. Instead of being seen as based solely on intrapsychic factors, the arrest is viewed as resulting from interaction of the psyche with specific interpersonal dynamics in the family. Although the mother–infant dyad is crucial in early development, the effect of the father also must be taken into account. The formation of the superego and ego, as well as the types of defenses employed, can also best be understood when one considers both the intrapsychic and the interpersonal dynamics.

CONCLUSIONS

A theoretical foundation for family therapy has been provided in this book that integrates many of the concepts and therapeutic procedures used in the field. It is a theory that is intimately connected to psychiatry and to psychoanalysis, in particular object relations theory. Presentation of this theory has been supported by empirical studies, laboratory findings, clinical case studies, and child development findings.

The family typology that was presented has long been sought after in the field, and brings together four specific patterns of family interaction that are related to four specific types of psychopathology. Basic to all four patterns is the fact that the child's developmental needs for self-object differentiation and separation are not appropriately responded to by the parents. Unconsciously, the child is used instead to satisfy and nurture parental narcissism and stabilize the parents' self-identities. Even though this role is performed at the expense of the child's own needs for nurturance, the child is induced into the role by the fear that the parent will be rejecting or will not survive psychologically. In the latter event, the child experiences itself as abandoned anyway. Projective identification is the primitive defense used by one or both parents whereby a good or bad aspect of the internal self or object is placed into the child. A symbiotic survival pattern results, with the child feeling responsible for the self-esteem and survival of the parents. This lack of family constancy in turn prevents self and object constancy from developing in the schizophrenic or borderline patient.

Object relations theory has been used to provide an understanding of family dynamics, in particular the diverse family therapy concepts such as the double bind, enmeshment, homeostasis, the identified patient, pseudomutuality, the rubber fence, scapegoating, transgenerational alliances, and triangulation. Even the effectiveness of certain treatment techniques in family therapy, such as reframing (redefining the patient's behavior or symptoms so that they no longer have a negative connotation), changing the family structure, and offering paradoxical interventions, can best be understood in terms of disrupting the family's use of the primitive defenses of splitting, projective identification, idealization, and devaluation.

As we sharpen our knowledge and understanding, we can intervene more accurately in our therapeutic efforts. The measure of the effectiveness of any form of psychotherapy is whether it enhances the patient's growth toward autonomy. If the patient is still symbiotically bound to the family, working with the familial context may be essential for movement in the patient to occur. The patient's strivings toward autonomy may require the therapist's helping the family to release the patient from a particular role. Thus, the patient is not bound into sustaining the narcissistic equilibrium of the parents or the stability of the family. The patient will not feel guilty or decompensate by separating or individuating from the family.

Effective therapy involves the therapist's being attuned to the psychological needs not only of the patient, but also of all the family members. The therapist can help resolve conflict and stabilize the personalities of others in the family. Thus, the whole process of separation and individuation is not simply left as a burden for the patient to shoulder. By the therapist's helping other family members to develop their own potential for growth, a new homeostatic balance is achieved, and the patient's progress will not be blocked or sabotaged. When working with a patient in individual treatment, one must be aware of the possible impact of the patient on others in the family and their influence on the patient.

Essentially, the most effective form of treatment is that which meets the needs of the patient as well as the family, whether it be individual, group, or family therapy. The form of treatment that will be most effective also varies greatly with the particular time. For example, individual therapy may reveal or lead into marital issues that require marital or family therapy. The reverse also may be true, with individual therapy being employed to consolidate the gains made in family therapy.

The typology and constructs developed in this book can also be an invaluable adjunct in working with patients in individual treatment. Indeed, individual therapy can be viewed as a form of family therapy, because the entire cast of characters from the patient's family, as well as their interaction, becomes internalized in the patient's psyche and continues to exert its powerful influence on the patient's present thoughts, feelings, perceptions, and actions.

REFERENCES

Abraham, K. (1911). Manic depressive states and the pre-genital levels of the libido. In *Selected Papers on Psychoanalysis*. London: Hogarth Press, 1965.

Ackerman, N.W. (1954). Interpersonal disturbances in the family: some unresolved problems in psychotherapy. *Psychiatry* 18:359–368.

Adler, A. (1917). *The Neurotic Constitution*. New York: Mofatt Yard.

Alarcon, R.D. (1973). Hysteria and hysterical personality: how come one without the other? *Psychiatric Quarterly* 47:258–275.

Alger, I., and Hogan, P. (1969). Enduring effects of videotape playback experience on family and marital relationships. *American Journal of Orthopsychiatry* 39:86–98.

Arieti, S. (1959). Manic depressive psychosis. In *American Handbook of Psychiatry*, vol. 1, ed. S. Arieti. New York: Basic Books.

——— (1962). The psychotherapeutic approach to depression. *American Journal of Psychotherapy* 16:397–406.

——— (1965). Conceptual and cognitive psychiatry. *American Journal of Psychiatry* 122:361–366.

Balint, M. (1953). *Primary Love and Psychoanalytic Technique*. New York; Liveright.

——— (1968). *The Basic Fault*. London: Tavistock.

Bateson, G. (1972). The science of mind and order. In *Steps to an Ecology of Mind*. New York: Ballantine.

——— (1979). *Mind and Nature: A Necessary Unity*. New York: Dutton.

Bateson, G., Jackson, D.D., Haley, J., and Weakland, J.H. (1956). Toward a theory of schizophrenia. *Behavioral Science* 1:251–264.

——— (1962). A note on the double bind. *Family Process* 2:154–161.

Beck, A.T. (1967). *Depression: Causes and Treatment*. Philadelphia: University of Pennsylvania Press.

Bell, S.M. (1969). The Development of the Concept of Object as Related to Infant-Mother Attachment. Unpublished doctoral dissertation, The Johns Hopkins University.

Bemporad, J.R. (1971). New views on the psychodynamics of the depressive character. In *World Biennial of Psychiatry and Psychotherapy*, vol. 1, ed. S. Arieti. New York: Basic Books.

Bibring, E. (1953). The mechanism of depression. In *Affective Disorders*, ed. P. Greenacre. New York: International Universities Press.

Bion, W.R. (1959). *Experiences in Groups*. New York: Basic Books.

——— (1970). *Attention and Interpretation*. London: Tavistock.

Blinder, M.G. (1966). The hysterical personality. *Psychiatry* 29:227–235.

Bonime, W. (1959). The psychodynamics of neurotic depression. In *American Handbook of Psychiatry*, vol. 3, ed. S. Arieti. New York: Basic Books.

Boszormenyi-Nagy, I. (1965). A theory of relationships: experience and transaction. In *Intensive Family Therapy*, eds. I. Boszormenyi-Nagy and J.L. Framo. New York: Hoeber Medical Division, Harper & Row.

Bowen, M. (1960). Family concept of schizophrenia. In *Etiology of Schizophrenia*, ed. D.D. Jackson. New York: Basic Books.

—— (1978). *Family Therapy in Clinical Practice*. New York: Jason Aronson.

—— (1982). Mental health and science. *American Family Therapy Association Newsletter* 10:Winter: 1–3.

Bowlby, J. (1958). The nature of the child's tie to his mother. *International Journal of Psychoanalysis* 39:350–373.

—— (1960). Separation anxiety. *International Journal of Psychoanalysis* 41:89–113.

—— (1969). *Attachment and Loss*. New York: Basic Books.

Brazelton, T.B., and Als, H. (1979). Four early stages in the development of mother-infant interaction. In *The Psychoanalytic Study of the Child*, eds. A.J. Solnit, R.S. Eissler, A. Freud, M. Kris, P.B. Neubauer. vol. 34, New Haven: Yale University Press.

Buirski, P. (1980). Toward a theory of adaptation of analytic group psychotherapy. *International Journal of Group Psychotherapy* 4:447–459.

Buirski, P., Kellerman, H., Plutchik, R., and Weininger, R. (1973). A field study of emotions, dominance, and social behavior in a group of baboons *(Papio anubis)*. *Primates* 14:67–78.

Buirski, P., Plutchik, R., and Kellerman, H. (1978). Sex differences, dominance, and personality in the chimpanzee. *Animal Behavior* 26:123–129.

Burnham, D., Gladstone, A., and Gibson, R.W. (1969). *Schizophrenia and the Need-Fear Dilemma*. New York: International Universities Press.

Canovan-Gumpert, D., Garner, K., and Gumpert, P. (1978). *The Success Fearing Personality: Theory and Research with Implications for the Social Psychology of Achievement*. Lexington, Mass.: D. C. Health.

Carothers, J.C. (1953). The African mind in health and disease: a study in ethnopsychiatry. World Health Organization Monograph Series 17.

Chodoff, P. (1954). A re-examination of some aspects of conversion hysteria. *Psychiatry* 17:75–81.

—— (1976). The diagnosis of hysteria: an overview. *American Journal of Psychiatry* 131:1073–1078.

Chodoff, P., and Lyons, H. (1958). Hysteria, the hysterical personality, and "hysterical" conversion. *American Journal of Psychiatry* 114:734–740.

Cleghorn, R.A. (1969). Hysteria: multiple manifestations of semantic confusion. *Canadian Psychiatric Association Journal* 14:539–551.

Cloninger, C.R., and Guze, S.B. (1970). Psychiatric illness and female criminality: the role of sociopathy and hysteria in the antisocial woman. *American Journal of Psychiatry* 127:303–311.

Cohen, M.B., Baker, G., Cohen, R.A., Fromm-Reichmann, F., and Weigert, E.V. (1954). An intensive study of 12 cases of manic depressive psychosis. *Psychiatry* 17:103–138.

Cohen, N. (1974). Explorations in the Fear of Success. Unpublished doctoral dissertation, Columbia University.

Cohen, R.O. (1977). The Effect of Four Subliminal Merging Stimuli on the Manifest Psychopathology of Schizophrenic Women. Unpublished doctoral dissertation, Teachers' College, Columbia University.

Dell, P.F. (1982). Beyond homeostasis: toward a concept of coherence. *Family Process* 21:21–41.

Deutsch, H. (1933). Zur Psychologie der manisch-depressiven Zustaende: Insbesondere der chronischen Hypomanie. *International Zeitschrift fur Psychoanalyse*, vol. 19.

Dewey, J., and Bentley, A.F. (1949). *Knowing and the Known*. Boston: Beacon Press.

Dicks, H.V. (1963). Object relations theory and marital studies. *British Journal of Medical Psychology* 36:125–129.

Easser, B.R., and Lesser, S.R. (1965). Hysterical personality: a reevaluation. *Psychoanalytic Quarterly* 34:390–405.

Eitinger, L. (1964). *Concentration Camp Survivors in Norway and Israel*. London: Allen and Unwin.

Emde, R.N., and Robinson, J. (1979). The first two months: recent research in developmental psychobiology. In *Basic Handbook of Child Psychiatry*, vol. 1, ed. J.D. Noshpitz. New York: Basic Books.

Epstein, H. (1977). The heirs of the holocaust. *New York Times Magazine* 14–77 June 19.

Epstein, N.B., and Vlok, L.A. (1981). Research on results of psychotherapy: summary of evidence. *American Journal of Psychiatry* 138:1027–1035.

Erikson, E.H. (1964). *Insight and Responsibility*. New York: Norton.

—— (1968). *Identity, Youth, and Crisis*. New York: Norton.

Escalona, S. (1953). Emotional development in the first year of life. In *Problems of Infancy and Childhood: Transactions of the Sixth Conference*, ed. M.J.E. Senn. New York: Josiah Macy, Jr., Foundation.

Eysenck, H.J., and Claridge, G. (1962). The position of hysterics and dys-thymics in a two-dimensional framework of personality description. *Journal of Abnormal Social Psychology* 64:46–55.

Fairbairn, W.R.D. (1952). *Psychoanalytic Studies of the Personality.* London: Tavistock.

—— (1954). *An Object Relations Theory of the Personality.* New York: Basic Books.

Ferenczi, S. (1913). Stages in the development of the sense of reality. In *Sex in Psychoanalysis.* New York: Basic Books, 1950.

—— (1920). The further development of an active therapy in psychoanal-ysis. In *Further Contributions to the Theory and Technique of Psycho-analysis.* London: Hogarth Press.

—— (1932). Confusion of tongues between adults and the child. Paper presented at the International Psychoanalytic Congress, Weisbaden, September.

Flavell, J.H. (1963). *The Developmental Psychology of Jean Piaget.* Princeton, N.J.: D. Van Nostrand.

Fraiberg, S. (1969). Libidinal object constancy and mental representations. In *Psychoanalytic Study of the Child,* vol. 26, eds. R.S. Eissler, A. Freud, M. Kris, S.L. Lustman, and A.J. Solnit. New York: International Universities Press.

Frank, R.L. (1954). The organized adaptive aspect of the depression-elation response. In *Depression,* ed. P.H. Hoch and J. Zubin. New York: Grune & Stratton.

Fraser, J.S. (1982). Structural and strategic family therapy: a basis for mar-riage or grounds for divorce? *Journal of Marital and Family Therapy* 8:13–22.

Freud, A. (1936). *The Ego and the Mechanism of Defense.* New York: Inter-national Universities Press, 1946.

Freud, S. (1900). The interpretation of dreams. *Standard Edition* 4/5:1–627.

—— (1905a). The fragment of an analysis of a case of hysteria. *Standard Edition* 7:3–124.

—— (1905b). Three essays on the theory of sexuality. *Standard Edition* 7:125–248.

—— (1909). Analysis of a phobia in a five-year-old boy. *Standard Edition* 10:5–149.

—— (1910). The future prospects for psychoanalytic therapy. *Standard Edi-tion* 11:141–151.

—— (1917). Mourning and melancholia. *Standard Edition* 14:239–258.

—— (1920). Beyond the pleasure principle. *Standard Edition* 18:3–66.

—— (1921). Group Psychology and the Analysis of the Ego. *Standard Edition* 18:67–143.

—— (1923). The ego and the id. *Standard Edition* 19:3–66.

—— (1926). Inhibitions, symptoms and anxiety. *Standard Edition* 20:75–174.

—— (1931). Libidinal types. *Standard Edition* 21:217–220.

Freud, S., and Breuer, J. (1895). Studies on hysteria. *Standard Edition* 2:19–305.

Fromm-Reichmann, F. (1948). Notes on the development of treatment of schizophrenics by psychoanalytical psychotherapy. *Psychiatry* 11:263–273.

—— (1959). *Psychoanalysis and Psychotherapy: Selected Papers of Frieda Fromm-Reichmann.* Chicago: University of Chicago Press.

Gaitonde, M.R. (1958). Cross-cultural study of the psychiatric syndromes in outpatient clinics in Bombay, India, and Topeka, Kansas. *International Journal of Social Psychiatry* 2:98–104.

Group for the Advancement of Psychiatry Report 78 (1970). *The Field of Family Therapy,* March.

Gibson, R.W. (1958). The family background and early life experience of the manic-depressive patient: a comparison with the schizophrenic patient. *Psychiatry* 21:71–90.

Gibson, R.W., Cohen, M.B., and Cohen, R.A. (1959). On the dynamics of the manic-depressive personality. *American Journal of Psychiatry* 115:1101–1107.

Giovacchini, P.L. (1975). Self projections in the narcissistic transference. *International Journal of Psychoanalytic Psychotherapy* 4:142–166.

Green, A. (1975). The analyst, symbolization and absence in the analytic setting. *International Journal of Psycho-Analysis* 51:1–22.

Greenberg, S. (1980). An Experimental Study of Underachievement: The Effects of Subliminal Merging and Success Related Stimuli on the Academic Performance of Bright, Underachieving High School Students. Unpublished doctoral dissertation, New York University.

Grotstein, J.S. (1981). *Splitting and Projective Identification.* New York: Jason Aronson.

Guntrip, H. (1968). *Schizoid Phenomena, Object Relations, and the Self.* New York: International Universities Press.

—— (1971). *Psychoanalytic Theory, Therapy, and the Self.* New York: Basic Books.

Guze, S.R. (1975). The validity and significance of the clinical diagnosis of hysteria (Briquet's Syndrome). *American Journal of Psychiatry* 132:138–141.

Haley, Jay (1982). An interview with Jay Haley. *American Family Therapy Association Newsletter*, September 1–3.

Harlow, H.F. (1958). The nature of love *American Psychologist* 13:675–685.

Hartmann, H. (1939). *Ego Psychology and the Problem of Adaptation*. New York: International Universities Press.

Hartmann, H., Kris, E., and Lowenstein, R.M. (1951). Some psychoanalytic comments on "culture and personality." In *Psychoanalysis and Culture*, eds. G.B. Wilbur and M. Muensterberger. New York: International Universities Press.

Heimann, P. (1950). On countertransference. *International Journal of Psycho-Analysis* 31:81–84.

Hollender, M. (1971). The hysterical personality. *Comments on Contemporary Psychiatry* 1:17–24.

Hoover, C. (1983). Obsessive-compulsives may have psychological problems similar to those found in depressives. *Psychiatric News* 18(8):9–28.

Horney, K. (1937). *The Neurotic Personality of our Time*. New York: Norton.

Jackson, D.D. (1957). The question of family homeostasis. *Psychiatric Quarterly* (Suppl.) 31:79–90.

—— (1965). Family rules: the marital quid pro quo. *Archives of General Psychiatry* 12:589–594.

Jacobson, E. (1954a). Contributions to the metapsychology of psychotic identifications. *Journal of the American Psychoanalytic Association* 2:239–261.

—— (1954b). The self and the object world. In *Psychoanalytic Study of the Child*, vol. 9, ed. R.S. Eissler, A. Freud, H. Hartmann, and E. Kris. New York: International Universities Press.

—— (1967). *Psychotic Conflict and Reality*. New York: International Universities Press.

—— (1971). *Depression*. New York: International Universities Press.

James, W. (1907). *Pragmatism*. London: Longmans, Green.

Johnson, A.M., and Szurek, S.A. (1954). Etiology of antisocial behavior in delinquents and psychopaths. *Journal of the American Medical Association* 154:814–817.

Jones, E. (1953). *The Life and Work of Sigmund Freud*, vol. 1, 1856–1900. New York: Basic Books.

—— (1955). *The Life and Work of Sigmund Freud*, vol. 2, 1901–1919. New York: Basic Books.

Jung, C.G. (1927). *The Psychology of the Unconscious*. New York: Dodd, Mead.

Kardiner, A. (1939). *The Individual and His Society*. New York: Columbia University Press.

Kardiner, A., Karush, A., and Ovesey, L. (1959). A methodological study of Freudian theory. II. The libido theory. *Journal of Nervous and Mental Disease* 129:133–143.

Kernberg, O.F. (1975). *Borderline Conditions and Pathological Narcissism*. New York: Jason Aronson.

Kety, S.S., Rosenthal, D., Wender, P.H., and Schulsinger, F. (1968). The types and prevalence of mental illness in the biological and adoptive families of adopted schizophrenics. In *The Transmission of Schizophrenia*, ed. D. Rosenthal and S.S. Kety. Oxford: Pergamon Press.

Khan, M.M.R. (1974). *The Privacy of the Self*. New York: International Universities Press.

Klein, D.B. (1981). *Jewish Origins of the Psychoanalytic Movement*. New York: Praeger.

Klein, M. (1932). Mourning and its relation to manic-depressive states. In *The Psychoanalysis of Children*. London: Hogarth Press.

—— (1948). *Contributions to Psychoanalysis, 1921–1945*. London: Hogarth Press and the Institute of Psychoanalysis.

—— (1950). A contribution to the psychogenesis of manic-depressive states. In *Contributions to Psychoanalysis*. London: Hogarth Press.

Klein, M., and Tribich, D. (1982). The short life and curious death of Sigmund Freud's seduction theory. *The Sciences*, 22:14–20.

Kohut, H. (1977). *The Restoration of the Self*. New York: International Universities Press.

Krystal, H., and Niederland, W.G. (1968). Clinical observations on the survivor syndrome. In *Massive Psychic Trauma*, ed. H. Krystal. New York: International Universities Press.

Laing, R.D., and Esterson, A. (1964). *Sanity, Madness and the Family*. London: Tavistock.

Langs, R. (1976a). *The Bipersonal Field*. New York: Jason Aronson.

—— (1976b). *The Therapeutic Interaction*, vol 2. New York: Jason Aronson.

Leff, J.P. (1976). Schizophrenia and sensitivity to the family environment. *Schizophrenia Bulletin* 2:566–574.

Levinson, D. (1964). Role, personality, and social structure. In *Sociological Theory: A Book of Readings*, ed. L.A. Coser and B. Rosenberg. New York: Macmillan.

Levy, D. (1943). *Maternal Overprotection*. New York: Columbia University Press.

Lewis, J.M., Beavers, W.R., Gossett, J.T., and Phillips, V.A. (1976). *No Single Thread: Psychological Health in Family Systems*. New York: Brunner/Mazel.

Lidz, T.A., Cornelison, A.R., Fleck, S., and Terry, D. (1957). The intrafamilial environment of schizophrenic patients. II. Marital schism and marital skew. *American Journal of Psychiatry* 114:241–248.

Lidz, T., Fleck, S., and Cornelison, A.R. (1965). *Schizophrenia and the Family*. New York: International Universities Press.

Lippitt, R., and White, R.K. (1958). An experimental study of leadership and group life. In *Readings in Social Psychology*, ed. E.E. Maccoby, T.M. Newcomb, and E.L. Hartley. New York: Holt, Rinehart and Winston.

Little, M. (1951). Countertransference and the patient's response to it. *International Journal of Psycho-Analysis* 32:32–40.

Ljungberg, L. (1957). Hysteria: a clinical prognostic and genetic study. *Acta Psychiatrica et Neurologica Scandinavia* (Suppl.) 32:112.

Loeb, A., Feshback, S., Beck, A.T., and Wolf, A. (1964). Some effects of reward upon the social perception and motivation of psychiatric patients varying in depression. *Journal of Abnormal Social Psychology* 68:609–616.

Mahler, M.S. (1952). On childhood psychosis and schizophrenia: autistic and symbiotic infantile psychosis. In *The Psychoanalytic Study of the Child*, vol. 7. eds. R.S. Eissler, A. Freud, H. Hartmann, and E. Kris. New York: International Universities Press.

—— (1958). Autism and symbiosis: two extreme disturbances of identity. In *The Selected Papers of Margaret S. Mahler*, vol. 1, pp. 169–182. New York: Jason Aronson, 1979.

—— (1964). On the significance of the normal separation-individuation phase. In *Drives, Affects, and Behavior*, vol. 2, ed. M. Schur. New York: International Universities Press.

—— (1965). On early infantile psychosis: the symbiotic and autistic syndromes. *Journal of the American Academy of Child Psychiatry* 4:554–568.

Mahler, M.S., and Furer, M. (1968). *On Human Symbiosis and the Vissicitudes of Individuation*, vol. 1. New York: International Universities Press.

Mahler, M.S., Pine, F., and Bergman, A. (1975). *The Psychological Birth of the Human Infant: Symbiosis and Individuation.* New York: Basic Books.

Marmor, J. (1953). Orality in the hysterical personality. *Journal of the American Psychoanalytic Association* 1:656–675.

Masson, J.M. (1984). *The Assault on Truth.* New York: Farrar, Straus & Giroux.

Matussek, P. (1975). *Internment in Concentration Camps and Its Consequences.* New York–Heidelberg–Berlin: Springer.

Meerloo, J. (1968). Dynamics of post-traumatic symptomatology and character changes. In *Massive Psychic Trauma,* ed. H. Krystal. New York: International Universities Press.

Miller, J.R. (1978). The Relationship of Fear of Success to Perceived Parental Attitudes toward Success and Autonomy. Unpublished doctoral dissertation, Columbia University.

Minuchin, S. (1974). *Families and Family Therapy.* Cambridge: Harvard University Press.

Mishler, E.G., and Waxler, N.E. (1968). *Interaction in Families: An Experimental Study of Family Processes and Schizophrenia.* New York: Wiley.

Mittelman, B. (1948). The concurrent analysis of married couples. *Psychoanalytic Quarterly* 17:182–197.

Modell, A.H. (1976). "The holding environment" and the therapeutic action of psychoanalysis. *Journal of the American Psychoanalytic Association* 24:285–307.

Niederland, W.G. (1968). The problems of the survivor. In *Massive Psychic Trauma,* ed. H. Krystal. New York: International Universities Press.

—— (1974). *The Schreber Case.* New York: Quadrangle.

Nissenfeld, S. (1979). The Effects of Four Types of Subliminal Stimuli on Female Depressives. Unpublished doctoral dissertation, Yeshiva University.

Oberndorf, C.P. (1938). Psychoanalysis of married couples. *Psychoanalytic Review* 25:453–475.

Peterfreund, E. (1978). Some critical comments on psychoanalytic conceptualizations of infancy. *International Journal of Psycho-Analysis* 59:427–441.

Piaget, J. (1954). *The Construction of Reality in the Child.* New York: Basic Books.

—— (1963). Realism and the origin of the idea of participation. In *The Child's Conception of the World*, ed. C.K. Ogden. Patterson,: Littlefield, Adams.

Provence, S., and Lipton, R.C. (1952). *Infants in Institutions: A Comparison of Their Development with Family Reared Infants During the First Year of Life*. New York: International Universities Press.

Rabkin, R. (1964). Conversion hysteria as social maladaptation. *Psychiatry* 27:349–363.

Racker, H. (1953). A contribution to the problem of countertransference. *International Journal of Psycho-Analysis* 34:313–324.

—— (1957). The meanings and uses of countertransference. *Psychoanalytic Quarterly* 26:303–357.

Rado, S. (1927). The problem of melancholia. *International Journal of Psycho-Analysis* 9:420–438.

Rakoff, V., Sigal, J.J., and Epstein, N.B. (1967). Children and families of concentration camp survivors. *Canada's Mental Health* 14:24–26.

Rangell, L. (1959). The nature of conversion. *Journal of the American Psychoanalytic Association* 7:632–662.

Reichard, S. (1956). A re-examination of studies of hysteria. *Psychoanalytic Quarterly* 25:155–177.

Reiss, D. (1971). Varieties of consensual experience. III. Contrasts between families of normals, delinquents, and schizophrenics. *Journal of Nervous and Mental Disease* 152:73–95.

Remmling, G.W. (1967). *The Road to Suspicion: A Study of Modern Mentality and the Sociology of Knowledge*. New York: Appleton-Century-Crofts.

Reusch, J. (1957). *Disturbed Communication*. New York: Norton.

Reusch, J., and Bateson, G. (1951). *Communication: The Social Matrix of Psychiatry*. New York: Norton.

Rinsley, D.B. (1981). Dynamic and developmental issues in borderline and related "spectrum" disorders. *Psychiatric Clinics of North America* 4:117–132.

Satir, V. (1964). *Conjoint Family Therapy*. Palo Alto: Science and Behavior.

Scheflen, A.E. (1963). Communication and regulation in psychotherapy. *Psychiatry* 2:126–136.

—— (1964). The significance of posture in communication systems. *Psychiatry* 27:316–331.

Searles, H.F. (1965). *Collected Papers on Schizophrenia and Related Subjects*. New York: International Universities Press.

Seligman, M.E.P., and Maier, S.F. (1967). Failure to escape traumatic shock. *Journal of Experimental Psychology* 74:1-9.

Seligman, M.E.P., Maier, S.F., and Gear, J.H. (1968). Alleviation of learned helplessness in the dog. *Journal of Abnormal Psychology* 73:256-262.

Shapiro, E. (1975). The influence of family experience on borderline personality development. *International Review of Psycho-analysis* 2:399-411.

Silverman, L.H., Lachman, F.M., and Milich, R.H. (1982). *The Search for Oneness*. New York: International Universities Press.

Silverman, L. (1971). An experimental technique for the study of unconscious conflict. *British Journal of Medical Psychology* 44:17-25.

—— (1975). On the role of laboratory experiments in the development of the clinical theory of psychoanalysis: data on the subliminal activation of aggressive and merging wishes in schizophrenics. *International Review of Psycho-analysis* 2:43-64.

Slater, E. (1965). Diagnosis of "hysteria." *British Medical Journal* 5447:1395-1399.

Slipp, S. (1969). The psychotic adolescent in the context of his family. Paper presented at the annual meeting of the American Medical Association, and In *The Emotionally Troubled Adolescent and the Family Physician*, ed. M.G. Kalogerakis. Springfield, Ill.: Charles C. Thomas, 1973.

—— (1972). A review of symbiotic relatedness. *Journal of Psychoanalysis in Groups* 4:1-6.

—— (1973a). Family therapy with disorganized poor families. *Journal of Psychoanalysis in Groups* 5:3-13.

—— (1973b). The symbiotic survival pattern: a relational theory of schizophrenia. *Family Process* 12:377-398.

—— (1976). An intrapsychic-interpersonal theory of depression. *Journal of the American Academy of Psychoanalysis* 4:389-409.

—— (1977). Interpersonal factors in hysteria: Freud's seduction theory and the case of Dora. *Journal of the American Academy of Psychoanalysis* 5:359-376.

—— (1981). The conflict of power and achievement in depression. In *Object and Self: A Developmental Approach, Essays in Honor of Edith Jacobson*, ed. S. Tuttman, C. Kaye, and M. Zimmerman. New York: International Universities Press.

Slipp, S., Ellis, S., and Kressel, K. (1974). Factors associated with remaining in or dropping out of conjoint family treatment. *Family Process* 13:413-426.

Slipp, S., and Nissenfeld, S. (1981). An experimental study of psychoanalytic theories of depression. *Journal of the American Academy of Psychoanalysis* 9:583–600.

Smith, J.H. (1971). Identificatory styles in depression and grief. *International Journal of Psycho-Analysis* 52:259–266.

Spiegel, H. (1974). The grade 5 syndrome: the highly hypnotizable person. *International Journal of Clinical Experimental Hypnosis* 22: 303–319.

Spiegel, J.P. (1971). *Transactions: The Interplay Between Individual, Family, and Society.* New York: Science House.

Spitz, R.A. (1945). Hospitalism: an inquiry into the genesis of psychiatric conditions in early childhood. In *Psychoanalytic Study of the Child,* vol. 1, ed. A. Freud, H. Hartmann, and E. Kris. New York: International Universities Press.

—— (1965). *The First Year of Life.* New York: International Universities Press.

Stern, D., and Sander, L. (1980). New knowledge about the infant from current research: implications for psychoanalysis. *Journal of the American Psychoanalytic Association* 28:181–198.

Stierlin, H. (1969). *Conflict and Reconciliation.* New York: Science House.

—— (1974). Psychoanalytic approaches to schizophrenia in the light of a family model. *International Review of Psycho-analysis* 1:169–178.

—— (1976a). *Adolph Hitler: A Family Perspective.* New York: Psychohistory Press.

—— (1976b). The dynamics of owning and disowning: psychoanalytic and family perspectives. *Family Process* 15:277–288.

Stolorow, R.D., and Lachman, F.M. (1980). *Psychoanalysis of Developmental Arrests: Theory and Treatment.* New York: International Universities Press.

Stone, M.H. (1981). Borderline syndromes: a consideration of subtypes and an overview: directions for research. *Psychiatric Clinics of North America* 4:3–24.

Sullivan, H.S. (1953). *The Collected Works of Harry Stack Sullivan.* New York: Norton.

Suttie, I. (1952). *The Origins of Love and Hate.* New York: Julian.

Szasz, T. (1961). *The Myth of Mental Illness.* New York: Hoeber.

Thomas, A., and Chess, S. (1980). *The Dynamics of Psychological Development.* New York: Brunner/Mazel.

Thompson, C. (1950). *Psychoanalysis: Evolution and Development.* New York: Grove Press.

Towne, M., Messinger, S., and Sampson, H. (1962). Schizophrenia and the marital family: accommodations to symbiosis. *Family Process* 1:304–318.

Vahia, N.S. (1963). Cultural differences in the clinical picture of schizophrenia and hysteria in India and the United States. *Transcultural Psychiatry Research Review* 14:16–18.

Veith, I. (1965). *Hysteria: The History of a Disease*, vol. 3. Chicago: University of Chicago Press.

Volkan, V. (1973). Transitional fantasies in the analysis of a narcissistic personality. *Journal of the American Psychoanalytic Association* 21:351–376.

Von Bertalanffy, L. (1968). *General Systems Theory*. New York: George Braziller.

Waelder, R. (1951). The structure of paranoid ideas. *International Journal of Psycho-Analysis* 32:167–177.

Watzlawick, P., Beavin, J.H., and Jackson, D.D. (1967). *Pragmatics of Human Communication*. New York: Norton.

Waxler, N.W. (1974). Parent and child effects on cognitive performance: an experimental approach to the etiological and responsive theories of schizophrenia. *Family Process* 13:1–22.

Wells, R.A., Dilkes, T.C., and Trivelli, N. (1972). The results of family therapy: a critical review of the literature. *Family Process* 11:189–207.

Wender, P.H., Rosenthal, D., and Kety, S.S. (1968). A psychiatric assessment of the adoptive parents of schizophrenics. In *The Transmission of Schizophrenia*, ed. D. Rosenthal and S.S. Kety. Oxford: Pergamon Press.

Whitehead, A.N. (1948). *Science and Philosophy*. New York: Philosophical Library.

Whitehead, A.N., and Russell, B. (1910). *Principia Mathematica*. Cambridge, Eng.: Cambridge University Press.

Wiener, N. (1954). *The Human Use of Human Beings: Cybernetics and Society*. New York: Doubleday.

Winnicott, D.W. (1949). Hate in the countertransference. *International Journal of Psycho-Analysis* 30:69–74.

—— (1965). *The Maturational Process and the Facilitating Environment*. New York: International Universities Press.

Wrong, D.H. (1964). The oversocialized conception of man in modern sociology. In *Sociological Theory: A Book of Readings*, ed. L.A. Coser and B. Rosenberg. New York: Macmillan.

Wynne, L.C. (1965). Some indications and contraindications for exploratory family therapy. In *Intensive Family Therapy*, ed. I. Boszormenyi-Nagy and J.L. Framo. New York: Hoeber Medical Division, Harper & Row.

Wynne, L.C., Ryckoff, I.M., Day, J., and Hirsch, S. (1958). Pseudomutuality in the family relations of schizophrenics. *Psychiatry* 21:205–220.

Wynne, L.C. and Singer, M.T. (1972). Principles for scoring communication defects and deviances of parents of schizophrenics in psychological test transactions. In *Annual Report Mental Health Intramural Research Programs, Division of Clinical and Behavioral Research and Division of Biological and Biochemical Research*, Vol. 2. Bethesda, Maryland: National Institute of Mental Health.

Zetzel, E. (1968). The so-called good hysteric. *International Journal of Psycho-Analysis* 49:256–260.

Ziegler, D.K., and Paul, N. (1954). On the natural history of hysteria in women. *Diseases of the Nervous System* 15:301–309.

INDEX

N